W9-CUG-133

REMNANTS OF BELIEF

REMNANTS OF BELIEF

Contemporary Constitutional Issues

LOUIS MICHAEL SEIDMAN
MARK V. TUSHNET

New York *Oxford*
OXFORD UNIVERSITY PRESS
1996

Oxford University Press

Oxford New York
Athens Auckland Bangkok Bombay
Calcutta Cape Town Dar es Salaam Delhi
Florence Hong Kong Istanbul Karachi
Kuala Lumpur Madras Madrid Melbourne
Mexico City Nairobi Paris Singapore
Taipei Tokyo Toronto

and associated companies in
Berlin Ibadan

Published by Oxford University Press, Inc.
198 Madison Avenue, New York, NY 10016

Oxford is a registered trademark of Oxford University Press

Library of Congress Cataloging-in-Publication Data
Seidman, Louis Michael.
Remnants of belief : contemporary constitutional issues /
Louis Michael Seidman, Mark V. Tushnet.
p. cm.
Includes bibliographical references and index.
ISBN 0-19-509979-6 (cloth).—ISBN 0-19-509980-X (pbk.)
1. United States—Constitutional law. I. Tushnet, Mark V., 1945– .
II. Title.
KF4550.Z9S37 1996
342.73'02—dc20
[347.3022] 95-23835
CIP

2 4 6 8 9 7 5 3 1

Printed in the United States of America
on acid-free paper

LMS: to Judith Mazo
MVT: to Naida Tushnet and Judith Broder

PREFACE

This book is the result of conversations that began when we both served as clerks to Justice Thurgood Marshall in 1972–73. Over the course of more than two decades of discussion and debate, we began to notice an odd feature of our own behavior.

Both of us love to argue about the Constitution and feel strongly about the arguments we make. The positions we hold on constitutional issues, though, rarely seem to be dictated by the arguments we formulate to defend them. Rather, it seems that we usually start with those positions and then use lawyers' skills to develop arguments to support them. By now, both of us are good enough at the game that we can see how the very arguments we care passionately about could be reversed to favor the opposite position.

It would be silly to generalize too broadly about the country as a whole based solely upon the experience of two law professors. We are nonetheless convinced that our own reactions are not completely atypical. Americans are preoccupied with constitutional argument even though they know that very few people are actually persuaded by the arguments they make. Until recently, constitutional argument has survived and flourished in an intellectual environment where its predicates have been destroyed.

This book represents our effort to investigate and explain this phenomenon. We want to understand why most constitutional argument is so weak and why we are drawn to it even when we know that it is weak.

We have omitted the usual scholarly apparatus in favor of a bibliographical essay identifying, in particular, the scholarly and popular discussions that have influenced us or that we think worth reading as exemplars of the type of analysis we criticize. The names of the cases we discuss in the text are provided with full citations in the Table of Cases.

We are grateful to participants at faculty workshops at the Georgetown University Law Center, the University of Virginia Law School, Harvard Law School, and the University of Chicago Law School, who put us through four grueling afternoons that were enough to convince us that the problems we discuss are authentically hard. Many colleagues read and commented on our work. Special thanks go to Rebecca Tushnet, who reviewed the entire manuscript, and to Tom Krattenmaker, who read and made detailed comments on most of the chapters. Anita Allen, Gregg Bloche, Mary Anne Case, Mike Klarman, John Mansfield, Earl Mazo, Eban Moglen, Roy Schotland, Girardeau Spann, Carlos Vasquez, and Ted White also provided useful comments on portions of the manuscript. Larry Tribe, Cass Sunstein, and David Strauss demonstrated extraordinary generosity in attempting to improve the book, including the portions that criticize their own work. Nathan Judish and Tamara Thompkins provided outstanding research assistance and, perhaps more significant, wise advice.

We would particularly like to acknowledge the faculty, administration, and staff of the Georgetown University Law Center, who have provided an intellectual environment that encouraged our work in a way we believe would not have been possible elsewhere.

Washington, D.C.
May 1995

L.M.S.
M.V.T.

CONTENTS

REMNANTS OF BELIEF

1

Introduction: Hard Questions, Easy Answers

Constitutional rhetoric is the language of American politics. Politicians regularly invoke the Constitution to support arguments on all sides of virtually every public question. Throughout our history, they have reflexively transformed policy controversies into constitutional problems.

Earlier generations saw disputes about alcohol consumption, wage and hour legislation, federal taxation, and state regulation of private markets as implicating our foundational document. Today there are concerted efforts to constitutionalize issues as diverse as federal fiscal policy, family law, school discipline, the practice of medicine, and even the most insignificant aspects of police–citizen interaction.

Many have lamented this tendency, and it certainly has sometimes produced unfortunate outcomes. Even when the debate has been about subjects that ought to be worthy of constitutional analysis, the result has not always been salutary. At the beginning of the twentieth century the Supreme Court relied on the Fourteenth Amendment's Due Process Clause to prohibit both the national government and state governments from alleviating some of free-market capitalism's worst excesses. By the 1930s this practice had led the country to the brink of disaster. Earlier, when the Supreme Court tried to "settle" the slavery question by finding that the Constitution barred Congress from regulating slavery in the national terrritories, the Court helped push the country over the brink and into civil war.

And the debate has not always been about subjects that ought to be discussed in constitutional terms. From today's perspective, the Prohibition experiment strikes many as a national embarrassment that trivialized the Constitution. Future generations may come to have similar views about the current constitutional disputes over term limitations, congressional pay raises, and balanced budgets.

Despite all this, the constitutionalization of our politics has not been entirely bad. Our tendency to express political disagreement in constitutional language has meant that the fundamental character of our country has remained continually up for grabs. Two centuries after our founding, we are still debating precisely what kind of country the United States is and what it stands for at the core. Paradoxically, contested efforts to fix a particular vision of America in our Constitution have given our politics a dynamism and a fluidity lacking in some other political cultures.

Moreover, our insistence on relating even relatively unimportant issues to these questions of national self-definition suggests a refreshing seriousness of purpose. To be sure, constitutional rhetoric sometimes deflects us from the issue at hand. It sometimes turns arguments about what we should do now into arguments about what the framers intended two hundred years ago. But such rhetoric can also give moral force to political argument that, at least occasionally and at least for a while, can be transformative. For example, the civil rights movement benefited enormously from its leaders' ability to frame the issues in constitutional terms.

More might be said on both sides of this question, but for now we prefer to put the discussion to one side.[1] Even if the constitutionalization of American politics were an unalloyed evil, the habit of thought it reflects is too deeply ingrained to change. For better or worse, we are stuck with a system in which constitutional argument will continue to play a central role in political debate.

For exactly that reason, we think it important to focus on the quality of that argument. Unfortunately, for the most part, its quality has been very poor indeed. There has been a persistent tendency to treat constitutional questions as if they were easy and the answers as if they were obvious. It naturally follows from this belief that one's opponents are foolish, or evil, or dangerous extremists bent on fundamentally transforming bedrock constitutional principles.

1. We return to the issue, in a somewhat different context, in chapter 9.

In this book, we attempt to investigate this phenomenon. Our aim is to explain why so many constitutional questions are hard and why so many commentators pretend that they are easy. Some representative examples of the sort of constitutional argument we are talking about—drawn from the popular press, public discussions, and the law reviews—will help frame our argument.

Let us first consider the style in which Nat Hentoff and George Will, two leading popular commentators on constitutional questions, present their views. Like an actor who has played a role so many times that he "owns" it, Hentoff has claimed permanent title to the persona of the beleaguered civil libertarian mourning the loss of our constitutional heritage and battling on the ramparts for what little is left. His regular columns on constitutional issues are populated by a colorful cast of bigots, know-nothings, and autocrats on one side and lonely and courageous freethinkers and nonconformists on the other. There is no room for ambiguity in these op-ed morality plays and precious little room for serious constitutional analysis.

One of Hentoff's forays into the arcane world of search-and-seizure law provides an example. Hentoff was upset that Congress was considzzering an expanded version of the "good faith" exception to the Fourth Amendment's exclusionary rule. The exception would permit the prosecution to introduce illegally seized evidence in cases where the police acted in "good faith." There are, of course, perfectly good reasons why Hentoff might oppose this change in the law. It is not hard to marshal persuasive arguments for why a "good faith" exception is a bad idea, although much can be said on the other side as well.

Unfortunately, however, Hentoff has no interest in making those arguments. Instead of focusing on how American police behave today, he castigates the behavior of British troops under King George III two hundred years ago. Responding to King George's abuses, Hentoff asserts, the framers drafted the Fourth Amendment, which was "the most precise [and] specific of all the amendments." That amendment, he asserts, plainly means that "searches cannot be made unless there is a warrant." Moreover, "the Framers chose not to substitute 'good faith' for 'probable cause.'"

It follows that the issue before Congress could not be simpler. The drafters of the legislation Hentoff opposes have decided to *celebrate* "the 200th anniversary of the Bill of Rights by acting as if it is time to replace most of them.'' The issue to be decided is ''whether the Fourth Amendment, however battered through the years, will continue to deter the police from invading homes and offices as if George III still ruled—or whether the Fourth Amendment will become so diluted that . . . it will be remembered only in the monographs of highly specialized scholars.''

All of this may be good rhetoric, but it is not persuasive argument. Hentoff's position proceeds from the undefended premise that we *ought* to be bound by what the colonists thought in a very different social setting two hundred years ago, rather than by what seems right to us now. Moreover, even if we were originalists, Hentoff's conclusions are still off base. The Fourth Amendment is hardly the study in precision he imagines. On the contrary, it is filled with ambiguities that have puzzled generations of scholars and judges. The amendment clearly prohibits ''unreasonable'' searches and seizures (whatever that means) and explicitly states that warrants must be supported by probable cause. But does it mean that the police must get warrants or that searches without warrants must be supported by probable cause? It certainly does not say so. And, of course, it does not say anything at all about what to do if the police do search unlawfully. Nothing in the constitutional text even hints that the framers contemplated or intended an exclusionary rule of any kind, much less an exclusionary rule without a good faith exception.

This does not mean that Hentoff's *conclusions* are wrong. The best historical evidence indicates that the framers probably did not intend to require warrants, but some scholars have advanced sophisticated arguments tending to show that warrants are the modern equivalent of eighteenth-century protections. No reputable scholar maintains that the framers meant to mandate an exclusionary rule, but perhaps the rule, like the warrant requirement, is a permissible judicial implication designed to give force to the textual requirements.

But these arguments are at best contested and uncertain. Reasonable people on the other side have made honest efforts to read the same history and have come to different conclusions. Not all of these people are bent on repealing the Bill of Rights or reestablishing the British monarchy on this side of the Atlantic.

Whereas Hentoff has assumed the role of the doughty nonconformist battling for freedom of thought, George Will presents himself as the patrician intellectual surveying the American scene with bemused condescension. Despite their differences in tone and political orientation, both authors see themselves as lonely defenders of forsaken values fighting with certitude and moral righteousness against the forces of evil.

For example, Will attacked the decision of an Arizona judge to place an abusive mother on probation on the condition that she use some method of birth control for the rest of her life. The mother, a drug abuser since age eleven, had had two children by age seventeen. She left her infants, aged eighteen months and six months, alone for three days in a sweltering apartment without air conditioning. The children nearly died. The mother was arrested, and while in jail she gave birth to a baby girl.

Although sympathizing with the sentencing judge, Will insists that the sentence starts us "down a dangerous path." He strongly implies that the judge's actions are unconstitutional[2] and is certain that they are "morally repellent." This is so because the "compel[led] . . . use of a drug is an intrusive act" that touches on "personal identity." The sentence is "a step toward treating an offender as a creature devoid of the essence of humanity" and "chemically nullifi[ed] the need for . . . her to make moral choices."

Once again, there are surely some things to be said for this view, and we will say some of them in chapter 4. But Will's commentary fails to so much as mention some obvious counterarguments that seriously weaken his position. Will thinks that the judge should have sent the defendant to prison. Arizona, like most states, does not permit conjugal visits for its inmates, a policy that, to our knowledge, Will has never attacked as "morally repellent." Imprisonment, which Will expressly endorses, would also nullify the defendant's "need . . . to make moral choices" about sexuality and reproduction.

Moreover, how was the defendant's opportunity for choice constricted by the court's decision? Arizona does not force prisoners to accept probation conditions; they can accept a prison term if they prefer. Thus, instead of foreclosing moral choice, the judge's sentence offered the defendant an additional option that Will would make unavailable. The sentence offered her a choice between prison and probation with the

2. Will does not quite say that the sentence is unconstitutional: "When government tampers, surgically or chemically, with sexuality, it is touching personal identity. In light of the recent elaboration of a woman's privacy rights, as defined in constitutional law concerning abortion, it is hard to imagine Forster's sentence withstanding scrutiny in an appeals court. . . . Forster is a Catholic, so the sentence may violate not only the privacy right, but the guarantee of free exercise of religion."

use of birth control. Offering this choice may make the defendant worse off or treat her as "devoid of the essence of humanity," but that claim has to be backed up by argument.

Finally, even if the sentence does tamper with reproductive choice and preserving such choice is important, Will's conclusions hardly follow. On the facts of the case, the likely alternative to compelled tampering with reproductive choice (either through birth control or imprisonment) was the compelled torturing of defenseless infants—also a serious matter that is surely "morally repellent." Will's entire argument rests uneasily on the undefended premise that the state is fully responsible for the sentence it imposes but not responsible at all for the consequences that would predictably flow from the failure to impose such a sentence.

It is not just that Will takes hard and complicated questions and treats them as if they were simple. He is also completely unfazed by contradiction. Consider, for example, Will's position on the need for judicial restraint in constitutional cases. In his column on mandatory birth control, Will suggests that the judge's sentence should be reversed because it violates the defendant's constitutional right to privacy. In this context, he seems untroubled by the fact that this right is notoriously lacking in textual support in the Constitution. Elsewhere Will presents himself as a strict textualist who would not allow mere policy preferences to influence constitutional interpretation. For example, although Will is a proponent of gun control, he says that the principled position is to insist on the repeal of the Second Amendment rather than to enact statutes infringing the constitutional "right to bear arms."

Sometimes Will's argument for judicial restraint seems to be premised on respect for democracy. On the subject of flag burning, Will argues that the Supreme Court was wrong to intervene because "democratic values require respect for the majority in close calls." But for reasons that are nowhere explained, this devotion to majority rule and principled unwillingness to allow policy considerations to influence constitutional decision making do not extend to affirmative action programs enacted by the political branches. Not only is there no textual support for the invalidation of these programs; the primary motivation behind the Fourteenth Amendment was a desire to *protect* the nineteenth-century analogue of affirmative action programs from constitutional attack. Yet Will wants the Supreme Court to outlaw them nonetheless because they are a "swamp" into which the country has "waded waist-deep."

Will opposes affirmative action because it violates "the constituting doctrine of all open societies[:] Rights belong to individuals, not groups." But his defense of individualism, like his defense of democracy, is selective. He opposes constitutional protection for flag burners as a manifestation of "a social atmosphere saturated with a philosophy of extreme individualism." In the flag-burning context, Will believes that the Supreme Court has wrongly preferred individual rights over "the community's right to nurture and act on the collective values that give it meaning and vitality." Yet somehow these collective values lose their force when the community attempts to prevent child abuse. Compelled birth control is wrong because the government is violating the woman's individual right of privacy and "touching personal identity."

One might, perhaps, forgive these lapses in light of the medium in which columnists like Will and Hentoff work. It is hard to lay out a carefully qualified argument in a seven-hundred-word op-ed piece. Unfortunately, the tendentiousness that Hentoff and Will exhibit is not restricted to newspaper pundits. It has become a hallmark of our constitutional debate.

Consider, for example, former federal judge Robert Bork and Harvard law professor Laurence Tribe. Like Hentoff and Will, Judge Bork and Professor Tribe are political opponents who oddly mirror each other across an ideological divide. Although they have come to be seen as champions of the "liberal" and "conservative" constitutional positions, respectively, each presents his theory as if it were neutral, noncontroversial, and wholly nonideological. Yet each manages to produce a theory that generates results agreeable to his ideological allies.

Judge Bork has attacked Professor Tribe's constitutional theory for "tak[ing] whatever form is necessary at the moment to reach a desired result. . . . [H]is writings are almost entirely an attempt to convert the Constitution to his political views." In contrast, Bork presents his own theory of original intent as entirely apolitical: "My philosophy of judging . . . is neither liberal nor conservative. It is simply a philosophy of judging which gives the Constitution a full and fair interpretation."

Bork does not deny that he has strong political views, and he is not reticent about expressing them. Indeed, his vision of political struggle borders on the apocalyptic. He describes a "war in our culture" begun by unprovoked attacks from "left activists" who have "contempt for the limits of respectable politics'' and who adhere to a ''restless and unprogrammatic radicalism that does not share but attacks traditional values and assumptions.''[3]

Judge Bork believes that his version of the ''rule of law'' stands as a bulwark against the ''restless and unprogrammatic radicalism'' he decries. But his position's logic requires him to deny that he has chosen his theory *because* it does so. If he did not deny that, he would have to give up his claim that his method of constitutional adjudication is politically neutral. We are therefore asked to believe that it is no more than a lucky coincidence that the theory produces politically desirable outcomes.

Judge Bork is a clever and resourceful lawyer who succeeds more often than one might expect in making this inherently dubious claim seem plausible. Occasionally, however, we catch a glimpse of the behind-the-scenes pulling and hauling necessary to make things come out the right way. Judge Bork's positions on the Equal Protection Clause of the Fourteenth Amendment and the Cruel and Unusual Punishment Clause of the Eighth Amendment provide an instructive example. (We discuss the death penalty debate at greater length in chapter 7.)

Bork's views on the constitutionality of the death penalty are simplicity itself: The constitutional text and the framers' statements and practice show that they did not mean the Cruel and Unusual Punishment Clause to outlaw the death penalty. Since the only legitimate function of a judge is to enforce the intent of the framers, the Court has no business banning capital punishment.

This view is presented as if it had nothing whatever to do with Judge Bork's own beliefs about the death penalty. On the contrary, he insists, the judicial opponents of capital punishment have wrongly read their own values into the Constitution. The Eighth Amendment's capacious phrasing might encompass some sort of ''evolving standard of decency,'' but, for Bork, this means only that

> society itself, not the judges, but the American people itself have evolved their moral views so that this thing becomes wrong. If that is true, statutes will reflect that fact and the death penalty will be repealed. If it is not true, then judges ought not to apply their own evolving morality.

3. We note that Judge Bork makes a passing critical reference to one of us but does not consider our work a target worth sustained discussion.

Unfortunately, this analysis creates difficulties for Judge Bork when it is applied to the equal protection context. Statements and practice by the Fourteenth Amendment's framers show that they no more intended to outlaw racial segregation and gender discrimination than the Eighth Amendment's framers intended to ban the death penalty. Indeed, the Fourteenth Amendment *introduced* gender discrimination into the Constitution, and feminists of the time opposed its enactment for precisely this reason. Yet, while strongly attacking the justices who invalidated the death penalty, Judge Bork approves of constitutional decisions striking down segregation and at least certain forms of gender discrimination. How can these views be reconciled?

Judge Bork may believe that racial and gender discrimination are morally and politically wrong, whereas the death penalty is desirable, or at least justifiable. His theory of original intent, though, means that he cannot rely on this straightforward argument. Instead, he must explain that the moral rightness of the race and gender decisions is no more than a fortunate but unintended by-product of neutral interpretation of the Constitution.

Bork manages to support the modern Court's general approach to race and gender while preserving the neutrality of his theory of original intent by manipulating the level of generality at which the theory is applied. He argues that the framers' specific intent regarding segregation is beside the point. The framers did not intend to outlaw racial segregation, but they did intend to provide for equality between the races. When the Supreme Court decided *Brown v. Board of Education* (1954), it had to transpose this general purpose into a world the framers had not imagined. Its decision correctly vindicated the framers' general intent at the expense of their specific expectations.

Similarly, Bork argues, it would be wrong to transpose directly into modern society the framers' specific expectations regarding the appropriate roles of men and women. He seems to endorse a kind of "evolving standards" approach to this problem:

> Distinctions based upon gender will rarely be reasonable because, in our society, as we now view the place of women in society, only extreme cases based upon biological differences would probably be upheld. . . .
>
> Now I am sure that the framers of [the] 14th amendment did not think that the way women were treated in those days was unreason-

able. That was seen to them very natural. Now, as women's place in society has changed, all of those distinctions that they made and thought were entirely reasonable now look to us unreasonable. That's the way constitutional doctrine evolves.

Standing alone, this interpretive technique is certainly defensible, but it cannot be reconciled with Judge Bork's narrower reading of the Eighth Amendment. He never bothers to explain why it is right to focus on the general standard the Fourteenth Amendment's framers constitutionalized while focusing solely on the narrow application of the Eighth Amendment standard. Nor does he explain why judges can use evolving standards to invalidate gender discrimination laws but not laws imposing the death penalty.

Judge Bork's many critics have fastened on inconsistencies such as these to argue that his claim to political neutrality is a fraud and that "original intent" is no more than a cover for judicial implementation of the Right's political program. Many of these critics, though, cannot resist the temptation to offer similarly tendentious arguments.

Professor Tribe's testimony before the Senate Judiciary Committee opposing Judge Bork's nomination to the Supreme Court provides a case in point. It would be a serious mistake to suppose that there is a kind of moral equivalence between Judge Bork and Professor Tribe. When he has not held government positions, Judge Bork has spent much of his time producing polemical writings seemingly designed to curry favor with his conservative patrons. Professor Tribe, in contrast, has devoted his not inconsiderable energy and ingenuity to the development of legal arguments that, by our lights, further the cause of social justice. In many respects, his career is a model of responsible and committed public engagement.

Despite these important differences, Bork and Tribe are, in other respects, alter egos. Although he is closely identified with "liberal" views on constitutional adjudication, Tribe, like Bork, insists that the political results produced by his constitutional theory are the merest happenstance. His theory is emphatically "not a cover for whatever liberal political views I might hold" and is "neither particularly instrumental nor reflective of any specific philosophy." Testifying against Bork before the Senate Judiciary Committee, Tribe went to some lengths to make clear that his opposition to Judge Bork had nothing whatever to do with Bork's "political philosophy." Instead, it was rooted in the belief that Bork's appointment "seriously threatens constitutional values that have proven fundamental in American history."

Professor Tribe also shares Judge Bork's habit of demonizing his opponents and presenting his own views as if they were the only conclusions a fair-minded person could reach. His testimony against Judge Bork was studded with references to the obvious correctness of his own position. "The problem," he asserted, "is very simple." Judge Bork's views are in direct conflict with "a 200-year-old tradition." Bork fails to comprehend what "[e]very law student knows" and "[differs] sharply from what virtually all commentators with whom I am familiar understand [our] jurisprudence to be." Bork's approach is "essentially lawless."

When he got down to specifics, Tribe sharply criticized Bork's approach to both substantive due process and equal protection. Regarding due process, Tribe attacked Bork for denying that "people retain certain unspecified fundamental rights that courts are supposed to discern and to defend" and made the startling assertion that "not one of the 105 past and present Justices of the Supreme Court has ever taken a view at odds with this basic axiom of our Constitution."

With regard to equal protection, Tribe attacked Bork's advocacy of a "reasonable basis" test rather than a more stringent level of scrutiny to evaluate classifications affecting women and the poor. We discuss these technical doctrines a bit later but note for now Professor Tribe's tone. He argued that the Court's use of more structured scrutiny "has led us predictably toward equality" and that a "reasonable basis test" was "open-ended, free-floating, [and] essentially lawless." Judge Bork's insistence on the test was "a request for a blank check." It asked "women and other vulnerable groups . . . to gamble [on Judge Bork's] personal notion of what is 'reasonable' according to his sense of community standards."

As should be apparent by now, we do not count ourselves among Judge Bork's fans. On balance, we think that the Senate was right to reject his nomination. Still, one can endorse the substance of some of Professor Tribe's criticisms of Judge Bork's positions while also regretting its hyperbolic and reductive tone. How, for example, could Professor Tribe square his assertion that Judge Bork's position is contrary to that of every serious constitutional thinker with the fact that numerous such thinkers, who appear to have absorbed "what every law student knows" and seem to be equally devoted to our "200-year-old tradition,'' testified in support of Bork's nomination?[4] How could it be that Bork's philosophy is inconsistent with that of all 105 former and sitting justices when former and sitting justices publicly endorsed his nomination?[5]

Professor Tribe's attack on Judge Bork's textualist approach to the Due Process Clause is seriously misleading. He may be correct when he asserts that virtually all previous justices have, at one time or another, defended the judicial articulation of nontextual values. However, he fails to mention that some of these justices thought that those values protected slavery and prohibited minimum wage laws. Nor does he mention that virtually all the previous justices have also claimed at one time or another that the legitimacy of judicial review rests upon judicial adherence to the Constitution's text and the framers' intent. One of the peculiarities of modern constitutional argument, which we will explore shortly, is that almost everyone holds both of these inconsistent views. Professor Tribe chooses to focus on one side of the inconsistency. Had he been a defender of Judge Bork, he could easily have focused on the other.

Tribe's critique of Judge Bork's equal protection jurisprudence is similarly misfocused. He complained that Judge Bork would abandon ''structured scrutiny,'' which has ''led us predictably toward equality'' in gender and wealth discrimination cases. This assertion reverses the historical record. At one time, the Court adhered to ''structured scrutiny,'' under which legislation was rigidly sorted into two discrete categories—''suspect'' and ''ordinary social and economic''—and more or less automatically upheld or invalidated laws according to which category was involved. Professor Tribe's liberal allies on the Court rebelled against this structure and argued that a looser ''sliding scale'' approach would provide greater protection for minorities. Eventually, the liberals won on this point, and it was only with the freeing up of equal protection review that the Court began to invalidate statutes based upon gender discrimination.

More fundamentally, Professor Tribe's critiques of Judge Bork's due process and equal protection jurisprudence are at war with each other.

4. Distinguished legal academics such as Michael McConnell, Henry Monaghan, George Priest, and Richard Stewart did so.

5. Former Chief Justice Warren Burger testified in support of the nomination, and Justice John Paul Stevens endorsed it in a speech to the Seventh Circuit Judicial Conference.

He attacks Bork's equal protection approach because it is "open-ended," "free-floating," and a request for a "blank check." Yet, it is precisely to avoid this problem that Judge Bork resisted the invention of nontextual rights under the plastic rubric of substantive due process. Professor Tribe never explains why he is so worried about judicial discretion in enforcing equal protection rights, yet so resistant to textual limitations on that discretion when it comes to privacy rights.

To be sure, there is an obvious explanation for this discrepancy. There was good reason to fear that Judge Bork would use the discretion built into his equal protection methodology to cut back on the protection afforded to disadvantaged groups, whereas the modern Court had already used the discretion built into its due process jurisprudence to expand the privacy rights Professor Tribe favors. But Professor Tribe could not advance *that* argument without giving up his claim that his opposition to the Bork nomination was unrelated to Judge Bork's "political philosophy." In order to retain the veneer of neutrality and apolitical, "principled" opposition, Professor Tribe was forced into a conspicuous contradiction that seriously weakened the force of his argument.

Our last pair of examples is drawn from the academic literature on constitutional law. Although the argumentative failings we identify are perhaps least consequential in this context, they are also the least excusable. Law review articles reach a tiny audience and rarely have much direct impact on public policy. The authors of these articles trade off the possibility of direct influence for the freedom that comes with not having to appeal to a mass audience and for the hope—realized in the case of the legal realist scholars we discuss in chapter 2—of influence in the long run. Within the sheltered world of grey text and endless footnotes, they are free to follow complex legal arguments wherever they lead.

The best academic work takes advantage of this freedom and avoids many of the pitfalls we have discussed. The work tends to be more fair-minded and qualified, less simplistic and tendentious than articles and speeches intended for broader distribution. (Professor Lani Guinier discovered that these more qualified arguments do not translate well into the world of sound bites and op-ed articles.) Unfortunately, even the best of this work also exhibits some of the failings we have already identified.

In particular, much of the work is marred by a theoretical stance that purports to place the author at a distance from the conclusions "the theory" generates. This theoretical posture has obvious strategic advantages. Authors can insist that they have reached beyond disagreements on the merits and can claim that their positions must be accepted by all honest individuals regardless of those disagreements. Still, the transparent ways in which the theory is manipulated to achieve the "right" results dissipates the argument's rhetorical force.

Moreover, the claim of disinterested neutrality has the corollary that those who disagree with the author are biased and unprincipled. This corollary, in turn, results in an odd and unfortunate paradox. The theoretical stance is designed to reach a wider audience by speaking to those who might disagree about the merits of a contested political issue, yet can agree on a theoretical perspective abstracted from those issues. In fact, theoretical argument tends to produce the opposite result. The assertion that the author alone is speaking from principle slides easily into a demonization of intellectual opponents and a failure to engage them on their own terms. The result once again is the kind of "preaching to the choir" that characterizes so much constitutional argument in nonacademic settings.

Consider, for example, an article by Michael McConnell published in the *Harvard Law Review*. McConnell is probably today's most sophisticated conservative constitutional scholar. His article uses the examples of religion and abortion to address the vexing problem of "selective funding."

The selective funding problem arises when the government chooses not to subsidize constitutionally protected activity even though it does subsidize a substitute for that activity. The Medicaid program reimburses poor women for some childbirth expenses, but for many years Congress has insisted that Medicaid dollars not be used to fund abortions. Similarly, public schools are funded out of tax dollars, but Supreme Court decisions sharply limit the extent to which the government can use tax money to subsidize religious education.

As we discuss at greater length in chapter 4, Supreme Court decisions addressing the selective funding problem have not been a model of consistency, and scholars have failed to make much headway in developing a coherent theory to deal with it. McConnell suggests that part of the difficulty stems from an unwillingness to abstract from "liberal" and "conservative" commitments. He complains that people reason "backward from the desired result," and he chooses the abortion and religion examples deliberately to "mitigate this tendency, in myself as well as others." A coherent, "neutral" theory of selective funding, he says, must reach consistent results in both the abortion and the religion contexts.

> It would be naive to believe that complex constitutional theory is a perfect constraint on politicized judging, but I am confident that a judge forced to develop doctrine that would govern *both* abortion *and* religious education will be more constrained, dispassionate, and fair-minded than one who decides what seems fair in each case as it comes.

In sixty pages of closely reasoned text, McConnell purports to develop such a theory. In many ways, his article is a model of legal argumentation. Unlike some of the work described earlier, it is sophisticated, thoughtful, and original.

There are, nonetheless, significant difficulties with McConnell's claim for his theory's virtues. McConnell would have the reader believe that his work is entitled to respect as "more constrained, dispassionate, and fair-minded" because he has avoided "reasoning backward" from his substantive positions on abortion—which he opposes—and religious education—which he supports—to a more general theory about selective funding. There are two problems with this assertion.

First, why is "reasoning backward" a bad idea? Why is it wrong to start with positions about the desirability of allowing choice as to abortion and about the merits of religious education and to reason from those substantive commitments to a theory about selective funding consistent with them? After all, no matter how elegant and aesthetically pleasing, a constitutional theory is presumably only as good as the results it yields. McConnell himself concedes that any theory of selective funding would have to incorporate some substantive account of the right pressured by the failure to fund. He fails to see that this concession undermines the very point of the exercise he undertakes.

Moreover, McConnell's own efforts to formulate and apply his theory undermine the claims he makes for it. McConnell claims that a theoretical approach "[yields] results that can be assessed objectively" and contrasts this with "conclusory or subjective approach[es that] invite ad hoc decisionmaking and unfairness." Yet when he actually deploys his elaborate theoretical construct and runs the abortion and religious education problems through it, the outcome precisely tracks his own "subjective" predispositions. Remarkably, it turns out that "neutral" selective funding theory not only allows the state to fund religious education; it probably compels such funding.[6] In contrast, the state is constitutionally permitted, and perhaps even constitutionally compelled, to *abstain* from funding abortions.

This denouement is more than a touch ironic. Professor McConnell begins by claiming that neutrality and objectivity will be advanced by testing a selective funding theory against both the religious education and the abortion funding problems. The need to produce consistent results in both cases supposedly guards against special pleading by either the Left or the Right. But one is surely entitled to wonder just how much constraining influence Professor McConnell's theory has exercised when the consistency requirement ends up producing results that, at least to the untutored eye, seem radically inconsistent. It is barely possible that the extraordinary confluence between these outcomes and Professor McConnell's substantive commitments is nothing more than a fortuitous coincidence. Moreover, it is a tribute to his persuasive powers that he makes plausible what would otherwise seem like the most obvious of gerrymanders. But the end product of McConnell's efforts can hardly be counted as evidence in favor of the constraining force of theory.[7]

In effect, Professor McConnell's resort to theory allows him to have his cake and eat it too. He gets to occupy the high ground and to chastise his opponents for making unprincipled and result-oriented arguments, all the while sacrificing nothing in terms of his position on the merits.

Right-wing scholars are not the only ones who use theory instrumentally and unconvincingly. David Strauss and Cass Sunstein, McConnell's colleagues at the University of Chicago Law School, are political liberals who have publicly expressed their unhappiness with many Su-

6. Although the main thrust of Professor McConnell's argument is to require state funding of religious education, he does acknowledge that if the Supreme Court were to adopt an ''anti-coercion'' perspective, funding would be optional. Under current doctrine, funding is sometimes prohibited.

7. We note as well that Professor McConnell's theory has the convenient attribute of removing from the political process the issue on which his side is unlikely to prevail (because today's legislatures are likely to be quite reluctant to spend much money on religious education). In its weak form, it requires political resolution of the issue—abortion funding—on which his side is likely to prevail. In its stronger form, it guards against even the unlikely possibility of a political victory by his opponents on abortion.

preme Court decisions handed down during the Rehnquist years.[8] Like McConnell, they are among the most thoughtful and sophisticated constitutional scholars at work today. In an article in the *Yale Law Journal,* written before Bill Clinton defeated President George Bush in the 1992 presidential election, they argue that the Senate should play a greater role in selecting Supreme Court nominees. The Senate should not limit itself to ensuring that a nominee is morally fit and intellectually competent, they argue. Rather, it should investigate the nominee's judicial philosophy and "insist that the next nominee be a 'liberal' or a 'moderate.'"

Like McConnell, Strauss and Sunstein say that their argument is independent of their own political commitments. They claim that their reasons for supporting an enhanced senatorial role have nothing whatever to do with their distaste for the ideology of the justices chosen by successive Republican administrations. Indeed, they assert that one advantage of their proposal is that it will make the judicial selection process less partisan and ideological. Their reasons for insisting on a more active senatorial role are rooted, not in politics or ideology, but in the Constitution's structure and text and in the nature of the judicial function.

Strauss and Sunstein demonstrate remarkable erudition and considerable rhetorical ability in arguing for this position. Once again, however, an application of supposedly apolitical theory somehow ends up producing outcomes consonant with its advocates' political views.

It hardly requires a political scientist to understand that under the political conditions that existed at the time they wrote, an enhanced senatorial role would have tended to produce justices more sympathetic to the kind of liberal constitutional law that Strauss and Sunstein favor. Not satisfied with even this result, the authors go on to argue that their "neutral" theory produces liberal results under even changed political conditions:

> Things would be different if one party controlled both the Senate and the Presidency. For example, there would be little need for a Democratic Senate to undertake an independent investigation of the nominee of a Democratic President—not because the Democratic view is "correct," but because there would be a reduced need for the Senate to serve as an ideological check on the President.

8. We are coauthors with Professor Sunstein of a casebook on constitutional law.

Given this position, one might suppose that the authors would at least have to concede that a Republican Senate should be similarly deferential to a Republican president. But no—it turns out that this configuration raises yet "another question" and that, under this scenario, at least some of the arguments against senatorial assertiveness "would cease to be compelling."

Thus, the end result of the "neutral" and "apolitical" Strauss and Sunstein theory is that the argument for senatorial assertiveness is exactly calibrated to the likelihood that such assertiveness will produce a more liberal Supreme Court. What their position amounts to is a claim that Republican but not Democratic presidents must answer to the Senate Judiciary Committee.

Preserving a veneer of ideological neutrality allows Strauss and Sunstein to claim that even conservatives should be persuaded by their argument. But does anyone seriously believe that many conservatives will in fact be moved? Like McConnell's selective funding theory, their argument is too self-serving, the gerrymander too transparent, to persuade anyone who needs to be persuaded.

Strauss and Sunstein are not only diligent and careful scholars; they are also brilliant and resourceful lawyers. One cannot help admiring the skill with which they marshal evidence and deploy their arguments. Yet, in the end, one is left with the same troubling questions about their efforts that plague the other works we have discussed:

- What purpose is being served by all of the intellectual pyrotechnics?
- Whose mind is being changed?
- How is the dialogue about our foundational document being advanced?
- Why, in the end, does constitutional argument always turn out to be so bad?

Our examples illustrate four common problems with the way we talk about constitutional issues. First, constitutional argument is disembodied. Constitutional advocates rarely assume direct responsibility for the results they advocate, and they go to great pains to demonstrate that their reasoning is not driven by a desire to reach any particular outcome. Instead, they say that the outcome is dictated by some neutral and apolitical principle independent of both the advocate who relies on it and the results it produces. When those results in fact coincide with the advocate's policy preferences (as they almost always do), the reader is asked to believe that this is a happy coincidence.

Second, constitutional argument is reductionist. Modern constitutional advocates believe they must be hyperbolic if they are to persuade. They are convinced that nonlawyers will not understand arguments acknowledging ambiguity or doubt. Instead, everything is a matter about which reasonable and right-thinking people simply cannot disagree. It follows from this stance that those who in fact disagree are either dangerous extremists or unprincipled opportunists acting nonneutrally, politically, and in bad faith. Their disagreement manifests a willful refusal to apply a bedrock principle in order to secure short-term advantage.

Third, constitutional argument is tendentious. Constitutional advocates are generally unwilling to come to grips with counterarguments advanced by their opponents. Sometimes these arguments are mischaracterized; sometimes they are treated as so obviously wrongheaded as not to merit a response; most often they are simply ignored.

Finally, constitutional argument is unconvincing. The problem is not just that complex matters are treated as if they were simple and obvious counterarguments ignored or mischaracterized. The core difficulty is that these moves are made so ineptly and transparently that virtually no one is fooled by them. Constitutional advocates seem to have lost interest in actually persuading anyone. At best their arguments serve to rally the already committed. They rarely reach out to the uncommitted and virtually never throw new or interesting light on the problem.

These four deficiencies in modern constitutional discourse raise a broader problem. In a diverse society, people will disagree about particular constitutional decisions. Some will think society will be better off if the courts strike down certain laws, and others will disagree. Constitutional law offers itself as a way of resolving that disagreement.

But, surely, it cannot be enough for one partisan simply to assert that because society will be better off if her side prevails, the Constitution requires that result. To say that is to use the magic words "the Constitution" to endorse her position. And, of course, constitutional discourse does not have quite so obvious a form. Rather, partisans say that if we accept a particular way of thinking about the Constitution, it will turn out that the partisans' desired result just happens to follow.

Why should their opponents accept that way of thinking? Maybe because, after taking everything into account, society as a whole will be better off if we adopt that way rather than some other. Even if a particular approach to constitutional law produces some unattractive results, it might produce better results overall than its competitors. Moreover, attempting to eliminate the results we do not like may introduce others we dislike more.

An instrumental argument along these lines might convince someone who did not like a particular result produced by a general approach to constitutional interpretation to support the approach nonetheless. On this level, instrumentalism is not only coherent but, perhaps, inevitable. We believe, however, that much modern constitutional discourse is instrumental in a more bothersome way: Many participants in constitutional debate seem unwilling to live with an approach that generates *any* result they find unattractive.

The abortion debate provides a useful illustration. Later in this book we discuss John Hart Ely's representation reinforcement theory of judicial review. According to that theory, the courts appropriately step in when people who do not have a fair chance of getting a legislature to respond to their concerns are involved. Ely himself was an early critic of the Supreme Court's abortion decisions.[9] He understood that they might be defended on representation reinforcement grounds, as responses to the disadvantages women faced in legislatures. But, he argued, the other "group" adversely affected—fetuses—was at an even worse disadvantage.

Over the succeeding years, scholars have worked out more complete representation reinforcement defenses of the abortion decisions; hints of those defenses can be found in the Court's most recent pronouncements (e.g., *Planned Parenthood of Southeastern Pennsylvania v. Casey,* 1992). We believe that they are at least as good as the representation reinforcement arguments Ely makes for careful judicial attention to laws adversely affecting the interests of racial minorities. Notice, though, the consequence: For those who find the representation reinforcement argument persuasive, the theory no longer generates a result that its adherents find unattractive. Those who do not—who continue to believe that the theory does generate an unattractive result—can be excoriated for failing to care enough about women's interests to see that the argument favoring abortion rights is just as persuasive as the argument opposing school segregation.

9. We do not know Ely's current views on the question.

It is tempting to ascribe the failures we have discussed in this chapter to personal deficiencies in the individuals we have criticized. But this will not do. We have deliberately chosen scholars, journalists, and public figures at the top of their professions, and they are properly there. Their failings are troubling precisely because they are the failings of our most skilled and thoughtful constitutional analysts.

In the rest of this book, we argue that the impediments to good constitutional argument are structural rather than personal. Although the problems at first seem quite disparate, in fact they are linked. All relate to the economic and social transformation that accompanied the New Deal half a century ago. These changes both facilitated and were facilitated by a shift in legal ideology that seemed to eliminate any plausible nonconstitutional baseline of natural rights against which claims of constitutional entitlement could be measured. Without such a baseline, constitutional argument cannot easily get off the ground.

If this were all there were to the problem, we might have simply assimilated this new knowledge and proceeded to talk about our differences in nonconstitutional terms. But, although the new critical techniques made old convictions less plausible, they did not succeed in eliminating the convictions themselves. Instead, they survive as remnants of belief, too central to our worldview to be abandoned, yet too tattered to serve any real purpose. The upshot is that constitutional advocates cannot help deploying old forms of argument in an environment where the arguments have lost the capacity to persuade.

Our position is likely to be attacked from two opposing directions. First, skeptics may advance a position more extreme than ours. They might maintain that the sorts of problems we identify are neither historically located nor confined to constitutional discourse. Rather, these skeptics would contend, the problems are inherent in *any* normative enterprise.

Second, sanguine constitutionalists may see us as the extremists. They might deny the existence of the pathologies we describe and maintain that constitutional argument makes an important contribution to public debate by injecting serious moral concerns into ordinary political discussion.

Our position is between these two claims. We are less pessimistic than the skeptics, less optimistic than the sanguine constitutionalists. We share the latter's hopes for the *possibility* of normative discourse. The position we defend refers only to the way a particular kind of normative argument has operated in a particular historical and intellectual setting. Precisely because we are optimists, we make some suggestions in chapter 9 for ways to reformulate constitutional argument that might make it useful again.

But we hope not to confuse potential with reality. We therefore share the skeptics' pessimism about how constitutional argument actually functions today. Our legal culture's continuing ambivalence about the critical techniques that came to the fore during the New Deal period has, at least for now, seriously weakened the ability of constitutional argument to persuade. Until it is reformulated, it will serve mostly to divide and anger.

Our strategy in elaborating these points is to proceed from the general to the particular. In chapter 2 we begin by describing the New Deal revolution and its ambiguous legacy. In chapters 3 and 4 we argue that this legacy produced two central, interlocking, and ultimately unresolvable problems that bedevil virtually all of constitutional law: the "state action" problem and the "unconstitutional conditions" problem. Chapters 5 through 8 trace these difficulties through a series of particular constitutional issues: race discrimination, the control of pornography and of campaign finance, the use of capital punishment, and the division of power among the three branches of the federal government and between the federal government and the states. In chapter 9 we make some suggestions for how constitutional discourse might be reconstructed to make it useful again. We argue against disclaiming either the skepticism born of our New Deal experience or the normative commitment prized by constitutionalists. Instead, these two contradictory impulses must be integrated in a way that reaches out to our adversaries while also validating our own sense of moral purpose even as it recognizes the contingent character of that sense.

Some readers may find our approach to these questions more than a little frustrating. They will wonder what we believe to be the "correct" solutions to the particular constitutional controversies we discuss and will want to engage us on the merits. Of course, we have views about these matters, and neither of us has been particularly reticent about expressing them elsewhere. But it would be preposterous to claim that we alone have managed to escape the problems that have bedeviled commentators as thoughtful and diverse as Hentoff, Will, Bork, Tribe, McConnell, Sunstein, and Strauss. Our claim in this book is that virtually all modern constitutional advocacy, including our own, is deficient.

In this book, then, we will spare the reader our own efforts to manipulate constitutional argument. Perhaps foolishly, we leave for another day the task of again persuading readers about the rightness of our substantive views in light of the critique we advance here.

2

The Origins of the Current Situation

Early in the twentieth century Virginia began to develop an apple-growing industry. As the industry took an important place in Virginia's economy, growers discovered that its future was threatened by a plant disease called cedar rust. Cedar rust spends its first phase on red cedar trees, which it does not harm. In a later phase, though, the cedar rust destroys the leaves and fruit on apple trees. From the apple growers' point of view, the remedy was obvious: Cut down all the cedar trees and thereby eliminate the threat. They persuaded the Virginia legislature to enact a statute letting apple growers petition the state entomologist to inspect cedar trees growing near apple orchards. If the entomologist found cedar rust infestation, the statute said, he or she could order the cedar trees' owners to cut them down.

Cedar trees, although not as important to Virginia's economy as apple orchards, were worth something to their owners. They could be sold for ornamental use or lumber. Cedar tree owners challenged the Virginia statute as a violation of the constitutional provision barring governments from "taking" private property for public use without compensating the owners. After all, they pointed out, the government was going beyond telling them how they might use their property by insisting that they completely destroy it. Worse, the destruction did not serve any truly public purpose; it simply made it easier for apple growers to earn profits. If Virginia thought that its economy was better off overall with a prosperous apple-growing industry, that was fine, but the Constitution meant that the cost of maintaining that industry had to be distributed among all of Virginia's citizens through the taxes they would pay to compensate cedar tree owners; the cost could not be borne by the cedar tree owners alone.

The cedar tree owners' challenge reached the Supreme Court in 1928 (*Miller v. Schoene*). The Court treated it as an easy case. Justice Harlan Fiske Stone, later to be named chief justice by President Franklin Roosevelt, wrote an opinion whose brevity hides its analytic importance. To Stone and the Supreme Court, "the state was under the necessity of making a choice between the preservation of one class of property and that of the other. . . . It would have been none the less a choice if, instead of enacting the present statute, the state, by doing nothing, had permitted serious injury to the apple orchards . . . to go unchecked." The Constitution, according to the Supreme Court, did not bar the state from deciding to destroy the property that was less valuable to the state's economy.

All this might seem simple enough: Either apple trees or cedar trees were going to be destroyed—the former by the cedar rust or the latter by order of the state. The outcome would be the result of choices made by government, either to let nature run its course or to intervene. The Constitution was indifferent to which choice the government made.

By seeing government "choice" everywhere, however, the cedar tree case undermined the conceptual structure that had made sense of constitutional law. And, unlikely as it may seem, some of the difficulties with the arguments we discussed in chapter 1 can be found in the implications of Justice Stone's insights. George Will's discussion of offering birth control as an alternative to imprisonment for child abusers, for example, faces a rather direct challenge from the proposition that *refusing* to offer that alternative is "none the less a choice" that dramatically affects the life chances of the abuser's children.

The arguments we discussed in chapter 1 characteristically purport to be "neutral"—based on premises that are independent of the political preferences of those who make them. What, however, is "neutrality"? It must be something independent *both* of political preferences *and* of constitutional conclusions—the former for obvious reasons, the latter because neutral premises are supposed to generate constitutional conclusions. Where, then, do the neutral premises come from? The natural answer is that they come from someplace else—perhaps text, history, tradition, or philosophy. But by suggesting that law is everywhere, that everything in social life results from a choice by government, Stone's insight eliminates the possibility of going somewhere else for our neutral premises. Without that possibility, the resources of constitutional discussion are dramatically impoverished.

The point can be made in many ways, both in the context of the cedar tree case and elsewhere. It was not enough for Virginia to define "private" property rights and let the market operate "freely," for in allocating property rights the government was choosing. Suppose Virginia did not have a statute like the one the cedar tree owners challenged, and suppose the apple growers sued the cedar tree owners for creating a "nuisance" by maintaining their cedar trees. If the Virginia courts decided that the cedar trees were *not* a nuisance, they would be deciding that merely raising cedar trees near apple orchards was an inherent right of private property. (And, not so incidentally, they would be forcing the apple growers to buy the right to be free of the threat of cedar rust by buying the cedar trees.)

On the other hand, if the Virginia courts decided that the cedar trees *were* a nuisance, they would be deciding that the right of private property did not include the right to threaten neighbors' property by ordinary uses of property. At the same time, they would be finding that the apple growers had a legal privilege to be free of the threat of cedar rust. (And, again not so incidentally, they would be forcing any cedar tree owner who wanted to stay in business to buy the right to do so from neighboring apple growers.) Either decision would be "none the less a choice."

Suppose the apple growers simply went onto their neighbors' land and cut down the cedar trees that threatened their prosperity. The cedar tree owners would then sue the apple growers for damages from the trespass. The state courts would have to choose between awarding the cedar tree owners damages and allowing the apple growers to "defend" themselves against the threat of injury.

The cedar tree owners' constitutional objections rested on the view that the Constitution took property law rules as the settled background: They argued that the Constitution bars the government from changing the rules (without paying for the change). The Supreme Court's decision brings the background rules of property law into the foreground and makes them completely subject to redetermination at any point—or, more precisely, to *determination* at any point, for, as the trespass example shows, even in deciding ordinary property law questions the state is nonetheless making a choice.

We can compare the cedar tree case to one decided by New York's highest court seventeen years earlier (*Ives v. South Buffalo Rail. Co.*, 1911). New York had enacted a workers' compensation statute. Instead of suing employers for injuries they received at the workplace, workers had to go to a commission, which would decide whether their injuries were related to their work; if they were, the commission would award a fixed amount. The theory behind workers' compensation statutes was that they substituted a relatively cheap and certain remedy through the commission, providing relatively low payments to workers, for the more expensive system of suing employers, which might provide workers with greater recovery but which was much less certain. New York's highest court called the statute "revolutionary" and held it unconstitutional because it displaced the judge-made common law of industrial accidents. Under the judge-made law, employers had to pay only when they were at fault and their workers were not. Under the statute, however, employers had to pay even if they were free of fault (and even if the injured worker had been negligent). According to the New York court, the judge-made law requiring fault was part of the constitutionally mandated background property law. If the legislature could displace *that* law, the New York court asked, why couldn't it displace every other aspect of property law, including the right of the wealthy to accumulate and use more wealth?

> Many persons have more property than they can use to advantage and many more find it impossible to get the means for a comfortable existence. If the legislature can say to an employer, "you must compensate your employee for an injury not caused by you or by your wealth," why can it not go further and say to the man of wealth, "you have more property than you need and your neighbor is so poor that he can barely subsist; in the interest of natural justice you must divide with your neighbor so that he and his dependents shall not become a charge upon the State?"

The Supreme Court had already rejected this view of workers' compensation statutes when it decided the cedar tree case. The responsibility for workplace accidents was not inherent in the job; it resulted from government choices defining property rights and could be allocated by the government to whomever government thought best suited to bear it.

Once government was seen everywhere, even in the ordinary exercise of purely private property rights, previous understandings of the Constitution were undermined. Under the cedar tree decision, for example, government was responsible for *outcomes,* not merely for processes.

The implications of that position are indeed unsettling. Today many would respond with a bored "So what?" to the New York court's observation that the principle justifying legislative shifts of responsibility for accidents—that the background rules of property can themselves be changed by the legislature—would also justify taking property from the rich to give to the poor. After all, to say that the Constitution permits legislatures to do some things is not to say that they certainly will do them, or that it would be a good thing if they did.

Consider, however, the implications of Justice Stone's statement that "it would have been none the less a choice if . . . the state, by doing nothing, had permitted serious injury." By saying that "doing nothing" is "permitting" injury, Stone eliminated the possibility that the Constitution could constrain *any* government action—or, alternatively, established the proposition that the Constitution determines in detail what government *must* do. Let us consider the latter point first. The Constitution bars states from "deny[ing] any person . . . the equal protection of the laws." The Equal Protection Clause was adopted after the Civil War and clearly has something to do with barring governments from engaging in racial discrimination. What about private discrimination, however? Under Stone's formulation, if a state fails to enact a comprehensive civil rights statute, that is "none the less a choice," a "doing nothing" that permits a serious injury to flow from the exercise of the private property rights that the state itself has created. More generally, under the "none the less a choice" understanding, every constitutional provision that purports to limit government power—which is to say, almost every constitutional provision—actually *mandates* the exercise of government power.

The alternative is no less disturbing. In the cedar tree case, the implication of the "none the less a choice" understanding was that the Constitution imposed no limits on the government's action. Against the New York court's fear, this seems reasonable enough: Legislatures can adopt laws taking wealth from the rich to give to the poor, if they want to. (But what about the claim that giving the wealthy the right to use their wealth however they wish is "none the less a choice" that violates the principles of equality embedded in the equal protection clause?)

However, let us again consider race discrimination. In a famous argument, Columbia University law professor Herbert Wechsler raised questions about *Brown v. Board of Education,* the Supreme Court decision holding segregated education unconstitutional. Imagine that, without a segregation statute, public schools would be operated as neighborhood schools, with the degree of racial integration depending on the degree of integration in each neighborhood. Imagine, too, that a majority of a state's white people believe that they suffer an injury when they associate with African-Americans, and they persuade the state legislature to enact a segregation statute.

Under the cedar tree case, the constitutional ban on uncompensated takings was not violated when the legislature decided that the apple growers did indeed suffer a serious injury. Either the apple growers would be hurt or the cedar tree owners would, and the legislature could choose which group it wanted to suffer. Why, Wechsler asked, was segregation different? Of course African-Americans would be hurt by segregation, but whites apparently believed that they would be hurt by integration. If the legislature could choose whom to hurt in the cedar tree case, why couldn't it choose whom to hurt in the segregation case?

As we will see, scholars later developed responses to Wechsler, although we argue that the responses were not completely effective. For now, our point is only that the "none the less a choice" understanding forces constitutional law into a new mold. Without that understanding, lawyers could find neutral premises for constitutional analysis in the background of judge-made property law or in a notion of what the laws of nature require. With it, we need something else. For several generations judges and scholars have struggled to come up with the alternative. They have failed.

Justice Stone's analysis in the cedar tree case was part of a more general development in early twentieth-century legal thought called American legal realism.[1] The legal realists reacted against two trends in legal thought, which they believed to be related. First, they criticized existing legal theory as excessively "formalistic." According to the realists, formalism specified some quite general abstract principles, such as freedom of contract and liability based solely on fault for accidents, and then deduced particular results from those principles, such as the proposition that workers' compensation statutes violated the fault principle.[2] Formalists disagreed over the ultimate source of the fundamental princi-

1. There is a different school of legal realism associated with Scandinavian legal thinkers.

2. And, incidentally, freedom of contract as well, because the statute prohibited workers and employers from agreeing to let workers bear the costs of injury.

ples—some found them in natural law, others in the traditions of the American people—but they agreed, so the realists said, on what those principles were.

Second, the legal realists criticized existing law because it was, in their view, too conservative. As realist thought developed, so did the Progressive movement in American political life, and most realists supported the Progressive agenda. They saw courts throughout the country invoking "freedom of contract" and "fault-based liability" as slogans to interfere with Progressive reforms such as workers' compensation, minimum wage and maximum hour laws, and collective bargaining by unionized workers.

The realists connected the two branches of their critique of existing law through their challenge to formalism. The challenge itself had two branches. First, the realists challenged assertions that the formalists' abstract principles were actually fundamental in American law. Against claims that the principles were rooted in natural law, the realists pointed out that the American people were deeply divided over what natural law and justice required. Against claims that the principles were founded in the American tradition, the realists insisted that the actual traditions of the American people were far more complex and accommodated principles that justified Progressive-Era reforms.

Second, and more deeply, the realists challenged the argument that particular results followed inexorably, by the rules of logic, from the specified principles. Even if "freedom of contract" were the ruling principle, the realists argued, judges had to have a firm understanding of what that principle meant before they could deduce anything from it. For example, even the most fervent adherents of freedom of contract agreed that contracts made under coercion, or through fraud, should not be enforced. But, the realists argued, once one starts to analyze the concept of coercion, alternative visions of social organization became obvious. Was a worker "coerced" into taking a risky job if no other jobs were readily available? If the answer was yes, many progressive reforms could fit into the "freedom of contract" principle. If the answer was no, the realists insisted that adherents of that principle explain in more detail what their concept of coercion was and why anyone should find it attractive. For the realists, whatever fundamental principles lay at the heart of the legal system were inevitably complex, and once their complexity was understood, no particular results could be "deduced" from them.

With this understanding of the law, the realists concluded that attacks on workers' compensation laws as inconsistent with fundamental principles had to be "merely" political. Their opponents presented conclusions as if they followed from agreed-upon premises. But the premises were contestable, and the conclusions did not really derive from the principles that their conservative opponents asserted. The only explanation for their opponents' claims that the realists could come up with was that they were disguising their conservative political beliefs behind the rhetoric of "the rule of law." The realists insisted on penetrating that rhetoric to see the real political aspects of the law.

In this phase of their argument the realists introduced the ordinary language of politics into legal analysis. By now we are all familiar with this vocabulary: We know that saying that Supreme Court justices are "conservative" or "liberal" means that they will vote for results that are roughly what conservative Republicans or liberal Democrats would vote for in Congress.

Familiar though the language is, however, it conceals an ambivalence that many realists themselves felt. They wanted to say that their opponents' positions were merely political, but they often wanted to claim something more for their own. The realists' ambivalence was exacerbated when many of them moved into administrative and legal positions during the New Deal. They wanted to claim that New Deal programs were somehow "above" the politics they had criticized, but their critical tools could be just as easily turned against them. Once the academic theory that was legal realism became embedded in the political program of those who led the nation, something had to happen.

We believe that the escalation in constitutional rhetoric discussed in chapter 1 results at least in part from the fact that today's legal thinkers know that they need something from outside law to justify their positions, and know as well that—because of the "none the less a choice" understanding—they will never find it. The alternative to the unconvincing formalism debunked by the legal realists is a nihilism that people exercising power in the United States are unlikely to find at all attractive.

Justice Stone's analysis of the cedar tree case was influenced by legal realism. The cedar tree owners relied on the fundamental principle of private property, which they correctly thought protected by the Constitution's ban on takings without compensation. Stone asked, however, what exactly *was* private property?

According to one view, it was a social institution designed to make sure that people were better off because they could use their property in the most productive way. The validity of Virginia's statute followed almost directly if one held that view, for, as Stone said, the people of Virginia, acting through their legislature, were in a better position to decide what made them all better off than were federal judges. According to another view, private property was an expression of individualism. But, Stone knew, society had always regulated private property to some extent—private owners could not use their property in ways that caused "public nuisances," for example. For Stone, the only way to understand the real-world institution of private property was to see the background law of property as always subject to social regulation. Even worse, if private property was an expression of individualism, the Court still had to decide *which* individual's rights to protect: the cedar tree owners' or the apple growers'? And, again, once the Court saw things that way, Virginia's statute would have to be constitutional.

Eventually this analysis threatened the ideal of the rule of law to which Stone and the realists were committed. The problem was that, without some fundamental principles on which the rule of law rested, no one could be confident that social policy represented anything more than the mere imposition of one group's power. Indeed, the realists' political criticism of conservative law took exactly that form: What the conservatives said were expressions of principle were actually—so the realists said—assertions of the power of the wealthy.

There was one apparent stopping point to the slide from law into politics. Recall that New York's highest court had to treat the principle of fault-based liability as fundamental to justify its invalidation of the state's workers' compensation statute. Yet, although it is relatively easy to find language in the Constitution making private property fundamental, it is almost impossible to find similar language about fault-based liability. It might have seemed, therefore, that the realist challenge could be sustained simply by acknowledging that legislatures had full power to modify the judge-made common law unless some relatively specific constitutional language stood in their way. As Progressive reformers, the realists believed that most of their agenda did not run up against such specific language.

This move had the advantage of accommodating the realist criticisms of formalism—which the realists had developed in connection with assertions about judge-made common law—to the Progressive agenda. It could not permanently salvage the rule of law from the realist critique, however.

The problem lay in the realists' attempt to preserve *some* domain for constitutional law by assuming that courts could enforce specific limitations on legislative power. Identifying constitutional provisions as specific and spelling out what they mean, however, requires a choice of baselines. Why is the Free Speech Clause more specific than the Due Process Clause, for example? Why should the entitlement conferred by the Free Speech Clause be treated as a baseline when the entitlements conferred by the common law are not? The entire notion of constitutional rights seems to require some idea of a background entitlement—the neutral premises found outside constitutional law, which conservatives call private property—that legislatures cannot displace. Once the realists showed that background entitlements were always open to redefinition, they could not readily defend the proposition that the Constitution protected transcendent individual rights.

On a less elevated plane, but probably one more important for public understanding of constitutional law, once the realists criticized their adversaries for being "conservative" and "merely political," people began to think about law in general in such political terms. An early warning of the problem was Charles Beard's notorious interpretation of the Constitution itself as designed to protect the interests of the wealthy. Some realists would say that judges had turned the Constitution into a conservative document; Beard argued that it was conservative from the beginning. As the language of politics pervaded discussions of the Constitution, it became natural for people to treat the realists and their Progressive allies as "liberals" in the same sense that the realists called their opponents "conservatives." Some realists might have believed that a traditional notion of law as distinct from politics could be salvaged, perhaps by relying on constitutional law. Their rhetoric, however, made it easy to reduce all law to politics.

Realism's jurisprudence converged with political developments in the 1930s. For several decades realism had been the language used by legal scholars to criticize conservative Supreme Court decisions. When President Franklin Roosevelt advanced the Progressive agenda through the New Deal's responses to the Great Depression, the Supreme Court seemed to stand in the way. In a series of decisions the Court reverted to a formalist understanding of the limits on government power. It interpreted the scope of Congress's power narrowly, threatening New Deal legislation designed to advance unionization. It invalidated state minimum wage and maximum hours laws, which Progressives continued to regard as essential to improving social welfare. The rest of the story is well known. After the 1936 elections endorsed the New Deal, Roosevelt proposed a "Court-packing plan" that would have allowed him to appoint enough new justices to ensure that the Court would uphold his programs. Although Congress rejected the Court-packing plan, the Court understood the lesson, and in decisions beginning in 1937 it rejected the formalism that it had only recently accepted.

The transformation of constitutional law during the New Deal was eased because the realist jurisprudence that provided its foundation was already in place. Indeed, as the cedar tree case shows, some of the Court's decisions had already accepted realism's premises before 1937. Realism's triumph, however complete, nonetheless left constitutional law in an unsatisfactory state. In particular, realism made the distinction between law and politics problematic, and the New Deal transformation of constitutional law did nothing to solve that problem. The Court replaced the conservative *content* of constitutional law with a progressive one, but within the realist framework, that simply meant that the politics of constitutional law had changed, not that law had replaced politics.

The realists needed a strategy to save law from politics. Sometimes, of course, politics—understood now to mean no more than the sheer imposition of power by one group against another—was a perfectly acceptable means of making the choices realists saw everywhere. Few realists, however, were prepared to give up entirely on a domain of law insulated from politics. Figuring out when sheer politics could rule and when something else had to be the basis for choice proved difficult. Moreover, even if these areas could somehow be sorted out, the realists still had to explain what that "something else" might be.

For a while, some realists thought they had found the "something else" in what they called "policy." Rather than the assertion of power, policy was the application of scientifically informed judgment to problems of social life. Justice Oliver Wendell Holmes wrote in 1897 that the lawyer of the future "is the man of statistics and the master of economics," and the realists took Holmes's prediction to heart. Lawyers, including judges, who immersed themselves in social science could devise solutions to social problems that transcended politics because they were expressions of reason and science rather than power.

The realists' attempt to substitute science for politics in lawmaking never really took hold. In many ways the effort reproduced the defects of the formalism the realists had criticized. For example, policy-oriented realists sometimes tried to identify the policies lawmakers should pursue, but their lists were pitched on a highly abstract level, just as formalists' concepts had been. The policy-oriented realists never adequately connected those high-level abstractions to particular policies in a "scientific" way. Their conclusions, therefore, seemed to reflect their "merely political" preferences, not their scientific deductions. The policy-oriented realists made some headway in the 1950s and 1960s, but—at least it seems today—only because that was the era social scientists have identified with achieving a particular ideological consensus on the wisdom of New Deal and Progressive policies. When that consensus dissolved, assaulted from the Left in the 1960s and 1970s and from the Right in the 1980s, the pretension that policy analysis could eliminate politics from lawmaking also disappeared.

The policy science approach to law suffered from another difficulty. The realists' political criticism of the conservative Supreme Court was that the Court denied the people of the country, acting through the democratic process, the power to do what they wanted. Law as policy science, however, was equally undemocratic: The technocratic language of science replaced the elitist language of conservatism, but truly popular participation in lawmaking was denied in both versions.

We have already mentioned another technique for restricting the domain of politics. Individual rights, it was said, had to be determined by law, while politics could determine economic matters. This allocation solved the immediate problem facing realists during the New Deal because they found it easy to describe New Deal programs as implicating economic matters and not individual rights. For them, the consequence was that the Old Court's approach, seeking legal constraints on public power, was simply misplaced.

Events rapidly overtook this solution, however. The reconstituted Supreme Court soon had to face questions about the regulation of picketing by labor unions. Some New Deal judges thought that picketing was similar to traditional political demonstrations and therefore ought to be protected as an individual right through the Free Speech Clause of the First Amendment. Other New Deal judges argued that the point of labor picketing was quintessentially economic and that picketing could therefore be regulated by political decisions.

The Court stumbled its way through this particular area, but its difficulties foreshadowed even more serious ones that arose as the scope of the welfare state gradually expanded. By the 1960s public assistance to the poor had become an important component of government activities. Previously seen as a substitute for private charity, public assistance began to be reconceived as an individual right. After all, according to good legal realist thinking, the poverty of those receiving public assistance resulted from the macroeconomic choices made by the public as well as from broadened definitions of private property rights. And, if the wealthy had a "right" to their property—which, again, resulted from public choices—so should the poor have a right to assistance. Once again, the line between individual rights and economic rights became obscure.

The New Deal solution of allocating politics to one domain and law to another had deeper problems, as well. It merely deferred the difficulty of distinguishing law from politics within the domain of individual rights. Many scholars have devoted careers to explaining how the courts can develop and apply legal standards to limit the government's choices in the area of individual rights, and just as many others have devoted careers to explaining why the proposed solutions fail. We will not rehearse the solutions and criticisms in detail here, although in later chapters we will scrutinize some aspects of these controversies. Instead, we offer an introductory overview of several solutions to which people have been attracted.

Recall that the problem is to identify lawlike constraints on the government's choices so that courts can confidently say that they are acting differently from legislatures, which are merely political bodies. Probably the most obvious constraints are the *words* of the Constitution themselves, understood in light of the meaning given to them at the time they were written. Legislatures might reflect the political preferences of popular majorities, but courts enforcing the Constitution's terms would be enforcing law.

If the Constitution's words are not enough, perhaps the courts could step back from day-to-day politics and say that it does not matter what choices the government makes so long as the *processes* by which it chooses are fair. So, for example, the Court's decision invalidating school segregation might be defended on the ground that African-Americans had been barred from voting in the states that had segregation. Similarly, statutes limiting free speech might be questionable because they deprive the public of information it might find useful in deciding what choices it wants its representatives to make.

Third, constitutional law might place *substantive* limits on the government's choices. The Constitution, it would be said, aims at securing justice. If segregation is unjust, for example because it perpetuates a regime of racial hierarchy, it might be unconstitutional—even if the words of the Constitution do not explicitly invalidate it and even if African-Americans had simply been outvoted when segregation statutes were adopted (or had been unsuccessful in their legislative attempts to get those statutes repealed).

Finally, constitutional law might be "law" rather than politics simply because courts offer *reasons* for what they do, while legislatures can act on the basis of what the majority wants without considering its reasons for having those desires.

Offering one-paragraph criticisms of these ways of ensuring the "lawness" of constitutional law would come close to parody. Scholars have developed standard responses to each argument, and proponents of the arguments have responded in turn. For our purposes, only two points need be made.

First, the "none the less a choice" understanding makes every proposed solution problematic. If the text protects property, it turns out that every government action destroys someone's property. In general, in determining what the text means, a government official is making a choice, which helps some and hurts others. The procedures a government follows lead to substantive results, and where the results would have been different had a different procedure been followed, the government, having chosen its procedure, is responsible for the outcome. Procedure, that is, cannot be disentangled from substance. Defining which substantive individual rights to protect also involves choices, as Wechsler's argument made clear.

Second, the arguments about how to interpret the Constitution have to be developed in detail to meet obvious criticisms. As they are fleshed out in the face of criticism, they become complicated enough that they simultaneously are drained of much of their initial appeal and become more readily characterized as efforts to dress up political preferences in the language of law.

Consider, for example, one common question raised about textualism (or, in some versions, an "original intent" approach to constitutional interpretation). The framers and ratifiers of the Constitution, this objection goes, were faced with a particular set of problems about governing their society. The Constitution they wrote—the words they used—were suitable, in their view, to deal with those problems and others they would have understood to be comparable. Today's problems, and today's society, are very different, however. How can we know what the framers and ratifiers would have thought about developments that they could not have anticipated and might have regarded with some distaste? The usual example is wiretapping, but as our discussion of Judge Bork's position in chapter 1 indicated, the problem also arises in connection with such matters as changes in social judgments about the appropriate relationship between men and women.

Like Judge Bork, defenders of text-based (and text-limited) interpretation typically respond that the Constitution's words were designed to address some generic *types* of problems. If the modern problem falls within the class the framers and ratifiers addressed, the Constitution "applies." If it does not, the Constitution leaves the matter to political choice. By moving to this higher level of generality, however, the argument already abandons the words of the Constitution, treating them as examples of some higher purpose that the framers and ratifiers sought to achieve.

Finally, identifying that higher purpose is inevitably controversial. Consider the wiretapping case, which is said to fall within the category of concern for privacy in the home that is addressed by the ban on unreasonable searches. If that is the higher purpose of the ban, however, why don't the words of the Constitution also protect the use of contraceptives in the home? One might respond that the constitutional ban on unreasonable searches addresses intrusions on what we might call informational privacy (and that wiretapping similarly violates informational privacy), while the prohibition of contraceptive use intrudes on a different aspect of privacy. But although many have tried, no one has yet come up with a compelling explanation of why we should move away from the words of the Constitution to one rather than to another level of generality.

Without such an explanation, in attempting to respond to an intuition that the Constitution ought to address an obvious modern problem such as wiretapping, the text-based approaches move to a higher level of generality. In doing so, they open up the possibility that the Constitution addresses the more controversial problem of a government ban on contraception.

Similar difficulties arise in connection with all the other approaches to constitutional interpretation. It is easy to agree, for example, that the Constitution ensures that politics be conducted according to fair procedures. What, however, *are* those procedures? Do restrictions on the financing of political campaigns enhance or impair the fairness of the election process? Suppose we learn that apparently fair procedures systematically generate results that trouble us: Legislation that adversely affects the interests of racial minorities might be enacted even if the election process were completely open, and yet such legislation might be thought to contribute to the continued racial subordination of those minorities. Are the procedures ''fair'' nonetheless, or need we search for defects in the procedures that we think will ''explain'' why the bad results occurred?[3]

Alternatively, if we take a substantive approach to constitutional interpretation, we must determine exactly what ''justice'' requires. Perhaps it is possible to generate wide agreement on highly abstract principles of justice, but the very abstraction that makes agreement possible deprives the principles of much real use in practice. It is relatively easy, for example, to get people to agree that a system of racial subordination is unjust. That agreement, however, does not help resolve disputes over whether affirmative action programs tend to eliminate or perpetuate racial subordination.

Discussions of approaches to constitutional interpretation have a predictable course. Proponents of one approach claim that their approach alone serves to distinguish the lawlike aspects of constitutional law from the preference-driven character of politics. They support this claim by pointing to examples where their law-based approach would produce different results from those yielded by a preference-driven one. An original-intent theorist, for example, might argue that the Supreme Court's abortion decisions could not be justified on such a theory and that the decisions therefore rest on politics rather than law. In their initial presentations, this claim has some intuitive appeal.

The next step is taken by those who support the ''preference-driven'' result that has come under fire. These critics might point out some problems with the proposed theory. They might ask, for example, how an original-intent theory can apply the Fourth Amendment's ban on unreasonable searches and seizures to wiretapping or the Fourteenth

3. According to one view, this was the shoal on which Lani Guinier's nomination foundered. Her scholarly articles proposed procedural solutions because of perceived substantive problems, and, because the procedural solutions she offered were manifestly inadequate to the task of eliminating the substantive problems, her critics readily—and erroneously—concluded that she actually had a more radical hidden agenda.

Amendment's Equal Protection Clause to school segregation. The proponents might reply by elaborating on their theory. As we have seen, they could say that wiretapping is a modern version of the *type* of problem to which the Fourth Amendment is addressed and that the Fourteenth Amendment was concerned with establishing racial equality in light of accurate factual information about how segregation operates.

At this point, the critics have two options. First, they can point out that exactly the same moves—to a higher level of generality or to an invocation of social facts—can justify the purportedly lawless result they support, all within the initial lawlike theory. Defenders of the Court's abortion decisions, for example, might argue that the Fourteenth Amendment, understood at an appropriate level of generality, was designed to secure equality on the basis of gender as well as race (as indeed Judge Bork came to argue) and that an accurate understanding of social reality demonstrates that freedom of choice with respect to abortion is essential to secure women's equal citizenship (as Judge Bork did not argue).[4]

Alternatively, critics of particular constitutional theories can argue that the elaborate theory, with all its gewgaws and special rules for special cases, no longer has much intuitive appeal. The Ptolemaic theory that the sun and planets revolved around the earth may have been simple and appealing. Once it was made more complicated to deal with uncomfortable facts, it became clear that what was going on was an effort to save the theory. Similarly in constitutional law: In response to criticism, simple theories become elaborate, to the point where it becomes clear that they are just as preference-driven as those criticized by their proponents.

As we will demonstrate in later chapters, we do not level these charges merely against original-intent theories. They can be brought against any of the general approaches to constitutional law we discuss. We think it will become apparent that what drives constitutional analysis is not some abstract concern about ensuring that constitutional law be law but a particular set of policy preferences that cannot be distinguished from the preferences expressed in other political forums.

4. Our aim here is not to provide the full-scale argument on these matters but only to sketch how the abortion decisions might be defended within an original-intent approach that has been elaborated to deal with the problems of wiretapping and school segregation.

We are hardly the first observers to notice that the changes in legal thought associated with the New Deal created problems for constitutionalism. After the Warren Court restored the good name of active judicial review, many scholars have tried to justify such activism while also taking into account the critique the realists advanced. Two of these efforts, embodied in the work of Cass Sunstein and Bruce Ackerman, are especially instructive. Both Ackerman and Sunstein recognize the destabilizing potential of legal realism, but they also attempt to preserve the possibility of a postrealist constitutional discourse separate from politics. The similarities between these works and ours mean that highlighting the differences will bring our arguments into sharp relief. For, although the efforts of Sunstein and Ackerman are provocative, each ultimately promises more than it delivers and each in a different way threatens to reproduce the problems of constitutional discourse that it is designed to escape.

Sunstein describes a constitutional revolution of 1937, when the Supreme Court came to understand that it could not use the common law as a baseline for measuring whether legislatures had made a choice. He also points out that similar problems attend many common understandings of constitutional rights. Many arguments, he points out, criticize legislation as improperly departing from the neutrality that we should desire but fail to note that the criticism implicitly takes the status quo as embodying a desirable neutrality.

Sunstein acutely identifies the problems with modern constitutionalism, but we believe that the difficulties he discusses go deeper than his presentation suggests.[5] Sunstein offers two interlocked solutions to the problems of modern constitutionalism. First, he suggests, the real difficulty with constitutional neutrality is not the aspiration to neutrality but the erroneous identification of neutral baselines. If we could come up with the proper baselines, we would be able to identify laws that really were impermissible departures from neutrality. In this argument Sunstein echoes one aspect of the legal realists' challenge to "conservative" constitutional law; like them, he would substitute correct baselines for erroneous ones.

Sunstein's second suggestion builds on a version of process-oriented approaches to law. After World War II, legal scholars led by the Har-

5. We have emphasized legal realism instead of referring to a "revolution of 1937" in part to suggest that these problems could not be solved by the Supreme Court's post-1937 approach to constitutional law.

vard law professors Henry Hart and Albert Sacks developed what they called the "legal process" theory of law, which we discuss at greater length in chapter 8. Acknowledging that it had proved impossible to develop substantive legal rules on which everyone could agree, Hart and Sacks argued that if legal scholars moved to a higher, more procedural level, they could gain agreement on which institutions should decide which questions. So, for example, they argued that legislatures were better than courts at investigating complex social problems and devising solutions that responded appropriately to that complexity. The idea that legislatures should deal with economic issues and courts with individual rights is a pale shadow of these legal process concerns.

As we have argued, the "none the less a choice" perspective makes it impossible to sustain that particular distinction and, with it, the distinction between law and politics. Sunstein transforms the legal process approach by arguing that although both courts and legislatures have a constitutional duty to ensure that the social order actually respects appropriate baselines, courts often lack the institutional capacity to perform this function effectively. It follows that legislatures, like courts, must sometimes transcend politics and be guided by law.

This aspect of Sunstein's argument avoids one problem with the legal process response to the legal realist challenge. It does not, however, address the deeper issues raised by legal realism. Sunstein insists that legislatures must be guided by law, but the realists had argued that the entire idea of being guided by law was misconceived. Even courts could not be so guided; how could legislatures? Furthermore, if recent experience is any guide, the constitutionalized politics Sunstein advocates would likely consist of people confronting each other in the Constitution's name, rather than working together to achieve the common good.

Sunstein understands the problem, but his responses are in the form of intellectual IOUs: He is confident that reasons *could be* developed to support the baselines he thinks appropriate, but he never actually develops the reasons in much detail. The upshot is that the reader is left with the concern that his baselines, like those of his pre-1937 adversaries, are generated by political preferences.

As we have suggested, and argue in more detail in chapter 9, we have no quarrel with the underlying position Sunstein takes on what philosophers call the metaethical question of whether there are morally appropriate or required norms. Our concern is narrower: Modern constitutional argument, including Sunstein's, has done little to convince others of the moral necessity of the particular norms favored by the advocate. Until Sunstein actually provides the reasons supporting his preferred baselines, we remain skeptical about his solution.

Ackerman, too, has offered a program for adjudication after the New Deal revolution. His argument on this point is embedded in a complex effort to explain why courts can properly invoke the Constitution to override the wishes of today's political majority. Briefly put, Ackerman distinguishes between normal politics, which produces the laws subject to judicial review, and what he calls constitutional moments, periods when the public has an intensified concern about fundamental aspects of the social order, comes to a profound judgment about how to organize society and its government, and embeds that judgment in the Constitution. When the courts invalidate statutes produced during periods of normal politics, they are acting in the name of "the people" who themselves acted in a constitutional moment. Because the people have a heightened constitutional consciousness during such moments, judgments reached at such times should be given greater weight than those arrived at during periods of ordinary politics.

For Ackerman, the judgments made during constitutional moments go beyond the words of individual constitutional amendments. He asserts that the Reconstruction amendments adopted after the Civil War embodied a judgment about the importance of national power in preserving individual liberty, not just a series of discrete judgments about the status and rights of African-Americans. Most dramatically, Ackerman treats the New Deal as a constitutional moment that validated the expansive exercise of government power comprehensively, even though that judgment was not embodied in any constitutional amendment.

Finally, Ackerman argues, the Supreme Court's task is to construct a coherent constitutional narrative, one that assembles all the constitutional moments into an account of the government we have now. After the New Deal constitutional moment, the Court had to reconcile the expansion of government power with the preservation of individual liberty that was the accomplishment of the Reconstruction amendments.

Ackerman's general account of constitutionalism is promising, but at least as articulated so far, his approach fails to solve the problems that legal realism identified. There are two overlapping difficulties. First, the impoverishment of constitutional discourse in the modern period has brought the possibility of creating a constitutional moment into question. Ackerman believes that sustained and contentious popular reflection on fundamental values characterizes constitutional moments and that the nature and quality of that reflection justifies overriding the views of today's majorities. Perhaps Ackerman has accurately described past constitutional moments, but unless the vocabulary of constitutional discourse is somehow reconstructed, constitutionalizing our politics under modern conditions is likely to produce no more than a shouting match.

Ackerman might concur. He need not be understood as recommending that now is a good time for another constitutional moment. He might be troubled, however, by the possibility that the nature of contemporary constitutional discourse forecloses the possibility of our living through another constititutional moment. Paradoxically, the exercise of judicial review that Ackerman commends provokes the contentiousness of today's constitutional discourse and reduces the possibility that we could have a constitutional moment again.

This problem is exacerbated by a second feature of Ackerman's argument: What Ackerman provides looks more like a menu of political positions he favors than a worked-out account of why those positions are legally obligatory.[6]

For Ackerman, as for Sunstein, the revolution of 1937 eliminated easy recourse to common-law baselines to define the sphere of individual liberty. According to Ackerman, the Court since then has had the task of working out the proper domain of individual liberty in a world where exercises of expansive government power are generally valid.

Ackerman provides two sketchy examples of how the Court performed that task well, and they are not encouraging. He argues that *Brown v. Board of Education* should be understood as the Court's reconciliation of the activist post–New Deal state with the principles endorsed during Reconstruction. There is nothing remarkable about invoking the principles of Reconstruction to explain *Brown*. Nor, in one sense, is it hard to see the activist state at work. Ackerman points out that the Supreme Court, in upholding a state law mandating segregation in railways and streetcars in *Plessy v. Ferguson* (1896), argued that we could see "enforced separation of the two races" as "stamp[ing] the colored race with a badge of inferiority . . . solely because the colored race choses [*sic*] to put that construction upon it." But, Ackerman argues,

6. We note as well the difficulty of identifying when a constitutional moment has occurred. Ackerman develops an elaborate set of criteria to do so, but his account seems clearly gerrymandered to ensure that the New Deal was a constitutional moment and the so-called Reagan Revolution was not.

after the New Deal we must see the government everywhere, and segregation's interpretation as a badge of inferiority cannot be treated solely as a matter of individual choice.

The difficulty with this argument is that it overlooks the potential role of the market in promoting equality. The streetcar owners were perfectly happy to maintain unsegregated cars; they were forced to segregate by law. Their market-driven decisions were, in this sense, consistent with the equality principles of the Reconstruction period. In repudiating the naturalness of the market, New Deal constitutionalism took away that defense of equality. Because he sees government implicated everywhere, Ackerman must come up with some alternative defense.[7]

He attempts to do so by describing the Court's development of a jurisprudence of constitutional privacy, culminating in the abortion decisions. The original Constitution sought to promote individual liberty by preserving a domain defined by common-law rights of property and contract. New Deal constitutionalism eliminated property and contract as the way to define a domain of individual liberty. But, Ackerman suggests, the jurisprudence of privacy may "provide *us* with the most meaningful way of preserving these Founding affirmations of liberty in an activist welfare state."

There are several difficulties here. As we discuss in more detail in chapter 3, exploitation and domination occur in *any* private domain, not only the domain of the market. If New Deal constitutionalism was designed to allow the government to respond to exploitation, it will not do to displace the area in which such exploitation occurs from the market to some other private sphere.

Perhaps more important, there is no guarantee that the jurisprudence of privacy provides the best means of protecting liberty. The Court's approach therefore can be justified only by some substantive argument for privacy that Ackerman does not provide. Ackerman has published only the first of a projected three volumes laying out his approach, and perhaps the substantive argument will eventually come forward. But in treating New Deal constitutionalism merely as a repudiation of the naturalness of the market, Ackerman may be developing only the legal realists' attack on prior law as enforcing a bad set of policy choices. He

7. Our discussion takes Ackerman as attempting to justify the Court's actions. He might be attempting only to explain why the Court acted as it did. In that case, however, more standard explanations, for example treating the Court as a political actor, seem far more plausible.

has not yet confronted the deeper challenge posed by the legal realists, which undermined confidence that anyone could produce the kind of substantive argument needed to justify a jurisprudence of privacy.

As the examples of Ackerman and Sunstein illustrate, all of us are the heirs of the New Deal transformation and its realist jurisprudence. We believe that we need a Constitution to ensure that in appropriate domains—"individual rights"—political majorities will be unable simply to assert the power of numbers. They must adhere to fundamental law, rather than merely exercise power. The realist critiques have gone deep enough, however, that we always are unsure about how to distinguish between law and politics. Even more, the political dimension of realism has given us the vocabulary to express our uncertainty: Whenever someone asserts that a particular result is required by the Constitution, we know that critics will find it easy to claim that the result is merely the reflection of a political preference. The degree to which that claim is found to be persuasive will depend not on the underlying analysis but on listeners' prior agreement or disagreement with the political views at stake.

Our legacy, in other words, is a dialogue in which one side insists that it has the law on its side and that its opponents are advancing merely political views, whereas the other side responds in the same terms, simply switching the allegation of base political motives and claiming for itself the mantle of disinterested law. At present we appear to have no resources to break out of this unproductive discussion.

In the remainder of this book we try to work out some implications of this analysis. Chapters 3 and 4 show how the "none the less a choice" understanding and the collapse of the distinction between law and politics affect two fundamental building blocks of contemporary constitutional analysis: the distinction between public and private action and the distinction between free choice and coercion. Chapters 5 through 8 work out the implications by examining specific constitutional disputes.

3

The State Action Paradox

In Joshua DeShaney's first year of life, his parents divorced, and a court granted custody of the infant to his father, Randy DeShaney. For the next four years, the child lived through a nightmare of pain and violence. Randy DeShaney beat his son repeatedly and with increasing savagery. Eventually, the toddler fell into a life-threatening coma, and emergency brain surgery revealed injuries, inflicted over an extended period, that left Joshua permanently and severely retarded.

As these tragic events unfolded, many of them came to the attention of county officials in the Wisconsin community where the DeShaneys lived. A battery of judges, lawyers, pediatricians, psychologists, police officers, and social workers became involved in Joshua's case. With Kafkaesque efficiency, these functionaries performed their particular assigned task within the social welfare bureaucracy. They held hearings, filed reports, completed forms. Yet despite all the purposeful bustling and the show of activity and concern, no one actually intervened to stop the violence until it was too late.

After the damage had already been done, Joshua and his mother filed an action against the county in United States District Court. They argued that county officials had deprived Joshua of his liberty without due process of law, thereby violating his rights under the Fourteenth Amendment.

If government officials had beaten Joshua themselves, his suit—even against their employers—might well have succeeded. Supreme Court decisions have made it clear that government agents who unjustifiably inflict physical injury violate the Due Process Clause. But because Joshua and his mother could not claim that the injury was directly inflicted by state officials, the suit foundered on the so-called ''state action'' requirement. As Chief Justice William Rehnquist explained when the case reached the Supreme Court,

> [N]othing in the language of the Due Process Clause . . . requires the State to protect the life, liberty, and property of its citizens against invasion by private actors. The Clause is phrased as a limitation on the State's power to act, not as a guarantee of certain minimal levels of safety and security. It forbids the State itself to deprive individuals of life, liberty, or property without ''due process of law,'' but its language cannot fairly be extended to impose an affirmative obligation on the State to ensure that those interests do not come to harm through other means (*DeShaney v. Winnebago County Dept. of Social Services,* 1989).

The Court's decision prompted two sharply worded dissents. Justice William Brennan accused the majority of fundamentally mischaracterizing the issue. The question, he insisted, was not whether ''as a general matter, the Constitution safeguards positive as well as negative liberties.'' The focus should be ''on the action that Wisconsin *has* taken with respect to Joshua and children like him, rather than on the actions that the State failed to take.'' As Justice Brennan explained, Wisconsin had established an elaborate social welfare bureaucracy, and people could reasonably expect it to respond to child abuse.

> In these circumstances, a private citizen, or even a person working in a government agency other than [the Department of Social Services] would doubtless feel that her job was done as soon as she reported her suspicions of child abuse to [the Department]. . . . Conceivably, then, children like Joshua are made worse off by the existence of this program when the persons and entities charged with carrying it out fail to do their jobs.

In a separate dissent Justice Harry Blackmun accused the majority of ''sterile formalism'' reminiscent of that of the antebellum judges who justified slavery. Blackmun argued that existing precedent concerning the state action problem ''could be read more broadly or narrowly depending upon how one chooses to read them. Faced with the choice, I would adopt a 'sympathetic' reading, one which comports with dictates of fundamental justice and recognizes that compassion need not be exiled from the province of judging.'' In an extraordinary final paragraph to his opinion, Justice Blackmun lamented Joshua DeShaney's fate:

> Poor Joshua! Victim of repeated attacks by an irresponsible, bullying, cowardly, and intemperate father, and abandoned by respondents who placed him in a dangerous predicament and who knew or learned what was going on, and yet did essentially nothing except, as the Court revealing observes . . . ''dutifully recorded these incidents in [their] files.'' It is a sad commentary upon American life, and constitutional principles—so full of late of patriotic fervor and proud proclamations about ''liberty and justice for all'' that this child, Joshua DeShaney, now is assigned to live out the remainder of his life profoundly retarded.

It is not surprising that *DeShaney* sharply divided the Court. In recent years, ''liberal'' and ''conservative'' justices have repeatedly clashed over the scope and the nature of the state action requirement. A technical and confused doctrine, the state action requirement has fundamental importance because of its ''gateway'' function. Much of the Court's work defines the scope and meaning of various constitutional protections such as freedom of speech and religion and the rights to equal protection and due process. But, according to the conventional view, the effort to define and apply constitutional rights need not even begin unless the complaining party first demonstrates that some government entity was responsible for the violation of her rights.[1] That is the state action requirement. It shields conduct from *any* constitutional scrutiny. As *DeShaney* itself demonstrates, even the most outrageous activity is simply outside the scope of the Constitution unless it is ''connected'' with the state.

For this reason, the state action requirement obviously obstructs the judicial enforcement of some rights. In this chapter, we argue for the less obvious proposition that some sort of state action doctrine also is a necessary prerequisite to the enforcement of rights: Without a private sphere in which individual decisions are not attributable to the government, the very concept of an individual right loses its meaning.

Some of the Court's confusion about the doctrine stems from this dual

1. The statement in text is subject to a minor qualification. The Court has held that the Thirteenth Amendment prohibition against slavery applies to private, as well as public, actors.

function served by the state action doctrine. But the doctrine is confused for another reason: The New Deal revolution made a state action doctrine necessary because without it, all decisions by the political branches would come under judicial control. Yet the revolution also made the doctrine unconvincing because it undermined the "naturalness" of the boundary between the public and the private upon which the state action inquiry depends.

Faced with nagging uncertainty about the content and the meaning of the state action doctrine, the justices have acted defensively. They have attempted to shore up the doctrine's weak foundations by vociferously insisting that the state action inquiry is easy. It is not. *DeShaney* is a hard case because determining the meaning of the state action requirement is hard. The weaknesses of the various *DeShaney* opinions eloquently, if inadvertently, testify to this fact. Our analysis of each opinion provides the building blocks for these arguments.

Consider, first, Chief Justice Rehnquist's opinion. It argues that the Fourteenth Amendment's language clearly makes it apply only to injuries inflicted by the state. This position is untenable.

Of course the command contained in the Fourteenth Amendment Due Process Clause is addressed to the government. The clause prohibits the *state* from depriving individuals of life, liberty, or property.[2] This verbal formulation is entirely consistent with the view that the state *is* inflicting such a deprivation when officials organize their activities so that people fall prey to private violence. In the most literal sense, the state deprived Joshua DeShaney of his liberty when its employees went about their work without stopping the attacks directed against him.

The Fourteenth Amendment's legislative history further weakens Chief Justice Rehnquist's position. The amendment's clear purpose was to expand the government's power to contend with private acts of violence. In the wake of the Civil War, Congress feared that the states of the

2. The Fourteenth Amendment Due Process Clause provides: "[N]or shall any State deprive any person of life, liberty, or property, without due process of law." Interestingly, the parallel Due Process Clause in the Fifth Amendment (which applies on the federal, rather than the state, level) contains no reference to government invasions of the right. The Fifth Amendment provides: "No person shall be . . . deprived of life, liberty, or property, without due process of law." Yet no one—least of all Chief Justice Rehnquist—has suggested that this difference in phrasing means that the Fifth Amendment clause applies to private conduct.

recently defeated Confederacy would not do enough to ensure the freedom of the newly liberated slaves. The Civil Rights Act of 1866 provided direct federal protection for the freedmen. Among other things, the act guaranteed all citizens "full and equal benefit of all laws and proceedings for the security of person and property as is enjoyed by white citizens." This provision was intended to provide positive protection through law against the private acts of violence and domination that were replacing the old slave system. As the Supreme Court wrote in its first decision interpreting the Fourteenth Amendment, Congress believed that the lives of African-Americans in the South "were at the mercy of bad men, either because the laws for their protection were insufficient or were not enforced" (*The Slaughter-House Cases,* 1873).

Fearing that the Supreme Court might overturn the 1866 Act on the ground that the federal government lacked constitutional authority to intervene in these traditionally state matters, Congress proposed the Fourteenth Amendment. It expanded national authority in order to prevent the reenslavement of African-Americans.

In light of this history, it is hardly surprising that the amendment has often been read to require "the State to protect [individuals] from each other," despite Chief Justice Rehnquist's contention. Indeed, even he concedes that the amendment would be violated if Wisconsin announced that it was henceforth no longer providing African-American children with protection from child abuse. Even though the state would be doing no more than failing to "protect [individuals] from each other," this failure would violate the central prohibition of the Fourteenth Amendment.

Of course, such a policy would involve overt racial discrimination—an issue closer to the core concern of the Reconstruction Congress than the problem raised by *DeShaney*. But the Court long ago rejected the view that the Fourteenth Amendment was directed solely at race discrimination. Consider, for example, *Nollan v. California Coastal Commission* (1987). In *Nollan,* the Court held that the Due Process Clause had been violated when the state created a public easement along a private beach without compensating the property owner for the invasion. Creating an easement sounds like "positive" state action, and the Court did not even pause to think about whether there was a "state action" problem in the case. In fact, a public easement simply withholds the protections against private invasions state trespass laws usually afford. The Court's holding thus rests on the proposition that the state may not withdraw ''normal'' property protections without first providing adequate compensation.[3]

If text and history fail to support the *DeShaney* decision, perhaps a moral or political theory could. The decision raises troubling questions about the moral and political significance of the distinction between nonfeasance (''not doing'') and misfeasance (''doing badly''). As used in *DeShaney,* the distinction gives peculiar incentives to state officials. Social workers now know that they are best off not doing their jobs: The less they do, the more likely they are to escape constitutional liability.

Even apart from these practical consequences, why, as a matter of principle, would a sensible constitution distinguish between actively bringing about bad results and passively allowing them to happen? Imagine that well-meaning but overzealous social worker Alice is horrified by Joshua's living conditions and immediately acts to remove him from his home without going to a judge. The misfeasance–nonfeasance distinction makes this ''positive action'' subject to due process restrictions, and the action may well be a constitutional violation. Yet, if sadistic and cruel social worker Bennett, realizing that Joshua's father is about to inflict serious injury on him that Bennett can easily prevent, nonetheless deliberately leaves him in the home because he would like to see Joshua dead, the Constitution does not speak to this ''mere failure to act.''

There may be a plausible political or moral theory to justify these results—we explore that question later in this chapter—but Chief Justice Rehnquist does not suggest it. If the Fourteenth Amendment's text or legislative history clearly mandated these outcomes, we would require no theory other than constitutional originalism to justify them. Because

3. Perhaps *Nollan* can be distinguished on the ground that when the state created the easement, it not only withdrew ''normal'' property protections previously enjoyed by the original owner but promised to provide such protections to the public if the original owner attempted to interfere with the easement. In contrast, the state's failure to intervene in *DeShaney* was not coupled with an immunization of parents against future legal action by their abused children. However, at the time of the *Nollan* decision, the state had taken no positive action to enforce the easement. Nothing in the *Nollan* opinion suggests that the result in that case turned on the implicit threat of future enforcement action if the original owner attempted to interfere with rights created by the easement. Moreover, in a different context, the Court, in an opinion by Justice Rehnquist, held that the mere announcement of a property right, without actual state enforcement efforts, does not constitute state action. See *Flagg Brothers v. Brooks* (1978). It is therefore difficult to see why the hypothetical threat of future enforcement distinguished *Nollan* from *DeShaney*.

they do not, we ought to assume that the Constitution's drafters meant to do something sensible—that they were reasonable people who wanted to achieve reasonable goals. Chief Justice Rehnquist's opinion turns this assumption on its head.

In light of these weaknesses in the argument for requiring state action in *DeShaney,* one might have supposed that Justice Brennan's dissenting opinion would attack it. Instead, the opinion embraces it. Justice Brennan directs our attention to one of the central dilemmas of state action analysis. What appears to be "mere" state inaction is always embedded in a network of state action. Courts will always have to choose whether to focus on the network or the "inaction." By establishing a social welfare bureaucracy, Justice Brennan argues, the state discouraged private efforts that might otherwise have saved the boy. Justice Brennan focuses on the ways in which the state made Joshua DeShaney's situation worse.

Like Chief Justice Rehnquist, Justice Brennan looks for state action, rather than arguing that the state should be held liable for failure to act. Why does Justice Brennan choose to argue around the state action requirement, rather than directly confront it? That question is especially vexing because the argument for state action that Justice Brennan advances has its own problems.

It seems unfair to hold states responsible when they try to prevent injury but fail, but not when they do nothing at all. According to Justice Brennan's arguments, the state could not be liable if it abandoned the child welfare business completely. For him, the state's actions designed to provide at least some protection for abused children make those children worse off than they would be if left entirely to their own devices. That, however, runs against our strong intuitions.

The best that Justice Brennan can do is to claim that Joshua might "conceivably" have been better off in a world of no government intervention because in such a world, private parties would not have come to rely on the social welfare bureaucracy: Joshua's neighbors might have come to his aid if they knew no public agency would. As this qualified language suggests, the claim rests on sheer speculation. Maybe Randy DeShaney was deterred from even greater violence by the state's limited intervention. And maybe DeShaney's neighbors or acquaintances would not have intervened even if the state had remained passive.

One of the difficulties with this sort of counterfactual is that it is very hard to know, or even guess with some confidence, how people would act in the radically different alternative world we are asked to imagine. In a world with no social welfare bureaucracy and no laws against child abuse, what could concerned outsiders do? There would be no welfare worker to call and no law to invoke. Outsiders might attempt to take custody of Joshua by physical force, but why should we suppose that they would succeed?[4]

Moreover, how could we account for the unfamiliar social conditions that would cause a society to repeal all of its laws against child abuse? Such a society would value children much less than ours does. Thus, even if we could count on bystander intervention to rescue Joshua in a society with *our* values, it does not follow that bystanders would be so motivated in this alternative world.

This sort of speculation, which Justice Brennan's opinion invites, is profoundly beside the point. *DeShaney* is not about what the state did but about what it failed to do. In that sense alone, Chief Justice Rehnquist accurately stated the issue.

Suppose Wisconsin had clearly put bystanders on notice that they could not count on the state to intervene in child abuse cases. According to Justice Brennan's theory, that would eliminate the risk of private reliance on state action and eliminate the reasons for holding the state constitutionally liable for Joshua's injuries. But the state did, in fact, offer such notice. The Supreme Court held that the state had no *constitutional* duty to protect children from their parents, and Wisconsin, by the very act of resisting Joshua Deshaney's law suit, served notice that it would not assume the duty voluntarily. Even if the risk of state nonintervention was unclear before *DeShaney,* it became crystal clear afterward. Yet no one who agreed with Justice Brennan's dissent when it was written has suddenly come to think that it is constitutionally fine for social workers to continue to ignore cases like Joshua's.

Even if we treat *DeShaney* as a case about the state's actions, how-

4. One (concededly controversial) way to test these intuitions is by comparing an imagined world in which there are no laws against child abuse with our current world in which there are no laws against early abortions. In the absence of state regulation, antiabortion groups like Operation Rescue have attempted to use self-help to protect fetuses. Their success in these efforts has been mixed at best. Both sides of the abortion debate seem to agree that fewer fetuses would be aborted in a world with even inadequately enforced antiabortion laws than in our current world of almost complete deregulation. There is no reason to doubt this conclusion or to think that a different conclusion follows regarding the regulation of child abuse.

ever, Justice Brennan's dissent concentrates on state action having only the most marginal and doubtful relationship to Joshua's injury while ignoring the state action that really did cause it: that is, through its custody rules and decisions, the state gave Randy DeShaney the opportunity to wreak violence against his son.

The state rules distributing children among adult caretakers almost always "cause" child abuse in the sense that the abuse would not have occurred had the state made a different choice. This is a modern version of the cedar tree case we discussed in chapter 2. (Recall the DeShaney divorce and the state court decision awarding custody to Randy rather than to Joshua's mother.) Even if we ignore the judicial decree (entered by the court of a different state before the DeShaneys moved to Wisconsin), the Wisconsin custody rules still created what amounted to a brutal prison for Joshua. These rules can be taken as a paradigm of government action that violates due process. They allocate children to biological parents without any investigation of parents' fitness or any opportunity for a hearing. Once this initial allocation is made, it is backed up by all the state's coercive powers. If Joshua DeShaney were to run away from home, state officers would have returned him to his father. If other adults had attempted to rescue him, they would have been arrested for kidnapping. Why does Justice Brennan (as well as the rest of the Court) ignore this obvious state action?[5]

The briefest and most elliptical of the opinions, Justice Blackmun's dissent also raises the most troubling issues. For Justice Blackmun, the Court's effort to draw "a sharp and rigid line" between action and inaction is "formalistic" and unconvincing. He argues that the constitutional text and the Court's decisions leave the Justices with a choice to find state action or not. The Court should make this choice, Justice Blackmun writes, by adopting a "sympathetic" reading of the law that

5. Most people doubtless believe that children "naturally" belong with their biological parents. It may therefore seem fanciful to suggest that the state has made a "choice" in "allocating" children in this fashion. As we argue, however, this strongly held intuition demonstrates our incomplete assimilation of realist insights. In some contexts, it seems obvious enough that the state *is* choosing how to allocate children—when it approves or disapproves adoptions, resolves custody disputes after divorce, or decides issues regarding parental rights over children produced by artificial insemination, for example. In other contexts, however, we want to deny that the state is responsible for "leaving" children with their parents, just as prerealist judges might have denied that the state was responsible for letting the cedar rust attack the apple trees.

''comports with dictates of fundamental justice and recognizes that compassion need not be exiled from the province of judging.''

The great strength of Justice Blackmun's opinion is his honest acknowledgement of the legal rule's indeterminacy. Ironically, this strength makes apparent the weak undergirdings of all the opinions, including his own. By admitting that the Constitution affords the justices a considerable measure of freedom to rule either way, Justice Blackmun raises the most familiar problem of liberal constitutionalism. If he is right—if text and doctrine do not constrain—then judicial review leaves us at the mercy of the justices' unfettered intuitions about the ''dictates of fundamental justice.''

Additional problems emerge when Justice Blackmun attempts to tell us what the ''dictates of fundamental justice'' require in *DeShaney*. Instead of an argument of this score, Justice Blackmun concludes his opinion with an extraordinary lament concerning ''poor Joshua['s]'' fate. To the extent that this rhetoric is effective, it gains its power by making the consequences of the Court's decision concrete. It focuses the reader on Joshua's individual story and away from abstract and general theorizing.

The problem here is that arguments about justice are, necessarily, arguments about more than a particular individual. Doing justice always involves mediating between the general and the particular. A just outcome gives the individual his or her due according to some more general precept that one is prepared to apply over some range of similar cases. How ''general'' the rule must be depends on how we decide to characterize the particulars of the individual's situation.

Justice Blackmun's emphasis on the particular and his disregard of the general is especially anomalous in *DeShaney*. Money damages might make Joshua's life somewhat more comfortable, but no damage award, no Supreme Court decision, no constitutional doctrine will give him back his stolen future. The argument that a rule based on Joshua's case will serve justice must, we think, be mainly forward-looking. (In contrast, a criminal prosecution of Randy DeShaney would have a large backward-looking element.) Justice Blackmun's opinion makes sense only if a decision for Joshua and his mother will make social workers more careful in the future and prevent more such tragedies. That argument is not about any particular story. It is about the general, anonymous, and collective impact of legal rules.

Once we get away from Joshua's particular story, the dictates of justice—and the courts' authority to determine them—become less clear. Money damages awarded against social workers who fail to intervene when they suspect child abuse will certainly produce more intervention—where it is unwarranted as well as where it is appropriate. Social workers will act more quickly to remove children from homes where they are at risk. But they will also be quicker to remove children from their homes where there is no need to do so. As a social scientist might put it, a stricter liability regime will produce fewer "false negatives" at the expense of more "false positives." Whether this change would be a good thing depends on an empirical judgment about the numbers of each sort of mistake and a value judgment about which kind of mistake is more serious.

Nor is that the end. Even if we decide in favor of greater protection against child abuse, we can achieve it only by spending more money. If we are serious about earlier and more frequent intervention, we will need more training and supervision of social workers, more juvenile court judges, more foster parents, more group homes.

Perhaps our economic resources should be directed in this fashion, but we cannot be sure until we know where the money comes from. Do the benefits of using tax dollars this way outweigh the benefits of using them for other worthy programs like running public hospitals, providing police protection, or furnishing prenatal care to imporverished pregnant women?

It turns out, then, that the underlying issue in *DeShaney* is complex, not simple. It is the kind of question about which "policy wonks" write long and boring doctoral dissertations. To resolve it in a sensible fashion, we need to know many facts that, if available at all, are not likely to be in the trial record upon which the Supreme Court bases decision. And even if we had access.to these facts, we would still need to make a series of value judgments, about which reasonable people surely differ.

It is difficult to know how a Supreme Court justice should act in the face of this uncertainty. It does seem clear, however, that Justice Blackmun's focus on the single case of "poor Joshua" tends to distract us from the real and painful choices that confront the Court.

There is nonetheless something to be said for Justice Blackmun's rhetoric. His insistence that we pay attention to Joshua's individual story reminds us that all of life is not policy analysis. We tend to make fun of "policy wonks" precisely because their preoccupation with costs and benefits blinds them to facts that cannot be captured in bloodless statistics.

Although Justice Blackmun is right to remind us of this, the final irony is that the reminder serves to reinforce his opponents' position. To see why, it is helpful to compare Justice Blackmun's position in *DeShaney* with his defense of abortion rights. When Justice Blackmun wrote for the Court a generation ago to affirm a woman's constitutional right to an abortion, he said, in essence, that a woman should be allowed to make this decision as part of her own individual life story (*Roe v. Wade,* 1973). The decision is private precisely because it ought not to be judged on the basis of abstract policy analysis. A woman who chooses to have an abortion need answer to no one but herself. It is irrelevant whether someone else thinks the decision maximizes social welfare or protects some abstract notion of autonomy.

Justice Blackmun's lament for "poor Joshua" reminds us that an analoguous sphere of individualism and privacy surrounds child-rearing decisions. Most of us think that parental interaction with children is also an act of self-definition that forms a part of the life story individuals make for themselves. It is therefore important that the relationship between parents and children remain in the realm of individual autonomy. Most child-rearing decisions should be free of government control, even if some of the choices parents make—about what kind of education or what kind (if any) of religious instruction their children receive, for example—cannot be justified on general public policy grounds. Indeed, *Roe* itself relied heavily on a series of Supreme Court decisions creating constitutional protection for this sphere.

Of course, no one thinks that this sphere ought to include the right to beat a child senseless or to deny a child any schooling whatever. An unavoidable consequence of holding social workers liable for failing to remove children from their homes, however, is to encourage greater public supervision and control over a range of child-rearing decisions. Risk-averse social workers threatened by liability suits will not only be quicker to remove children from the home; they will also be quicker to threaten removal unless parents comport with state-approved child-rearing standards.

Such public processes will not—and ought not—focus on the individual stories of children and parents. Social welfare bureaucracies will formulate general policies thought to be in the interests of society as a whole. When Justice Blackmun focuses our attention on "poor Joshua," he reminds us of the risks that inhere in desiccated, dehumanizing generalizations that subsume the individual stories of real people. He fails to see that these risks provide the primary argument for keeping child-rearing in a private sphere free from government intervention—but, unhappily for constitutional law, defined by government institutions.

Each of the three *DeShaney* opinions is, in its own way, unconvincing. None provides a persuasive theory for sorting the public from the private. Unfortunately, these difficulties are not confined to the narrow problem of state responsibility for child abuse. No area of constitutional law is more confusing and contradictory than state action.

For example, in the famous case of *Shelley v. Kraemer* (1948), the Court held that judicial enforcement of racially restrictive covenants on real property constituted "state action" sufficient to trigger Fourteenth Amendment protections. On one level, state court enforcement of these provisions is obviously the action of the state; whose action could court enforcement be? A moment's reflection makes clear that all private action ultimately rests on the state's willingness to enforce the civil and criminal rules that facilitate that action. Writing a will that gives money to some people but not others or inviting some people but not others to dinner are familiar examples. The Court has never held—and, we are confident, never will hold—that courts cannot enforce wills according to their terms unless the courts are satisfied that the money is distributed fairly or that the police cannot help a homeowner eject an intruder from the dining room unless they are satisfied that the homeowner is not motivated by racial hatred. The Court has never explained why these cases are different from *Shelley*.

Analytic confusion of this sort, to which we could add many more examples, has led many commentators to suggest that the state action analysis ought to be abandoned altogether. Why not simply concede that state action is always present in some form and move directly to an analysis of whether the state action is constitutionally permissible? According to this view, the Court erred in *Shelley* in focusing on whether judicial enforcement of restrictive covenants was state action (it obviously was) instead of addressing the harder question of whether such enforcement violates the Constitution. Similarly, a court applying this approach in *DeShaney* would acknowledge that enforcing child custody rules was state action—or ignore the question entirely—and then move on to the question whether these rules, as applied in Joshua DeShaney's case, violated his constitutional rights.

In light of the confusion produced by the state action inquiry, this approach is certainly attractive. Unfortunately, however, it only shifts the problem without really solving it, because something like the state action doctrine—together with all the uncertainty and incoherence that accompanies it—is built into how we think about constitutional rights.

Consider again the constitutional right most closely associated with Justice Blackmun—the right to an abortion. *Roe v. Wade* stands for the proposition that there is a sphere of privacy within which each woman has a right to decide for herself whether she ought to have an abortion. As Justice Blackmun's *Roe* opinion makes clear, the state may not invade this sphere simply because it disagrees with the woman's judgment about the profound and difficult moral issues raised by abortion. Put simply, the choice must be left to the individual and cannot be exercised by the state.

It is hard to reconcile this position with Justice Blackmun's stance in *DeShaney*. Just as there are background facts that allow us to attribute Randy DeShaney's actions to the state if we are so inclined, so, too, a "sympathetic" Justice could attribute a woman's abortion decision to the state: Inadequate state efforts to provide counseling and health benefits for pregnant mothers and scandalously insufficient child services for new infants directly cause many decisions to abort fetuses in just the way that the state caused Joshua's injuries. But if the abortion decision is the state's responsibility, it cannot also be within a private sphere within which the woman can act without state interference.

As the abortion example illustrates, the state action problem cannot be avoided by focusing on the scope of the substantive constitutional right at stake. All substantive rights rest on the assumption that we can define a sphere of private conduct not attributable to the state. The effort to bound this sphere necessarily reintroduces through the back door all the confusion that surrounds state action analysis.

For example, Justice Blackmun's *DeShaney* dissent tells us that a judge deciding how to pay attention to these background facts should look to the "dictates of fundamental justice." But the core holding of *Roe* is that public officials (including judges) have no business deciding questions of "fundamental justice" with regard to matters, like abortion, that belong in the private sphere. We are thus left with this central contradiction: The abortion right rests on the premise that decisions about the justice of particular abortions should be left to the *private* sphere. But the very existence of the private sphere seems to turn on a *public* decision regarding the justice of decisions made within it.

Perhaps Justice Blackmun thought that the difference was between a public decision to *define* a protected private sphere and private decisions *within* that sphere. Still, the boundaries of the private sphere will inevitably be defined by a public determination that, overall, we are better off accepting some unfortunate private decisions than attempting to intervene whenever some other public body—the child welfare agency in *DeShaney*—notices a decision that it thinks wrong. A public assessment of the justice of particular decisions necessarily accompanies a decision to draw the private sphere's boundaries *here*—including this decision along with many others—rather than *there*—including only the other decision.[6]

Our analysis of the opinions in *DeShaney* shows that they begin by relying on a distinction between malfeasance and nonfeasance. That distinction in turn requires a moral assessment, cast in terms of an appropriate mediation between the general and the particular, of actions taken within a private sphere. Yet, the boundaries of that sphere must be drawn by the courts, either through a "state action" doctrine or through a definition of substantive constitutional rights. In this way, the "state action" inquiry is unavoidable.

It turns out, then, that the Court's problem articulating a convincing version of the state action doctrine is very serious indeed. Because some conception of individual action not attributable to the state is necessary to the existence of rights, the confusion associated with the state action doctrine threatens more than the coherence of the cases that the Court labels as posing "state action" problems. It brings into question the very enterprise of constitutional review. What stands in the way of developing a sensible set of principles that we might use to map the boundary between the public and private?

We can begin to answer this question by examining the history of the state action doctrine. When we do so, a striking fact emerges: Before the New Deal transformation of constitutional doctrine, the Court exhib-

6. Perhaps the public institution defines the protected sphere by referring to some "natural" rights of parents and children. We discuss difficulties associated with this solution later in this chapter.

ited little interest in the state action requirement, at least in the modern sense.

In a few cases growing out of Reconstruction, the Court applied something it called a state action requirement. The most famous of these, *The Civil Rights Cases* (1883), invalidated the Civil Rights Act of 1875 on state action grounds. Although the Court used the language of state action, the nineteenth-century requirement differed from the modern one.

The 1875 Civil Rights Act guaranteed to all persons "the full and equal enjoyment" of all public accommodations, inns, and public conveyances without regard to race or previous condition of servitude. Congress enacted the law under power granted in Section 5 of the Fourteenth Amendment, which authorized it to enforce the substantive provisions of the amendment by appropriate legislation. Writing for the Court, Justice Joseph Bradley held that the law exceeded Congress's powers because the acts of private individuals could not constitute a denial of fourteenth amendment rights.

The case differs from modern versions of the state action requirement in two ways. First, Justice Bradley did not assert, as Chief Justice Rehnquist did in *DeShaney,* that the states had no positive obligation to act against private individuals who threatened the constitutional rights of others. On the contrary, in private correspondence, Justice Bradley made clear his view that the Fourteenth Amendment

> not only prohibits the making or enforcing of laws which shall abridge the privileges of the citizen; but prohibits the states from denying to all persons within its jurisdiction the equal protection of the laws. . . . Denying includes inaction as well as action. And denying the equal protection of the laws includes the omission to protect, as well as the omission to pass laws for protection.

Justice Bradley's quarrel with the Civil Rights Act was not that it affirmatively protected rights from private violations. Rather, his claim was that these rights had not been violated *so long as the state stood ready to provide a remedy for private misconduct*. In his view, the Civil Rights Act was unconstitutional because it mandated federal intervention even where the states prohibited racial discrimination. The act

> does not profess to be corrective of any constitutional wrong committed by the states. . . . It applies equally to cases arising in States which have the justest laws respecting the personal rights of citizens, and whose authorities are ever ready to enforce such laws, as to those

> which arise in States that may have violated the prohibition of the [Fourteenth] [A]mendment. In other words, it steps into the domain of local jurisprudence and lays down sanctions for the enforcement of those rules, without referring in any manner to any supposed action of the State or its authorities.

Thus, if Justice Bradley had been confronted with the *DeShaney* problem, he might well have found a constitutional violation so long as Wisconsin did not allow Joshua and his mother to recover damages, under state law, from the social workers.

The nineteenth-century version of the state action doctrine differed from its modern counterpart in a second way. For Justice Bradley, the issue in *The Civil Rights Cases* was whether the federal government had the power to prohibit private discrimination in public accommodations. The holding was that no provision in the Constitution gave Congress this power and that a law purporting to exercise it was therefore unconstitutional.

The structure of Chief Justice Rehnquist's *DeShaney* opinion is very different. Wisconsin, and Congress as well, had the power to prevent Randy DeShaney from harming his son; the issue was whether the Constitution required either government to exercise this power.

These differences have important implications for the meaning of and justification for the state action requirement. Justice Bradley saw the doctrine as limiting the power of the political branches of the national government; Chief Justice Rehnquist understands that the power of those branches has already expanded and sees the doctrine as limiting only the power of the federal courts. For Bradley, the doctrine defined a prohibited realm where government could not act; for Rehnquist, it identifies a discretionary realm where governments are free to act or not as they choose without federal *judicial* intervention.

This change creates new problems in explaining why we should have such a requirement. If the government is constitutionally forbidden to intervene, then it is obvious that it should bear no responsibility for its failure to do so. Justice Bradley's version of the state action requirement therefore did not force him to confront the vexing moral and philosophical problem of distinguishing between responsibility for acts and omissions. Indeed, as Justice Bradley's correspondence makes clear, he thought this difference unimportant and viewed the Fourteenth Amendment as prohibiting government acts *and* omissions that harmed the newly freed slaves.

In contrast, the distinction between acts and omissions is central to modern articulations of the state action requirement. *DeShaney* leaves no doubt that Wisconsin had the power to do something about Randy DeShaney's violence if it chose to act. Chief Justice Rehnquist, unlike Justice Bradley, must confront the knotty problem of whether to attribute responsibility for "mere" failures to act. If Wisconsin could have prevented Joshua DeShaney's injury and chose not to do so, why should it not bear constitutional responsibility for its decision?

Although a handful of pre–New Deal cases foreshadowed a reformulated state action doctrine, the Court did not begin to develop the modern requirement until the New Deal. The modern state action doctrine emerged with the victory of the liberal Roosevelt appointees over the free market ideology of the Old Court. We cannot understand why state action issues are so hard without first coming to grips with the reasons why these liberals needed to create a state action doctrine and the ways in which the doctrine relates to the transformation of constitutional law that occurred in the wake of the New Deal.

A central element of the New Deal revolution was the systematic dismantling of the public–private distinction. The attack on the distinction proceeded on several levels. First, the old natural rights ideology that carved out a public sphere from a preexisting and natural realm of private economic freedom collapsed. When the Court repudiated *Lochner v. New York* (1905), it effectively eliminated constitutional impediments to government regulation of the economy. The extent of government intervention became a matter of discretion and policy, rather than of necessity and right.

Second, a powerful critique of the feasance–nonfeasance dichotomy emerged. The Court came to understand that inaction was a kind of action: The government was always confronted with the option of reallocating burdens and benefits or leaving them undisturbed. It could either destroy the cedar trees by its action or the apple trees by its inaction. Because both decisions were "public," there was no refuge from public responsibility for the outcomes.

Finally, the Roosevelt administration took advantage of the new powers granted to government to inaugurate the modern regulatory state. Broad areas of the economy that had previously been left to private contract were now subject to explicit government regulation. Obviously, the popularity of the New Deal transformed public attitudes about the importance of respecting a private economic sphere. Beyond these changes in public perceptions, however, the growth of government regulation threatened the very concept of a private sphere. Where government regulation was the norm rather than the exception, virtually all conduct came to be seen as, in some sense, resting on an entitlement created by government.

For these reasons, the New Deal constitutional revolution left the public–private distinction in tatters. But, although the story of its demise has been told many times, most renditions have ignored a remarkable paradox: At the moment when the distinction collapsed as a limitation on governmental power, it replicated itself as a limitation on federal judicial power. For the very reason that *Lochner*-like reasoning was rejected as a restraint on government intervention, it had to be accepted as a restraint on judicial intervention.

What would a post–New Deal world have looked like without a reformulated state action doctrine? The constraints that Justice Bradley perceived on what the government could do had been swept away. It was no longer true, as it had been in 1883 when *The Civil Rights Cases* were decided, that federalism prevented the national government from dealing with "local" problems. More broadly, no natural or preexisting private sphere prevented either federal or state governments from intervening to redistribute economic resources.

When this new empowerment was coupled with the critique of the feasance–nonfeasance distinction, in the absence of a state action doctrine courts would have been free to order a comprehensive allocation of resources on their own initiative. Since the government was now empowered to distribute goods in any way it chose, its failure to do so had to be treated as a governmental decision that was subject to constitutional review.

Miller v. Schoene again serves as an apt example. Taken to its logical conclusion, Justice Stone's reasoning meant not just that the government's destruction of the cedar trees was not a taking for constitutional purposes. It also meant that the *failure* to destroy the cedar trees *might be* a taking of the apple trees. Because inaction is a kind of action and because there was nothing "natural" or "preexisting" about the spread of disease from the cedars to the apples, the government's failure to destroy the cedars constituted a possible "taking" of the apples subject to constitutional review and judicial control.

Although this potential reallocation of power between the courts and the political branches was immanent in the New Deal revolution, it also contradicted one of its core premises. President Roosevelt and his allies insisted that the revolution was triggered by judicial arrogation of power properly exercised by the political branches. Turning every policy decision into an issue of constitutional law, to be finally resolved by unelected justices on the Supreme Court, would have made a mockery of the bitter struggle against the Old Court. Restraint of the judiciary was therefore necessary to make the space for the newly unrestrained political branches to engage in the vigorous government intervention at the heart of the New Deal.

We are now in a position to understand why Justice Brennan's *DeShaney* dissent accepts the state action requirement as a given instead of launching a frontal assault against it. Although they represent sharply conflicting judicial ideologies, both Chief Justice Rehnquist and Justice Brennan are heirs to the New Deal revolution. Both understand that most decisions of government are questions of policy and that the Constitution should be read to give the political branches broad discretion in resolving them. Both understand that a state action requirement shields these policy questions from constitutional review except where government conduct invades a protected private sphere.

We are now also in a position to understand why the opinions of the justices applying the state action requirement are bound to be unsatisfactory. The critique of the public–private distinction that made a reformulated state action doctrine necessary also makes it impossible. In the post–New Deal regime, the Court can no longer talk convincingly of the distinction between acts and omissions, or of a natural and preexisting private sphere not constituted by public decisions. It is therefore as difficult to utilize state action rhetoric as a restraint on judges as it is to utilize it as a restraint on government as a whole.

State action cases are hard because the New Deal revolution necessitated a newly formulated state action requirement to curb judicial power and simultaneously demolished the analytic tools that could have been used to articulate the requirement convincingly. In the modern period, without a natural and preexisting distinction between public and private, a state action requirement survives as a remnant of belief. The requirement is essential to prevent every policy question from becoming an issue for constitutional interpretation. But the death of the public–private distinction also dooms any effort to justify insistence upon the state action or to distinguish action from inaction.

The preceding discussion helps explain why constitutional rhetoric about state action is so unconvincing. It is not quite the whole story, however, for we still need to understand why all the Justices selectively use state action rhetoric. For example, why does Justice Brennan see state action in Wisconsin's establishment of a child welfare system but remain blind to the state's action when it chooses to allocate infants to their biological parents? Why does Justice Blackmun think that the government should accept responsibility for Joshua DeShaney's beating but not for Jane Roe's abortion? Why does Chief Justice Rehnquist think that withdrawing state protection from property is state action, while withdrawing state protection from child abuse is not?

It is tempting to attribute these inconsistencies to the cynical manipulation of constitutional doctrine to achieve ideological goals. Of course the justices have ideological presuppositions, but these presuppositions themselves rest on beliefs about the "naturalness" of differently defined private spheres. Without such a belief, it is hard to know how constitutional argument could proceed.

We can gain some insight into this problem by examining another of the contradictions in the New Deal revolution. Although the New Dealers were intent on upsetting the old order, they were hardly nihilists. They had absorbed the rhetoric and analytical tools of the legal realists, but they rejected the most radical and destabilizing implications of realism.

Nowhere is this ambivalence about the lessons of legal realism more apparent than in the post–New Deal treatment of a private sphere. As already noted, the realist assault on the public–private distinction played a crucial role in justifying the New Deal. Historically, the ideology of natural rights and of a private sphere had been used to justify the suppression of relatively powerless groups—primarily workers, secondarily women—within that sphere. For political liberals, committed to the welfare of the dispossessed, debunking this ideology was crucial. The legal realists helped explain why the government was responsible for outcomes in the private sector and why it was legitimate for the government to regulate "private" transactions.

Although the realist arguments were useful in dismantling the old order, they obstructed the effort to build a new one. Political liberals resented the use of privacy rhetoric to shield distributions of wealth and power from public criticism, but they could not make their own arguments for redistribution without relying on some normative vision of what people were "naturally" entitled to in a just society. New Dealers therefore could not wholly embrace the skeptical view that individual freedom was a myth. On the contrary, their ultimate aim was to create the material conditions that would free individuals to lead productive and happy private lives.

One strand of post–New Deal thought attempted to avoid this contradiction by reformulating the public–private distinction in pragmatic fashion. For them, the distinction is a human construct to be defined and employed in ways that are useful to achieving our ends.

This effort to tame the contradiction simply pushes it deeper. A pragmatic, instrumental manipulation of the public–private distinction presupposes that we have ends that we are trying to advance. If we were sure about those ends and in agreement with one another, perhaps there would be no need to do more than assert them. But most of us engage in critical reflection about our own ends, and we frequently find ourselves in conflict with others about them. In these circumstances, many feel a need to justify or explain these ends, and it is hard to mount such an explanation without resort to some ''natural'' normative framework.

The justices on the *DeShaney* Court are the uneasy beneficiaries of this confused legacy of the 1930s. Cursed with the knowledge that the public–private distinction is artificial and constructed, they cannot completely free themselves from a residual sense that something crucial would be lost if we gave it up.

The upshot is that all the justices selectively employ and ignore the state action requirement in ways that are impossible to reconcile. It could hardly be otherwise. Unless we want to give up altogether on the idea of individual rights, we must preserve in some form the notion that individuals can make some decisions without those decisions being attributed to the government. Yet unless we want to return to the pre–New Deal *Lochner* ideology, we must also understand that whenever we choose, we can see the world in a way that makes the government responsible for those decisions.

State action problems are authentically hard. The New Deal revolution has left us unable to believe in the naturalness of the public–private distinction, yet also unable to reconceive a system of individual rights without it. We want to repudiate state action rhetoric because we know that it blinds us to human suffering that the state might otherwise ameliorate. Yet we also want to embrace the concept of a private sphere because we know that it preserves a space for individual flourishing that the state might otherwise destroy.

In the face of this ambivalence, it is no wonder that the Supreme

Court's state action opinions are confused. The confusion is not the product of sloppy reasoning or unprincipled manipulation of doctrine. It is rooted in the fundamental difficulty in thinking about constitutional law in the legal culture we have inherited from the legal realists and the New Deal.

The distinction between public and private is not the only fundamental dichotomy threatened by this culture. A second building block of constitutional law is the distinction between freedom and coercion. The New Deal raised troubling questions about this dichotomy as well. Indeed, as chapter 4 demonstrates, the freedom–coercion problem is really no more than the public–private problem in different garb.

4

Burdens, Benefits, and Baselines

Michael T. McSpadden, 209th district judge of Harris County, Texas, doesn't mince words. In a 1992 speech he urged Texans to lobby for passage of laws that would allow castration of sex offenders "before every woman and child" is raped. If all 9,000 sex offenders currently jailed in Texas were castrated, he said, there would be only 450 repeat offenders.

Allen Butler, a twenty-eight-year-old defendant awaiting trial for rape, had more than an academic interest in Judge McSpadden's proposal. While on probation for performing an indecent act with a seven-year-old girl, Butler was accused of repeatedly raping another girl, aged thirteen. If convicted, he was likely to be sentenced to thirty-five years in prison.

When Butler heard that McSpadden favored castration for rapists, he offered the judge a deal: He would plead guilty to the charges in return for a sentence of probation and castration. After McSpadden agreed to accept the plea and approve the castration request and newspapers across the country carried accounts of his decision, a media circus began. Editorials denounced the judge. The Reverend Jesse Jackson arrived in Houston to protest McSpadden's decision. Butler's five sisters hired an attorney to block the castration. A state representative vowed to seek impeachment if the judge did not reverse himself.

Ultimately, McSpadden backed down. Butler's lawyer, who had brokered the plea, claimed that because of the publicity the case had generated, no doctor could be found who was willing to perform the operation. Then both she and Judge McSpadden withdrew from the case.

As these events demonstrate, Judge McSpadden's "modest proposal" breached contemporary norms concerning individual rights and the limits of government coercion. But whose rights were violated? How was anyone coerced? Didn't McSpadden's willingness to accept castration plus probation widen, not narrow, Butler's options? Before McSpadden agreed to the castration option, Butler faced thirty-five years' imprisonment. After McSpadden's decision, Butler was still free to accept imprisonment if he preferred. The court's decision simply gave him another choice, which he was free to accept or reject.

Viewed from another perspective, however, Butler's choice to undergo castration was not free at all. Butler certainly did not "want" this outcome. He accepted castration only because he was threatened with a thirty-five-year prison sentence if he did not acquiesce. He "voluntarily" chose castration only in the sense that a robbery victim "voluntarily" gives over his property when the robber says, "Your money or your life." Nor is it obvious that McSpadden's conditional offer made Butler better off than he would have been without the offer. How do we know that McSpadden would have imposed a thirty-five-year sentence if the castration option were foreclosed? Perhaps he threatened a more severe sentence for the very purpose of forcing Butler's acquiescence to castration.

Although much of the media commentary on the curious proceedings in Judge McSpadden's courtroom treated the events as a throwback to a less civilized era, there is something strikingly modern about the problem posed by the judge's actions. Indeed, implausible as it might seem, the bizarre decisions of this obscure Texas trial judge perfectly reflect a central dilemma that has dominated constitutional jurisprudence during the modern period.

The dilemma is so pervasive that sometimes we do not even realize it is present. Few Americans seem concerned about the fact that approximately 90 percent of all criminal cases are resolved by plea bargains, albeit more conventional ones. Typically, the defendant agrees to plead guilty in exchange for a reduced sentence. Ironically, most opposition to plea bargaining comes from people who fear that the bargain makes defendants better off than they would be if they were forced to go to trial. Yet these bargains always pressure defendants' constitutional rights in just the way that Judge McSpadden pressured Allen Butler's right not to be castrated.

To get the reduced sentence, the defendant must give up his Sixth Amendment right to a jury trial and his Fifth Amendment privilege against self-incrimination. True, the defendant does not have to accept the bargain. Allowing defendants to trade these rights for goods they would prefer (usually a shorter sentence) does make them better off in a sense. Still, it is not hard to envision bargains that almost everyone would agree are unconstitutional despite the defendant's "freedom" to reject them. Suppose, for example, a judge agrees to grant a defendant probation on the condition that he join the Catholic Church or that he never vote for a Republican candidate.

Problems with the same essential structure appear in areas of the law far removed from plea bargaining and criminal justice.

- The government has no constitutional obligation to provide assistance to families with dependent children. It chooses to do so but also provides that by accepting assistance, recipients consent to searches of their homes without warrants or probable cause.
- The government has no constitutional obligation to operate public parks. It chooses to do so but also provides that the parks may not be used for distributing political literature.
- The federal government has no constitutional obligation to subsidize highway construction. It chooses to do so but also provides that states receiving the subsidy must pass laws prohibiting those under eighteen years of age from purchasing alcoholic beverages.
- The government has no constitutional obligation to subsidize the arts. It chooses to do so but also provides that the money is not available for work that attacks organized religion.
- The government has no constitutional obligation to fund family planning clinics. It chooses to do so but also provides that employees of a clinic accepting the funds cannot recommend abortion as a family planning technique.

Each of these cases poses essentially the same problem. In each situation, the government has linked receipt of a benefit that it grants voluntarily to acceptance of a burden that it could not impose directly. By forcing the potential recipient to accept or reject the entire package, it provides incentives that mold behavior without the direct coercion that would clearly be unconstitutional.

Problems of this nature have produced more than their share of tendentious and question-begging constitutional argument. Supreme Court justices have taken inconsistent positions on the issue—positions driven, to all appearances, by their political commitments rather than by any principle that they are ready to apply across the board.

Consider, for example, the positions taken by Justices Antonin Scalia and William Brennan in cases arising during a single Supreme Court Term. When the Court used the First Amendment to strike down an Arkansas statute exempting newspapers and religious, professional, trade, and sports journals from the state sales tax imposed on general interest magazines, Justice Scalia dissented (*Arkansas Writers' Project v. Ragland,* 1987). He argued that the statute was simply a subsidy of the publications receiving the tax benefit and that mere subsidies violate no one's rights: "The reason that the denial of participation in a tax exemption or other subsidy scheme does not necessarily 'infringe' a fundamental right is that—unlike direct restriction or prohibition—such a denial does not, as a general rule, have any significant coercive effect."

During the same term, Justice Scalia had no analogous difficulty detecting coercion when the government conditioned the right to rebuild a beachfront home on the grant of a public easement across the property (*Nollan v. California Coastal Commission,* 1987). Justice Scalia conceded that the government had no obligation to allow the rebuilding, just as it had no obligation to grant a tax exemption for the favored publications in the Arkansas case. Yet in the beachfront home case, Justice Scalia was able to see that withholding of voluntary benefit coerced the property owner into sacrificing his constitutional right not to grant an easement without just compensation. In his view, the building restriction was "not a valid regulation of land use, but 'an out-and-out plan of extortion.'"

In the beachfront case, Justice Brennan dissented, arguing that "appellants were clearly on notice when requesting a new development permit that a condition of approval would be a provision ensuring [the easement]." Yet prior notice failed to satisfy Justice Brennan in another case decided during the same term. In that case the government conditioned provision of benefits under Aid to Families with Dependent Children on the willingness of the recipient family to assign to the government child support payments received from a noncustodial parent (*Bowen v. Gilliard,* 1987). In this context, Justice Brennan suddenly understood how withholding benefits could violate individual rights:

> In a society in which most persons receive some form of Government benefit, Government has considerable leverage in shaping individual behavior. . . . On certain occasions . . . Government intrusion into private life is so direct and substantial that we must deem it intolerable if we are to be true to our belief that there is a boundary between the public citizen and the private person.

It would be unfair to single out Justices Scalia and Brennan as especially inconsistent in dealing with this problem. None of the justices has figured out a general approach that would permit the cases to be resolved in a consistent fashion, and academic commentators have not done much better.

Almost everyone falls into the same trap. How many feminists who think that the Constitution is violated when the government subsidizes live childbirth but not abortion also think that it is violated when it subsidizes ballet but not nude dancing? How many religious conservatives who think that the Constitution requires support for private religious education so long as the public schools teach "secular humanism" also think that the Constitution requires support for sacrilegious art so long as government-supported art museums display religiously inspired paintings? Is there anyone who supposes that because the government subsidizes antidrug educational efforts it must devote any resources at all to a "just say yes" campaign? Why is it that although no one is troubled by this sort of discrimination, virtually everyone would be troubled by the use of tax dollars for an educational effort designed to get voters to support Democrats rather than Republicans?

If partisans on particular issues are to convince their opponents, they need a general theory that transcends views on the merits of the particular rights pressured by conditional offers. Then they could explain why one kind of condition is permissible while another is not. The theory might be "clause-specific," applying one approach to free speech questions and another to questions implicating religion. But surely the theory must treat subsidies to "good" and "bad" speech consistently. Lacking such a theory, the justices and other participants in constitutional debate are unable to transcend their political differences. They speak as if their dispute is over the coercive impact of conditional offers, but what really creates the disagreement is a political difference of opinion about the worth of the underlying right being pressured—or worse, a political difference about the merits of particular government actions. The kind of tendentious debate that has made constitutional argument so unproductive in the modern period is the result. We need a way to bridge the gap created by our political differences so that we can talk to each other about these problems in a common language. Yet despite the best efforts of our most thoughtful legal scholars, such a theory remains beyond our grasp. The next section explores some of the obstacles that such a theory would have to overcome. A final section discusses the relationship between these obstacles, the state action problem addressed in chapter 3, and the changes in constitutional thought that accompanied the New Deal revolution.

In a famous article on the conditional offer problem, the philosopher Robert Nozick proposed a distinction between "offers" and "threats." No one can complain, he argued, if he receives an offer. Offers are good because they expand the realm of freedom. Threats, on the other hand, restrict the realm of freedom.

Sometimes, the courts have attempted to make essentially the same distinction by differentiating between subsidies and burdens. In *United States v. Butler* (1936), a case decided on the eve of the New Deal revolution, the Court considered a constitutional attack on the first Agricultural Adjustment Act. The act taxed food processors to pay farmers who agreed to restrict their crop production.

Both the majority and the dissent assumed that Congress could not directly order farmers not to grow the crops.[1] The dissent claimed that the act was constitutional even so, because it involved a subsidy to farmers who consented to the crop limitation. The majority angrily disagreed, arguing that the statute imposed a burden on farmers who insisted on growing. Both sides were right. Failing to subsidize is no different from imposing a burden. Either way, the law made farmers who grew crops poorer and farmers who restricted production richer. Oddly, the Court had seen this point in the cedar tree case a decade earlier.

A half century after *Butler,* the Court was divided by a similarly pointless issue of characterization regarding the so-called Hyde Amend-

1. When the case was decided, existing precedent sharply limited the power of Congress to directly coerce individuals in this fashion. Under more recent decisions, there is no doubt that the Commerce Clause of Article 1 authorizes coercion of this sort.

ment restricting Medicaid funding for abortions (*Harris v. McRae*, 1980). Both sides conceded (at least for purposes of the case) that the government could not constitutionally restrict abortions. The Court's majority thought that the Hyde Amendment was constitutional because the government had no duty to subsidize abortions even though it could not prohibit them. The abortion restriction left pregnant women no worse off than they would have been without a Medicaid program.

In contrast, the dissent argued that the failure to pay for abortions when money was available to pay for medical expenses for childbirth burdened the abortion right. Pregnant women were effectively penalized when the government took away money to which they otherwise would have been entitled just because they exercised their constitutional right to abort their fetuses.

Once again, both sides were right. In a sense, the Medicaid statute together with the Hyde Amendment simply provides a subsidy for women who choose childbirth. Women choosing abortion are made no worse off just because women choosing childbirth are made better off. But there is also a sense in which the statutory scheme burdens women who now must bear their own costs when they choose abortion. Had they chosen live birth, they would have had money that they now must sacrifice because they have exercised their constitutionally protected abortion right.

Nozick is too sophisticated a philosopher to believe that this problem can be solved by the sort of arbitrary characterization the Court has used. Virtually any offer can be recharacterized as a threat. Suppose that Adam happens upon Bob, who is drowning. Adam can offer to rescue Bob in exchange for one hundred dollars, or he can threaten not to rescue him unless Bob gives him one hundred dollars. Obviously, there is no more than a verbal difference between the two transactions.

Nozick offers a theory to distinguish offers and subsidies from threats and burdens. He suggests that we look at the problem from the perspective of the recipient of the offer or threat before it is extended. If the recipient would want the offer/threat to be made, then it expands his or her freedom and should be characterized as an offer or a subsidy. If the recipient would prefer that it not be made, then it restricts his or her freedom and should be characterized as a threat or a burden.

Nozick's suggestion is helpful, of course, only if we know what people would prefer in a given situation. To figure this out, we need a baseline against which offers and threats can be measured. For example, if drowning people cannot ordinarily expect to be rescued, Bob would surely welcome Adam's offer. Even in the unlikely event that the rescue is not worth one hundred dollars to him, he is certainly made no worse off by being presented with this additional option. If the baseline is that drowning people can expect to be rescued, Bob is made worse off by Adam's threat. Now he must sacrifice one hundred dollars for something he otherwise would have received for nothing.

Thus, if Nozick's analysis is correct (we will introduce some doubts on that score later in this chapter), the trick is to figure out what baseline to use when measuring offers and threats. Unfortunately, this is no easy task. Our drowning hypothetical suggests that the baseline should be ordinary and expected practice. But this standard does not work well when we are talking about the constitutionality of government action. The government has a right to change ordinary and expected practice so long as it does not act in ways that are independently unconstitutional. Suppose, for example, that the government has provided Medicaid coverage for abortions or crop support for all farmers for years and that people have come to expect these benefits. Surely Congress can change its mind about these social programs and discontinue them. Put differently, the only *legitimate* expectation people have is that the funding will continue until Congress repeals the statute making it available.

Perhaps, then, the test should be whether some independent provision of the Constitution prohibits Congress from withdrawing the subsidy. Where the government has no obligation to provide the subsidy at all, it makes no one legally worse off by conditioning the subsidy on desired behavior. Under this test, however, the conditional-offer doctrine does no work: It would apply only when some substantive constitutional provision already required the subsidy. Even worse, this approach appears to give the wrong answers in some clear cases. Although the government has no constitutional obligation to provide sewer service, the First Amendment's free-exercise guarantee would be worth very little if the government could restrict this "subsidy" to practicing Christians.

Sometimes the Court deals with these difficulties by distinguishing between a permissible government choice to subsidize only certain activities and an impermissible effort to use government money to change citizen behavior unrelated to the funded program. According to this theory the government can refuse to provide Medicaid coverage for abortions—this is only a failure to subsidize. In contrast, the government cannot cut off all welfare benefits (or the sewer system) to any woman who has had an abortion—that would be a penalty, unrelated to the welfare program and designed to coerce.

In one case the Court held unconstitutional a statute denying all government support to public broadcasting stations that editorialized (*FCC v. League of Women Voters,* 1984). Earlier the Court had upheld a provision denying a tax deduction for contributions to an otherwise tax-exempt organization if a substantial part of the organization's activities involved efforts to influence legislation (*Regan v. Taxation with Representation,* 1983). The two cases were different, the Court said, because a charitable organization, as in the 1983 case, could create an affiliate to conduct its nonlobbying activities using tax-deductible contributions. Therefore, the government was doing no more than failing to subsidize an activity it did not wish to support (lobbying). In contrast, the federal government withdrew all its funding from the educational station that editorialized, thereby going beyond a mere failure to subsidize a certain activity (in this case, editorializing) and using money that would not have been spent on editorializing as a lever to extract unrelated concessions from the recipient.

Despite its intuitive appeal, this approach goes both too far and not far enough. Suppose the government offered funding to public television stations to support editorializing in favor of Democratic, but not Republican, candidates. This case involves a mere failure to subsidize, because stations endorsing Republicans would continue to receive federal support for their other activities. Yet few would doubt that this sort of selective subsidization is unconstitutional. Here the approach does not go far enough.

The approach goes too far, however, because it fails to explain how potential funding recipients are made worse off by the fact that others receive subsidies. No public television stations have a right to federal subvention.[2] Because Congress could terminate this program across the board, the appropriate legal baseline seems to be a world where there is no funding. Measured from this baseline, stations that editorialize are made no worse off even if they receive no money at all.

Some commentators have attempted to deal with this problem by

2. Some might deny this, asserting that under modern circumstances government has a constitutional obligation to subsidize public television. If so, however, analyzing the issue as raising a conditional funding question simply obscures the underlying claim about the government's duties.

establishing a baseline premised on predictions of what the government would do if it were not been permitted to condition its offer. For example, if we are really convinced that Judge McSpadden would sentence Mr. Butler to thirty-five years' imprisonment if the castration option were foreclosed, then Butler is made no worse off when that option is made available to him. On the other hand, perhaps McSpadden threatened a longer term of imprisonment than he otherwise would have imposed precisely to get Butler to agree to castration. Here Butler is made worse off than he would have been if the castration "offer" could not have been made. Similarly, if we conclude that Congress would have cut off all funding for public stations rather than include those that editorialize, editorializing stations are made no worse off by the failure to provide them with funds. On the other hand, if Congress would agree to include editorializing stations if faced with an all-or-nothing choice, then the condition on funding does make these stations worse off.

If we accept Nozick's basic distinction, using this sort of prediction as a baseline makes some sense. Unfortunately, the prediction approach raises some troubling questions about Nozick's distinction itself.

Consider the following problem. After *Brown v. Board of Education,* the city council in Jackson, Mississippi, chose to close its municipal swimming pools altogether rather than operate them on an integrated basis. In a 5-4 decision, the Supreme Court held that the closing did not violate the Constitution even though it was motivated by the desire to avoid desegregation (*Palmer v. Thompson,* 1971). This holding has been extremely controversial, but if the Court had used prediction as a baseline, it might have gone even further.

Using the prediction approach, the city's demonstrated willingness to close the pools meant that African-Americans would have had no ground for complaint even if the city continued to operate segregated pools (or, indeed, even if it operated no pools at all for African-Americans). True, African-Americans would not get a benefit that whites received and would therefore be treated unequally. But the City Council had convincingly demonstrated that, if forced to rectify this inequality, it would do so by abolishing the program altogether. The appropriate baseline is therefore a world in which neither African-Americans nor whites receive the benefit. A departure from this baseline making whites better off does nothing to make African-Americans worse off, at least with respect to swimming pools (we discuss another way in which they are worse off in the following paragraphs).

The Supreme Court has consistently rejected this logic, and for good reason. For example, several years ago, Congress amended the Social Security Act to extend certain benefits to women but not to men. Concerned that the courts might invalidate the law on equal protection grounds, Congress also included a provision stating that if the law were invalidated, neither men nor women would get the benefit. When a man sued to challenge the provision, the Supreme Court was faced with the argument that the plaintiff lacked standing to attack the discrimination, since his victory would result in terminating the entire program, leaving him no better off. The Court rejected this claim, and its holding seems clearly correct (*Heckler v. Mathews,* 1984). If the case had gone the other way, it would have provided powerful incentives for policymakers to attempt to shift the baseline by, in effect, playing a game of ''chicken'' with the courts. By promising to end the program altogether in the event of an adverse ruling, they could forestall such a ruling and continue the challenged discriminatory practice.

The Court's holding also suggests that there is an independent, constitutionally significant interest in equal treatment apart from either the material benefit that might be derived from that treatment or the coercive effects of conditional offers. When a subsidy is extended to some people but not to others, the people failing to receive it lose more than just the value of the subsidy. Even if they are not coerced, they may experience a sense of unjust exclusion. Depriving the benefited class of the subsidy might remedy this inequality even if the excluded class gains no material benefit. There is thus a real sense in which Jackson's African-Americans are better off with no swimming pools for anyone than they would be with segregated pools.

The swimming pool case involves racial discrimination, where equality claims are uniquely powerful. Many of the Court's conditional-offer opinions have argued against extending the logic of racial cases to situations where individuals are excluded from benefits because they have exercised constitutional rights.

The Court has failed to explain the basis for this limitation, however. The racial cases demonstrate that victims of conditional offers can be harmed by an unjust exclusion even if they are not forced to change their behavior, and similar harms occur in other contexts. Consider, for example, a statute requiring segregated municipal facilities for women who have had abortions. Even if the statute is not coercive (because the city would rather close down the facilities altogether than allow integration), surely the women suffer an injury of constitutional dimension.

There is another problem with Nozick's distinction. So far, we have uncritically assumed that people in the preoffer–threat situation will always prefer to be given more options. But choices are not always desirable, particularly when they are made under severe constraints. This point is powerfully illustrated in William Styron's novel *Sophie's Choice*. A concentration camp inmate, Sophie is made to choose which of her two children to send to death. Does anyone suppose that Sophie is better off because of her ability to make this choice or that she would desire to have this ability in the prechoice situation? The Nazis foist the choice upon her because they understand what Nozick's theory does not acknowledge—that choice under unjust constraints can be cruel and undesirable.

None of the conditional offers we have considered so far is as sadistic as the choice Sophie faced. Yet many share one psychological characteristic with it. By being forced to choose, individuals are, in effect, implicated in government policies they detest. To some extent, the policies are now shielded from criticism because the victims appear to have chosen them for themselves.

Consider, for example, a federal grant recipient who must "choose" to execute a form promising not to produce "indecent" art in order to receive federal subvention. In the preoffer situation, some artists might well prefer direct government coercion in the form of outright censorship to a situation where they would be tempted to sacrifice their own artistic integrity in exchange for badly needed benefits.

Similarly, if Allen Butler were simply sentenced to thirty-five years' imprisonment, he would surely lose his freedom, but he might maintain his self-respect. By "choosing" castration, he is forced to participate in his own mutilation in a fashion that, ironically, undermines his sense of autonomy and independence. By giving him a choice, the government effectively harnesses his will and turns it to its own purposes.

The answer to Sophie's choice, and the conditional offer problem, may lie in reframing it. Instead of asking whether, after being sent to the camp, Sophie would have desired to have the choice available to her, we might ask whether, years earlier, Sophie would desire to live in a society that, later on, would put that choice to her. That, however, is simply—but deeply—to say that the only answer lies in specifying the conditions of justice.

The conditional-offer problem resists easy solution. Before we can make any progress toward a satisfactory approach, we must find baselines from which burdens and benefits can be measured; yet no obvious method for generating such baselines suggests itself. Moreover, even if we could agree on the baselines, we would still need a method for resolving claims rooted in equality rather than coercion and for distinguishing between choices that make people free and choices that people would choose not to make. Because the problem is complex, it is little wonder that no one has satisfactorily resolved it. It is too bad, however, that so many people purport to have done so.

There is a good reason why our constitutional advocates engage in this practice. To concede the intractable nature of the conditional offer problem is to destabilize the entire structure of constitutional argument. It is to concede that all of the standard moves these advocates regularly make simply do not withstand analysis.

To see why this is so, we need to examine the connection between conditional offers, state action, and the New Deal revolution. The first step is to show that the conditional offer dilemma does not exist apart from the public–private distinction discussed in chapter 3.

The point can be illustrated by reversing the usual abortion funding problem. Suppose the government makes abortion criminal for any pregnant woman who fails to pay six hundred dollars for a special abortion license. Although this scheme seems clearly unconstitutional,[3] standard accounts of the conditional offer doctrine fail to explain why. The government seems to have made the very sort of conditional offer that the abortion funding cases uphold. In both cases, the government has not outlawed abortion outright. Instead, it has packaged the right to obtain an abortion with a willingness (or ability) to pay money in order to receive it.

What makes our hypothetical different from the real abortion funding cases is not that the offer is conditional but that the government seems to be acting rather than merely failing to act. In the real abortion funding cases, the government simply failed to take affirmative measures to make abortions available to women too poor to afford them. Under

3. A plurality of the Court now utilizes an "undue burden" test to evaluate the constitutionality of restrictions on abortion. Although the parameters of this test remain unclear, it would almost certainly be violated by the six-hundred-dollar fee, especially if the fee served no purpose other than to discourage women from having an abortion.

standard doctrine, it is no more obligated to intervene in this fashion than Wisconsin was required to protect Joshua DeShaney from his father. In contrast, in our hypothetical case the government has "acted." The special abortion licensing fee makes it more difficult for women to obtain abortions than it "naturally" would be in the private sphere. It is as if state officials themselves had beaten Joshua DeShaney.

In light of the this overlap between the conditional-offer problem and the state action problem, it is hardly surprising that the effort to sort out permissible from impermissible conditional offers is bedeviled by the same difficulties confronting courts trying to figure out whether there is "really" state action.

Recall, for example, Chief Justice Rehnquist's effort in *DeShaney* to explain why the state bore responsibility for acting but not for its failure to act. If the government could have prevented Joshua's injury, why isn't it responsible when it deliberately failed to prevent foreseeable harm? Precisely the same difficulty confronts those who try to explain why the government is responsible when it prevents abortions by criminalizing them but is not responsible when it prevents abortions by failing to subsidize them.

Justice Brennan's *DeShaney* dissent attempts to establish state responsibility without abandoning the basic state action requirement. He argues that the government has no constitutional obligation to intervene at all but that it is constitutionally responsible for making things worse for Joshua through its partial intervention. He then must explain how Joshua is made worse off by the government's efforts to help some other abused children.

This problem also parallels difficulties faced by opponents of conditional offers. Why does government intervention extending benefits to some people make things worse for those to whom the benefits are not extended? Justice Brennan responded to the problem in *DeShaney* by constructing elaborate counterfactuals suggesting ways in which the world might be better for Joshua if the government had not intervened at all. The prediction technique for thinking about conditional offers requires similar mental gymnastics. The technique requires us to imagine how the world might have been reconstructed if the government were put to an all-or-nothing choice.

Justice Blackmun's *DeShaney* opinion argues that the public–private distinction is meaningless and that the Court ought simply to do what is just. His problem lies in finding a way to explain how the concept of individual rights can survive the insight that the government is in some sense responsible for all choices.

Once again, there is a parallel difficulty in the conditional-offer context. Women may be coerced into having children by the government's failure to subsidize abortions, but it does not follow that those subsidies would leave them in a state of perfect freedom. After all, the government does not reimburse poor women for the full cost of raising a child. Subsidizing abortions without subsidizing child-rearing expenses might therefore coerce women into choosing abortion. The point can be generalized: In any complex society, individual choice is inevitably influenced by society's choices about which functions are to be performed (and to what degree) by government and which are to be left to the market. If all private decisions are shaped by this complex web of conditional offers, the very concept of individual rights existing within a nongovernmental sphere collapses.

Thus, the conditional-offer and state action problems turn out to be identical and to produce an identical set of destabilizing problems for constitutional argument. Surprisingly, however, the histories of the two doctrines are somewhat different.

In chapter 3 we argued that the modern state action doctrine was created by the liberal justices who claimed power in 1937. In contrast, the conditional-offer doctrine predated the New Deal. Long before the Court began rejecting claims to constitutional protection on the ground that there was no state action, it sometimes limited the reach of constitutional rights by finding that freedom had not been impaired by conditional offers.

This paradox is more apparent than real, however. Before the New Deal, a premodern state action doctrine anticipated, in reverse, the modern one. The pre–New Deal version directed courts to limit political institutions of the national government, while the modern one frees national and state political institutions from judicial supervision. The modern version bounds a discretionary sphere where the political branches are free to intervene or not as they choose; the premodern version bounded a mandatory sphere where the courts prevented the national political branches from acting.

Before the New Deal, the conditional offer doctrine functioned in a similar fashion. Prerealist judges had no trouble distinguishing between conditional offers granting discretionary benefits and conditional threats imposing impermissible burdens. They could make this distinction by referring to a natural baseline formed by the freedom individuals enjoyed within a mandatory private sphere.

From this perspective, there is nothing problematic about our abortion-funding hypothetical. The baseline is formed by the contract price, freely negotiated within a naturally private sphere, to perform the service. If the government imposes a burden on top of this price, it is distorting the market and precluding a transaction that both parties freely agreed to and, therefore, definitionally, made both parties better off. On the other hand, if the government refuses to pay for abortions, it is doing no more than leaving individuals undisturbed within this sphere of private freedom.[4]

The fact that a Court would surely resolve both cases the same way today demonstrates the hold this way of thinking still has on us. Yet the very existence of the New Deal destabilized the conceptual framework that justified these outcomes. The New Deal was a set of interventions into "private" markets designed to shift contractual baselines. These interventions subverted the old approach on both a practical and a normative level.

As a practical matter, the intricate web of subsidies, licensing schemes, and regulatory measures made it increasingly unrealistic to take a private contract negotiated between two autonomous individuals as a starting point. Of course, even before the New Deal, government coercion in the form of background contract and tort rules was necessary to allow the market to function. As a cultural and political matter, the New Deal brought these interventions into public view. In a regulatory state, all negotiations occur against a preexisting backdrop of government actions designed to encourage one or another outcome.

As a normative matter, the country's acceptance of the New Deal entailed a rejection of the view that private ordering was necessarily superior to ordering brought about by government action. New Dealers believed that the baseline provided by individual contracts was often

4. The abortion example serves to emphasize the fragility of the prerealist worldview. Obviously, pre–New Deal courts would have been untroubled with state restrictions on private contracts to perform abortions. These contracts were treated as outside the private sphere—perhaps because they fell within the state's traditional police power to enforce standards of morality, perhaps because the fetus was treated as a third party whose liberty interest was invaded by the contract. The perceived arbitrariness of distinctions like these ultimately contributed to the downfall of the natural-rights approach.

unjust and that decisions made by individuals in the private sphere were hardly free. When workers agreed to work long hours for low wages, they were not exercising natural rights. Rather, they were responding to an unfair economic order that the government had to (or at least could) rectify. Thus, the New Deal's central purpose was to shift the baseline through government intervention. The old natural-rights ideology treating contractual ordering as an aspect of freedom was dislodged and replaced by a pragmatic, policy-management approach that asked whether a particular distribution of resources best served the country's needs.

This revolution in legal ideology should have solved the conditional-offer problem. Once it was understood that all baselines were created by government decision, there was no longer a need to worry about whether a particular action constituted an offer or a threat. However characterized, government intervention inevitably influenced all private conduct. Hence, the only issue was how baselines might be manipulated to produce outcomes that advanced the government's policy goals.

In fact, however, the New Deal made the conditional offer problem much worse. As we discussed in chapter 3, most New Dealers were never able fully to accept the concept of completely manipulable baselines. To do so would necessarily have undermined the normative commitment to social justice that gave moral force to the New Deal. Any claim that a particular social arrangement is unjust implicitly requires a comparison between that arrangement and some other ideal arrangement against which it is being measured. Hence, even as they rejected the Old Court's effort to reason from natural baselines, New Dealers were erecting new natural baselines of their own.

Moreover, undermining the concept of natural baselines posed special problems for constitutional argument. New Dealers wanted to liberate the political branches to shift baselines for pragmatic purposes. How were the courts to approach constitutional argument in this new environment? Most New Dealers wanted to restrain judges. One approach, associated with Justice Black in the post–New Deal period and with Robert Bork in our own time, is the retreat to textualism. According to this view, judges have no business basing their decisions on their views about social policy or moral philosophy. Their only job is to enforce those rights embedded in the constitutional text.

For all its problems, textualism has the virtue of holding on to the idea of individual liberties while restraining judges in a culture where the old natural-rights approach has lost its plausibility. Unfortunately, however, the conditional-offer dilemma renders this approach largely useless. The problem is this: No matter how many rights are granted in a constitutional text, some things people very badly want or need will always fall outside the text's guarantees. The government will therefore always be able to undermine textually protected rights by threatening to withhold nontextually protected benefits unless the individual gives up the rights.

A constitutional text therefore cannot protect individual rights without some background assumptions about other, basic rights to which people are entitled. Textual rights are meaningful only if people have some set of nontextual entitlements that they can depend upon to shield them from pressures to yield their textual rights.

Yet the whole point of the New Deal's rejection of judicial supremacy was to prevent the courts from enforcing entitlements of this sort. Indeed, opponents of judicial activism were able to use conditional-offer analysis as a powerful tool for demonstrating why the case for these nontextual rights was incoherent. Because all individual decisions are inevitably made against the backdrop of a network of government offers and threats, the search for a state of nature in which people exercise their rights to make free and private decisions is pointless.

Thus, the changed perception of the baseline problem left constitutional argument in stalemate in the post–New Deal period. The regulatory state's ability to generate an endless array of conditional offers meant that the Supreme Court could neither limit itself to protecting textual rights nor take on the task of elaborating rights outside the text. Textual rights were hopelessly vulnerable to the conditional offers generated by the state, and nontextual rights lost their plausibility in light of the government's conceded ability to change what people chose by shifting the baseline against which the choice was made.

Of course, despite all of this, people have gone on making constitutional arguments. We want to make these arguments because we want to believe that it is still possible to appeal to a common set of assumptions that might unite us and provide a generally agreed-upon framework for settling our disputes. Moreover, whether we realize it or not, these arguments usually appeal to some natural baseline against which the impermissible coercion of individuals can be judged. No matter what the realists taught us, few of us are prepared to give up on baselines of this sort, for to do so is to give up on the possibility of normative judgment altogether.

What has been lost is the faith that arguments of this type will actually persuade. Although we are unable to let go of it, the intellectual apparatus that once gave substance to these arguments has lost its plausibility. It is therefore apparent to everyone that the arguments can be manipulated to advance the particular policy goal of the advocate who makes them.

As a result, constitutional argument in the modern period actually accomplishes precisely the opposite of the result intended. Instead of appealing to what unites us, constitutional argument is almost always divisive. Instead of a method for reaching out to one's opponents, it is a method for rallying one's own troops by dehumanizing one's opponents. Instead of a technique for settling disputes by resort to reason, it is a way of asserting power over others.

These unfortunate trends have infected constitutional debate on a wide variety of subjects. In the remaining chapters of this book we canvass a few of them.

5

Racial Equality and the Rhetoric of Nondiscrimination

Let us begin with our own summary of the "nondiscrimination principle":

> Racial discrimination is irrational, unfair, and inherently wrong. People should be judged on the basis of their individual merit rather than on the basis of racial stereotypes. The government should never allocate benefits or burdens on the assumption that individuals are likely to act in a particular way just because of the color of their skin.

For most of this country's history, most of its people denied the truth of these propositions. They were soundly rejected by the framers who wrote our founding document in 1787. Washington, Jefferson, Lincoln, and Wilson are only the most prominent presidents who did not accept them. For decades, the economy of half the country was organized around the explicit and brutal rejection of racial equality. Within the lifetime of many of us, the mere assertion of a belief in racial justice was, at least in certain contexts, a revolutionary act courting a violent response.

Remarkably, the very propositions that once defined a fringe position have now taken on the character of a central, unifying creed—an organizing postulate of our politics. Whatever else divides us, few contemporary Americans would deny the nondiscrimination principle.

This story might appear to provide a strong counterexample to our general thesis concerning the disutility of constitutional argument in the modern period. The extraordinary victory of the nondiscrimination principle seems to demonstrate that serious constitutional argument can indeed change minds about even deeply entrenched and emotionally charged positions.

This optimistic view, however, is true only if we confine the discussion to a very high level of generality. As soon as one tries to give the nondiscrimination principle specific content, soothing unanimity gives way to contentious argument. Although newly united in our commitment to racial justice, we remain as divided as ever concerning the meaning of this ideal.

Perhaps this disagreement reflects an unwillingness to accept the ideal on anything more than a rhetorical level. It is one thing to talk the language of racial equality and quite another to transform our politics and daily lives in a way that would make the language meaningful. Indeed, the widespread acceptance of equality rhetoric might even retard the movement toward a truly nonracist society by dulling our sensibilities to racist structures and practices.

Although we do not wish to deny the possibility that equality rhetoric masks continued adherence to old, racist assumptions, in this chapter we explore a different and, in some ways, even more unsettling claim: Disagreements about concrete applications of the nondiscrimination principle reflect an incoherence at its core.

In chapters 3 and 4 we argued that the transformation of American legal thought that accompanied the New Deal revolution created significant barriers to serious discussion of constitutional issues. The collapse of natural-rights theory and the partial triumph of legal realism generated the need for the delineation of a private sphere and the establishment of an extraconstitutional baseline for the measurement of rights, while simultaneously erecting obstacles to the achievement of those objectives. The resulting ambivalence has made it difficult for serious constitutional argument to get off the ground and has led to the posturing and oversimplification that characterizes so much modern constitutional debate.

This chapter develops these themes against the backdrop of Americans' supposed commitment to racial nondiscrimination. We argue that the state action and baseline problems prevent us from giving the principle meaningful content. As a result, despite its nearly universal acceptance, the principle fails to guide our politics. It has become no more than a rhetorical weapon used by each side to discredit the other.

Our analysis proceeds in three parts. First, we argue that efforts to apply the seemingly straightforward nondiscrimination principle produce results that nearly everyone would agree are incoherent and normatively unattractive. Second, we explore the ways in which current Supreme Court doctrine reflects this unhappy situation. Finally, we suggest reasons why defects in this doctrine are the inevitable consequence of the baseline and private sphere difficulties discussed in chapters 3 and 4.

The nondiscrimination principle seems so simple and so simply right that it is hard to believe that its application would cause serious difficulties. How can anyone believe that a person should be disadvantaged solely because of the color of her skin? Yet no area of constitutional law has generated more confusion and controversy.

Perhaps the most heated argument has centered around "affirmative action" programs that allocate scarce resources in a race-conscious fashion to overcome prior discrimination or to ensure racial diversity.[1] Opponents of these programs claim that they violate the nondiscrimination principle by disadvantaging whites solely because of their race. Advocates of the programs claim that they are required (or at least permitted) by the nondiscrimination principle because the application of a seemingly neutral standard against the backdrop of several hundred years of oppression in effect penalizes African-Americans because of their race.[2]

Although the affirmative action debate is central to modern controversy about racial equality, we postpone further discussion of it until

1. It is symptomatic of the polarization on this issue that one cannot even name such programs without committing oneself to a position on the merits. (A similar difficulty bedevils the effort to talk about conflicting positions on abortion in terms of "pro-choice" and "pro-life"). The term "affirmative action" implies that the existing norm, resulting in the exclusion of many African Americans, is neutral and uncontroversial and that one must act "affirmatively" to depart from this norm. Some advocates of race-conscious programs favor them precisely because they believe that existing norms are not neutral and manifest white dominance in our culture. We discuss this issue in more detail later in this chapter.

2. In fact, advocates advance a variety of arguments, not all of which are consistent. Some advocates claim that race-conscious programs do not violate the antidiscrimination principle either because the supposedly race-neutral standard is itself racially biased or because "affirmative" remedial measures are necessary to compensate for years of prior discrimination. Other advocates claim that even if such programs are racially discriminatory in some sense, discrimination against the dominant group has a different social meaning from discrimination against the oppressed group. These adherents assert that the nondiscrimination principle is a tool for ending a system of racial hierarchy and ought not apply to efforts by subordinated groups to end their subordination.

later in this chapter. We do so because it is not possible to get beyond the overheated rhetoric about that issue without understanding that it is really a symptom of a broader difficulty with the nondiscrimination principle. Popular debate about jury selection in the state trial of Los Angeles police officers accused of beating Rodney King provides a useful vehicle for addressing this difficulty.

The trial judge shifted the trial to Simi Valley, a mostly white suburb, after an appellate court found that pervasive pretrial publicity would prevent a fair trial in Los Angeles. The court's selection of Simi Valley was widely criticized as a blunder or worse. Many commentators found it incomprehensible that the judge could have been so insensitive as to arrange for the trial of this racially charged case before a nearly all-white jury. Indeed, the decision seemed to epitomize the lingering racism that still infects the judicial system. Yet paradoxically, if the judge had rejected a Simi Valley trial to avoid trying the case before an all-white jury, this ''racially sensitive'' decision would have violated the nondiscrimination principle.

The principle prohibits government officials from acting on the basis of racial stereotypes. It guarantees the right of individuals to be judged without regard to generalizations based upon skin color. The original selection of Simi Valley did not violate this requirement, at least if we are to take the trial judge at his word. The judge claimed that the choice was dictated by racially neutral factors, such as the availability of a large courthouse and proximity to Los Angeles.

Having selected the site for racially neutral reasons, a judge who refused to go forward with the trial there because of the likely racial composition of the jury would be violating the principle because that decision would rest on a deliberate effort to manipulate the jury pool to produce jurors of a particular race. The Supreme Court has repeatedly held that such government efforts violate a defendant's right to a fair and impartial jury. This is so, at least in part, because the selection of the jury pool should not be based on the racial stereotypes outlawed by the principle. The judge therefore cannot premise his decision on a belief that an all-white jury is less likely to adjudicate the case fairly.

Thus, the Constitution and the nondiscrimination principle seem to require the judge to act in the racially ''insensitive'' fashion widely attacked by critics who surely view themselves as strong believers in racial nondiscrimination.

Perhaps these critics are simply wrong. Perhaps they would change their views once they came to understand that these views conflict with the more fundamental principle of nondiscrimination they profess to believe in. Unfortunately, matters are not quite that simple.

Sometime stereotypes are factually accurate, but the nondiscrimination principle still prohibits the government from relying on stereotypes linked to race. An adherent of the principle must therefore concede at least the theoretical possibility that an all-white, Simi Valley jury would in fact be less likely to judge the case fairly—perhaps because white jurors could not put aside their own stereotypes about African-Americans like Mr. King.

If the facts turned out that way, the trial judge would be faced with a difficult dilemma. Moving the trial from Simi Valley would violate the nondiscrimination principle because the decision to do so would be based upon a racial stereotype about the ability of white jurors to judge the case fairly. Yet allowing the Simi Valley trial to go forward would lead to a jury verdict infected by a racial stereotype. If we are prepared to treat such a verdict as government action (or if the judge's action can be treated as a cause of the verdict), then the verdict would violate the nondiscrimination principle, and a judge who adhered to the principle would be obliged to move the trial to a location where a racially mixed jury could hear the evidence.

Is it any wonder, then, that the nondiscrimination principle ends up settling few arguments? Both sides can accuse the other of violating its terms, and both sides are, in a sense, right.

The paradox runs still deeper. Suppose the trial judge announces that he cannot go forward with a Simi Valley trial because there are likely to be too many whites on a Simi Valley jury and that he is therefore transferring the trial to a jurisdiction with a larger African-American population. Suppose further that the defendants are convicted in the new jurisdiction by a predominantly African-American jury. Should they be able to overturn their convictions on the ground that the judge violated the nondiscrimination principle?

The decision to move the trial out of Simi Valley would be premised on a racial stereotype about the behavior of white jurors that the nondiscrimination requirement prohibits. Yet an appellate decision that the defendants were harmed by the trial court's actions is also based upon a racial stereotype violating the nondiscrimination principle: The defendants are harmed only if the judge's actions reduced their chance of acquittal, and their chance of acquittal is reduced only if white jurors are in fact less likely to vote for conviction than African-American jurors.[3]

It turns out, then, that both the decision to move the trial and the reversal of that decision violate the nondiscrimination principle. Both the decision and the reversal are premised on impermissible generalizations about the likely behavior of black and white jurors.

How might we explain these paradoxes and contradictions? At the simplest level, they are manifestations of two interrelated problems with the concept of nondiscrimination.

The first problem arises out of the conflict between race consciousness and color blindness. The nondiscrimination requirement appears to embrace the ideal of color blindness. It is rooted in the liberal assumption (perhaps "hope" is a better word) that racism amounts to no more than a perceptual error, that people who believe that race correlates with various individual characteristics are simply mistaken. If only we could convince these people to put aside their prejudices and irrational predispositions, they would see that a person's race is never a relevant characteristic.

This assumption produces difficulties for the nondiscrimination principle because in our culture, it is almost certainly wrong. In late twentieth-century America, an individual's race often tells us something important about him or her. Membership in a racial group is part of an individual's cultural identity, and this identity correlates (albeit imperfectly) with a whole range of views and predispositions. Of course, racial generalizations are far from universally true, and racial prejudice causes us to exaggerate their accuracy. Nonetheless, we cannot escape the reality that race often matters.

Indeed, it is precisely because race does correlate with other attributes that we need the nondiscrimination principle. In this sense, the principle is rooted in the concept of race consciousness rather than color blindness. We do not generally insist on a principle of nondiscrimination for

3. The Supreme Court has sometimes attempted to avoid this contradiction by insisting that the "harm" produced by deliberate efforts to exclude a particular race from the jury pool is not to the defendant but to the excluded jurors or to society as a whole. In other cases, however, it has claimed that the defendant himself is denied equal protection by the deliberate exclusion of jurors of his race. At this stage of the argument, we make no claims about actual Supreme Court doctrine. We wish to establish only that attempts to apply the nondiscrimination principle lead to confusion. We discuss the extent to which the principle is incorporated in current doctrine later in this chapter.

individuals whose last names are at the end of the alphabet or for people who are left handed even though individuals belonging to these groups frequently suffer disadvantage because of group membership. In our culture, these are not socially significant groups. An important reason that they are not socially significant is that being left-handed and having a name at the end of the alphabet do not define cultural differences and therefore do not correlate with other important individual characteristics. In contrast, the nondiscrimination principle applies to race precisely because racial groups have the kind of social significance that liberal advocates of nondiscrimination want to deny to them.

It is easy to see how the nondiscrimination principle is caught between the desire to treat race as if it were irrelevant and the reality that it is not. The trial judge who moves the trial from Simi Valley for racial reasons must be reversed because the nondiscrimination principle requires him to treat the race of jurors as if it did not matter. He cannot proceed on the assumption that, as a group, white jurors are likely to vote differently from African-American jurors. Yet the reversal of his decision is premised on the belief that the jurors' race does matter. The defendants are harmed because white and African-American jurors are likely to react differently to the evidence.

Our ambivalence about treating race as a relevant characteristic also produces the second problem: The nondiscrimination principle is rooted in contradictory views about individual and group rights. On the one hand, the principle seems to be grounded in a rejection of group identity. An individual asserting the nondiscrimination principle claims that it is unfair to make generalizations about her or him on the basis of group membership. However other members of the group behave, she or he insists upon an entitlement to an individual determination that is based upon individual merit. Whereas advocates of color blindness deny that race correlates with attributes such as jury voting behavior, individualists claim that it is wrong for the state to characterize individual jurors based upon even accurate racial generalizations.

On the other hand, the nondiscrimination principle makes sense only because individuals belong to groups, and its protection seems to be primarily directed to groups. Even if its conduct is egregiously unfair, the government does not violate the principle when it misjudges the individual characteristics of a citizen. For example, the nondiscrimination principle is not violated if the government denies someone a job because some bureaucrat pulled out the wrong test results and mistakenly thought that the applicant lacked the qualifications for the job. The principle takes hold only when its actions cast aspersions on a group. Deliberate gerrymandering harms African-Americans as a group because the exclusion stigmatizes all African-Americans.

In theory, these contradictions might be resolved if we were willing to commit ourselves firmly to either the individualist, color-blind version of the nondiscrimination principle or to the group-rights, race-conscious version. We might convert the principle into a prohibition against categorization, one that would prohibit the state from relying on group generalizations of any kind. The principle would require the government to evaluate everyone solely on the basis of individual merit. Alternatively, we might convert the principle into a prohibition against caste that might obligate (and surely would permit) the state to take the measures necessary to end the subjugation of African-Americans as a group.

Each of these approaches, if seriously pursued, is normatively attractive in its own way. Most of us are drawn to the uniquely American idea that individuals should be free to construct their own identities without regard to accidents of birth. The notions that rewards should be apportioned according to individual merit and that it is deeply unfair to judge a person on the basis of preconceptions are firmly embedded in our culture. These intuitions pull us toward an anticategorization stance.

Many of us, however, also experience pride and a sense of identity from membership in ethnic or cultural groups. They play an important role in defining who we are, even though we did not choose to belong to them. Moreover, the degradation of certain groups and the seemingly permanent alignment of groups in a hierarchical relationship seem profoundly wrong. These intuitions pull us toward the anticaste position.

Unfortunately, the problem is not just that we are attracted to each of these contradictory ideals. The more serious difficulty is that we are unable fully to embrace either. Each position is difficult to reconcile with the structure of constitutional thought after the New Deal revolution.

Thus, a prohibition against categorization presupposes a version of individual freedom that is inconsistent with the New Deal revolution. The administrative state rests on the assumption that individuals acting alone are often not "free" in any meaningful sense. Moreover, collective intervention designed to ensure "real" freedom is possible only if the government is permitted to group people on the basis of general tendencies. A ban on categorization would therefore effectively prevent the sort of legislative intervention that was at the heart of the New Deal.

A prohibition against caste, while avoiding these problems, requires the specification of a "natural" order, which contradicts another aspect of New Deal jurisprudence. If the Court were to enforce the prohibition, it would have to make political outcomes conform to some preexisting natural-law baseline against which the actual alignment of groups could be measured.

The result is that the Supreme Court has been unable to give a convincing account of either version of the nondiscrimination principle. Instead, it has satisfied itself with watered-down, halfhearted accounts of both versions.

Viewed superficially, the modern Court appears to have firmly committed itself to the anticategorization version of the principle. It has emphasized individualism and color blindness at the expense of group rights and race consciousness. Thus, the Court has been extremely hostile to government actions that facially discriminate against African-Americans. For example, a statute that excluded all African-Americans from jury service clearly violates the principle and would certainly be invalidated. Such a statute is premised on the assumption that race is a relevant characteristic and precludes individualized judgments about each juror.

Of course, hostility to measures of this sort might also be explained by opposition to caste, since they have the effect of reinforcing the subservient status of African-Americans as a group. But two other classes of cases—concerning government policies that have a disproportionate impact on racial minorities and affirmative action programs—make clear that this is not the Court's predominant concern.

The Court's disproportionate-impact cases have generally upheld government actions that adversely affect African-Americans so long as the challenged statute or policy is facially neutral (that is, so long as the statute or policy does not by its terms discriminate along racial lines) and so long as it is not enacted for the purpose of disadvantaging African-Americans. For example, the trial judge's decision to relocate the King trial to Simi Valley for facially race-neutral reasons did not violate the principle even though it resulted in the exclusion of African-Americans from the jury.

The Court's decision in *Washington v. Davis* (1976) illustrates this position. Plaintiffs were African-Americans whose applications to join the District of Columbia police force had been rejected because the applicants had failed to achieve high enough grades on an examination designed to test verbal ability, vocabulary, and reading comprehension. They made no claim that the test was deliberately formulated to exclude African-Americans, but they asserted that it was nonetheless unconstitutional because it "had no relationship to job performance and had a highly discriminatory impact in screening out black candidates."

The Supreme Court firmly rejected this claim. Although acknowledging that the "central purpose of the Equal Protection Clause of the Fourteenth Amendment is the prevention of official conduct discriminating on the basis of race," the Court declined to embrace "the proposition that a law or other official act, without regard to whether it reflects a racially discriminatory purpose, is unconstitutional *solely* because it has a racially disproportionate impact."

Significantly, the Court justified this outcome with the rhetoric of individualism. The Court had "difficulty understanding" how a test requiring individualized judgments concerning each applicant according to racially neutral standards could be thought of as racially discriminatory.[4]

A court committed to a group-rights version of the nondiscrimination principle might be troubled by government actions of this sort. Even facially neutral statutes and policies can have the effect of maintaining the inferior status of African-Americans as a group if the basis for the statute systematically correlates with race. But because blacks and whites are given an individual opportunity to show that they satisfy the statute's requirements, the statutes and policies seem to satisfy individualist version of the nondiscrimination principle.

The Court's decisions concerning affirmative action form the second line of authority inconsistent with the anticaste version of the principle.

4. The Court reasoned as follows: "Had respondents, along with all others who had failed Test 21, whether white or black, brought an action claiming that the test denied each of them equal protection of the laws as compared with those who had passed with high enough scores to qualify them as police recruits, it is most unlikely that their challenge would have been sustained. . . . Respondents, as Negroes, could no more successfully claim that the test denied them equal protection than could white applicants who also failed. The conclusion would not be different in the face of proof that more Negroes than whites had been disqualified by Test 21. That other Negroes also failed to score well would, alone, not demonstrate that respondents individually were being denied equal protection of the laws by the application of an otherwise valid qualifying test."

A court committed to the anticaste position might permit, or even require, such measures on the ground that they are calculated to end black subjugation. The Court has instead subjected them to careful scrutiny because they disadvantage individual whites who are "unfairly" categorized on the basis of their group membership.

Washington v. Davis did not expressly discuss the affirmative action problem, but its approach obviously has important implications for this controversy. At a minimum, the holding meant that affirmative action was not constitutionally required. The plaintiffs' claim amounted to an assertion that the government had to adjust its facially neutral standard to produce an outcome favoring African-American applicants. By rejecting that claim, the Court was, in effect, rejecting judicially mandated affirmative action programs.

Of course, affirmative action might be constitutionally permissible even if it is not constitutionally required. *Washington v. Davis* did not directly address the constitutionality of voluntarily established affirmative action programs. Nonetheless, the Court's individualist rhetoric clearly presaged its subsequent decisions closely scrutinizing these programs. The Court suggested that the District of Columbia test was constitutionally permissible because it allowed for individualized judgments about an applicant's fitness for employment under a neutral standard. In contrast, affirmative action measures are usually justified by claims about the effect of government policies on racial groups—or, as the Court put it, on "other Negroes [who] also [fail] to score well." This is precisely the sort of argument that *Washington v. Davis* treats as illegitimate.

Washington v. Davis thus seems to embrace an approach to the nondiscrimination principle that treats race as an irrelevant characteristic and prohibits group generalizations. It is easy to be misled by the Court's confident tone, however. Despite some of the opinion's rhetoric, its endorsement of individualism and color blindness is highly qualified. It embraces these ideals to the extent that this version of the nondiscrimination principle allows it to reject the plaintiffs' claims. Yet it backs off from these commitments when they might entail judicial intervention to promote racial justice.

Clearly, the Court cannot be insisting upon a general requirement of individual evaluation. The District of Columbia police department did not pretend to provide such evaluations, and the Court was untroubled by that fact. The police department unashamedly categorized job candidates on the basis of their performance on the challenged examination. It was apparently not open to individual candidates to demonstrate that the examination failed accurately to measure their particular abilities or that a case-specific analysis of their individual attributes demonstrated that deficiencies in the areas tested were outweighed by strengths in areas not tested. Instead, it was enough for the city—and for the Court—that the test divided applicants into groups with general tendencies relevant to good police work even if reliance upon those general tendencies led to the inaccurate categorization of some individuals.

Of course, the disadvantaged group was not racially defined—at least, not in any obvious way. Perhaps, then, *Washington* can be understood as abandoning the individualist prong of the nondiscrimination principle but adhering to the color blindness prong. According to this view, the government may group people in ways that do not necessarily apportion benefits according to individual merit so long as it does not do so on a racial basis.

There are two problems with this approach. First, when so modified, the nondiscrimination principle loses much of its moral force. Once it is conceded that it is permissible for the government to make generalizations about individuals along a whole range of dimensions, some observers might question why we should retain a special rule prohibiting such generalizations on the basis of race. Indeed, the special hostility to group-oriented measures designed to improve the status of African-Americans in a context where group-oriented measures harming them are routinely accepted might, itself, violate the requirement of color blindness, although the nation's history of adopting programs in the name of assisting African-Americans that in retrospect appear to have harmed them might give us pause.

Second, closer analysis makes plain that the Court has abandoned the color blindness prong of the nondiscrimination principle in other respects as well. The problem here is to devise a satisfactory account of what it means for the government to be "blind" to color. Most obviously, it means that the government may not expressly use race as a criterion for apportioning benefits and burdens. For more than a hundred years, however, the Court has made plain that this is not all it means. Even if a statute or policy is facially neutral, it can still violate the color blindness prong of the nondiscrimination principle if it is gerrymandered—that is, if the line is drawn for the purpose of achieving a specific racial outcome. For example, even if the judge in the Rodney King trial claimed to be moving the case to Simi Valley because this location was convenient for witnesses, he would still be violating the nondiscrimination principle if his real purpose was to achieve an all-white jury.

The *Washington* Court was convinced that the District of Columbia's policy was not gerrymandered in this fashion. The Court thought it obvious that the police department was motivated by the desire to produce a more literate and responsive police force, not by the desire to exclude African-Americans.

Unfortunately, the Court's approach papers over a host of problems. It is not at all clear what it means to say that a collective institution, such as a legislature or an administrative agency, is motivated by one desire rather than another. What if some members vote for a measure for one reason, and others for another? What if members voted for a policy years ago for racial reasons but more recently have failed to repeal it for nonracial reasons? Suppose legislators are motivated by neither racial nor public policy concerns but simply by the desire to be reelected. Is the policy nonetheless unconstitutional if some of their constituents take race into account when they cast their ballots?

Even if we had answers to all these questions (and even if we could figure out a satisfactory way for a court to resolve factual disputes about the internal mental states of legislators, administrators, and voters), we would still not be at the bottom of the problem. Even if the police department did insist on the test solely because of a desire to produce a more literate police force—indeed, even if no one associated with this decision ever thought about race—the decision to impose the test still might violate the requirement concerning color blindness.

This is true for two reasons. First, the standard itself might incorporate white rather than African-American norms. Perhaps the test assumed familiarity with white institutions and culture or tested for linguistic and grammatical conventions common in the white but not the African-American community. Indeed, the very decision to treat literacy as an important requirement for a police officer might reflect a cultural bias. Why is the department testing for literacy rather than, say, for knowledge of the particular community to which the officer will be assigned? If the standard is inherently biased in favor of whites in this fashion, it seems obvious that judging applicants according to the standard is not color-blind.

Second, even if we assume that the standard itself is neutral, the decision to adopt it might nonetheless have taken race into account in the sense that administrators would not have adopted it if the costs of doing so had been differently distributed. Although administrators might genuinely prefer a more literate police force, there are surely some limits on the resources they are willing to expend to achieve this result. If administrators care less about the welfare of African-Americans than about the welfare of whites, it will seem to them that the costs of the program are relatively small if large numbers of prospective African-American police officers are disqualified by it but relatively large if a comparable number of whites are disqualified. Thus, even if the Court is right that the officials were genuinely committed to police literacy and did not use the test as a subterfuge to eliminate African-American candidates, they might still have rejected the test if it had resulted in a virtually all African-American police force.

The Supreme Court has cut off inquiries along these lines. It has ignored the possibility that government officials might unthinkingly accept white standards as neutral and natural when the standards are in fact culturally specific and contested by members of minority communities. And it has expressly rejected the claim that these officials violate the Constitution when their conduct is the result of selective indifference to the welfare of African-Americans. Thus, unless color blindness is taken to require no more than a prohibition against sadistic action motivated by the unadorned desire to make life worse for African-Americans, the Court's approach fails to embody that ideal.

The upshot of all this is that although the Supreme Court has endorsed individualism and color blindness on the rhetorical level, it has made only halfhearted efforts to follow through on the logic of these positions. It does not follow that this vacuum has been occupied by the competing anticaste version of the nondiscrimination principle, however. To be sure, a few of the Court's cases have been influenced by the group-rights, race-conscious approach. This line of authority forms a deviant countertradition that competes with the dominant one. Even when they are taken on their own terms, however, the anticaste cases suffer from a parallel failure to follow through on the implications of the Court's rhetoric.

The Court's best known anticaste decision is also one of the most famous and celebrated decisions in all of constitutional law—*Brown v. Board of Education*. Superficially, it might seem that *Brown*'s prohibition against legally mandated segregated schools fits easily within the color blindness–individualism approach embraced by *Washington v.*

Davis. The Court's central holding was that public officials could not take race into account (i.e., had to be "blind" as to color) when they assigned children to schools. That holding was premised on the belief that it was deeply wrong to deny individual African-American children the opportunity to fulfill their potential because of their membership in a disfavored group.

On closer analysis, however, it becomes clear that *Brown* is fundamentally incompatible with *Washington v. Davis*. Consider, for example, the best-known passage in Chief Justice Earl Warren's opinion for the *Brown* Court: "To separate [African-American children] from others of similar age and qualifications solely because of their race generates a feeling of inferiority as to their status in the community that may *affect* their hearts and minds in a way unlikely ever to be undone" (emphasis added). The *Washington v. Davis* Court was unmoved by the argument that the City's hiring policies had a bad *effect* on African-Americans. For Justice Byron White, the author of *Washington v. Davis,* government policy was unconstitutional only if it had the *intent* of discriminating against racial minorities. In contrast, there is not a word about intent in Chief Justice Warren's *Brown* opinion. Segregation is unconstitutional not because it is intended to hurt blacks but because, whatever its intent, it relegates them *as a group* to a permanently subservient position.

Of course, there are important differences between *Washington v. Davis* and *Brown*. The intent behind the system of segregation was patent—to maintain the subordination of African-Americans. Any claim by segregation's defenders that segregation benefited African-Americans would have reflected their perspective, not social reality. Further, whereas the District of Columbia hiring policy did not facially categorize people according to race, school segregation statutes did. One might therefore suppose that both *Washington v. Davis* and *Brown* endorse the requirement concerning color blindness.

But this formulation begs the central question in *Brown*. Defenders of segregation argued that segregated schools did not categorize people along racial lines. Blacks and whites alike were compelled by law to attend schools populated by children of their own race. The *Brown* court looked behind this argument from formal equality to the real impact that segregation had on African-American children. Although blacks and whites were equally denied the right to integrated education, this policy had a disproportionate impact on blacks—an impact that was inconsistent with the core aspirations of those who wrote the Equal Protection Clause. If disproportionate impact alone was sufficient to invalidate the formally equal segregation policies attacked in *Brown,* why was it not sufficient to invalidate the formally equal employment policies attacked in *Washington v. Davis*?

Brown's incompatibility with the requirement concerning color blindness became more apparent when the Court turned to implementation of the decision. Because *Brown*'s holding rested on the effect of segregated schooling on black children, it was a short step to the conclusion that the state had an affirmative obligation to end the harm that segregation caused. And it eventually became apparent that meeting this obligation required race-conscious remedies. Thus, the Court held that school boards that had violated *Brown*'s command were sometimes constitutionally obligated to assign children to public schools on the basis of race in order to eliminate the vestiges of legal segregation.

School boards resisting these decrees sometimes tried to rely on the principle behind *Washington v. Davis*. They argued that if their assignment policies were neutral on their face and not racially motivated, they could not be unconstitutional. Significantly, the Court generally rebuffed these efforts. For example, it held that a policy designed to produce neighborhood schools was unconstitutional, even if it was not racially motivated, if it failed to meet the state's affirmative obligation to end the harm caused by segregation.

Brown is also incompatible with the individualism strand of *Washington v. Davis*. Notice, for example, that the *Brown* Court did not pause to investigate whether segregation retarded the development of each individual African-American forced to attend all-black schools. It is implausible in the extreme that the Court's empirical assumptions about the effects of segregation were universally true. On individualist premises, it is wrong to deprive an individual African-American child of the right to show that he or she would be better off in a segregated environment on the basis of a generalization about the group to which he or she belongs. Yet the Court was completely unfazed by this difficulty. Plainly, Chief Justice Warren's concern was not with doing retail justice to individual students but with wholesale social engineering. *Brown* was intended to end the caste system that dominated American society.

With forty years' hindsight, it is obvious that *Brown* did not achieve this goal. There are many reasons for this failure, but one reason is that the Court itself largely abandoned the effort. The Court failed to deliver on *Brown*'s anticaste rhetoric in much the same way that it backed off from its anticategorization commitment.

Brown implies that the government has an affirmative obligation to take whatever measures are required to end the subjugation of African-Americans as a group. Ending legally imposed school segregation does not begin to exhaust the measures that must be taken to achieve this goal. Affirmative measures on many fronts—from welfare and tax reform, to drug and AIDS treatment, to job training and remedial education programs—would be required.

Today, no one within the political mainstream thinks that *Brown* mandates anything like such a program. Instead, *Brown* has been more or less confined to the specific setting in which the case was decided, and its reach has been sharply limited even within that setting. *Brown* now means that public institutions may not be deliberately segregated by race, and nothing more.

Brown was gutted in two steps. After creating an illogical distinction between the substantive right protected by *Brown* and the remedial measures necessary to implement that right, the Court interpreted these remedial measures extremely narrowly.

Brown itself spoke eloquently of the actual effect segregation had on African-Americans, and some post-*Brown* decisions required affirmative measures designed to create integration. More recently, however, the Court has confined the scope of these decisions by treating them as relating to the remedial discretion of judges charged with ending segregation, rather than as a component of the substantive right at stake.

According to this approach, once a school board is found to have committed a violation, a judge can order effects-based, race-conscious measures to remedy the violation. For example, the judge can assign students to schools according to race and order busing of students outside their neighborhood even if the school board's opposition to these measures is motivated by a good-faith desire to maintain neighborhood schools.

The violation itself, however, is now defined in terms more consistent with the *Washington v. Davis* approach. As an initial matter, school boards are not obligated to take affirmative measures to deal with the harmful effects of so-called de facto segregation. If these officials are not motivated by a desire to segregate students, the Constitution does not require them to do anything about the harm produced by the segregation.

This approach is illogical. If the Constitution, as a substantive matter, requires no more than the avoidance of deliberate segregation, what justification is there for a court's going beyond this requirement to remedy the violation? Logical or not, the bifurcation of right and remedy sharply limited the scope of *Brown*. It means that where there is no proof of an antecedent constitutional violation (defined in *Washington v. Davis* terms), the government need not act affirmatively to end black subjugation.

Even if one accepted this bifurcation, *Brown* might still have had some bite if the Court had adopted a more expansive approach toward the government's remedial obligations. For example, federal courts have held that the District of Columbia schools attended by many of the African-American police applicants who performed poorly on the *Washington v. Davis* examination were segregated by law. It does not require much imagination to see how this poor performance was caused by the antecedent constitutional violation. Why didn't the government have an affirmative obligation to remedy this violation by making appropriate accommodations for African-Americans on the examination?

In recent years the Court has sharply constricted the government's remedial duties. In contexts like *Washington v. Davis,* it has said that the government is under no obligation to remedy harms produced by unconstitutional segregation even though *Brown* held that the segregation was unconstitutional precisely because it produced those harms. Even more remarkably, in cases where jurisdictions have *voluntarily* undertaken affirmative race-conscious measures designed to remedy these harms, the Court has invalidated them.

If the argument we have outlined is correct, it is hardly surprising that invocation of the nondiscrimination principle does little to advance our ongoing debate about race. Advocates on all sides of racial issues try to claim the moral high ground by using the principle as a weapon against their opponents. Invocation of the principle is superbly effective in achieving this purpose, and its use is therefore all but irresistible. Unfortunately, the principle is a good deal less effective in actually changing anyone's mind. It is too confused, and our adherence to it too qualified, to do any real intellectual work. The nondiscrimination principle incorporates contradictory critiques of caste and categorization, and attempts to apply it therefore produce endless contradiction. Moreover, even when we try to embrace one or the other of these critiques, we have found ourselves unable or unwilling to follow through on that commitment.

Why has it proved so hard to articulate a coherent moral vision concerning the role of race? Why have we been so reluctant to implement whatever vision we have chosen?

One source of the difficulty is unwittingly revealed in the concluding passage of the constitutional discussion in *Washington v. Davis*:

> A rule that a statute designed to serve neutral ends is nevertheless invalid, absent compelling justification, if in practice it benefits or burdens one race more than another would be far reaching and would raise serious questions about, and perhaps invalidate, a whole range of tax, welfare, public service, regulatory, and licensing statutes that may be more burdensome to the poor and to the average black than to the more affluent white.

The clear implication of this passage is that the fact that a new approach would be "far reaching" and might necessitate invalidation of many of our current practices should, by itself, count heavily against it. The Court's apparent endorsement of this view provides ammunition to those who charge that the debate about the nondiscrimination principle is no more than a charade designed to mask the justices' unwillingness to do anything serious about a problem that would, in fact, require "far reaching" actions to extirpate.

Typically, it is at this point in the argument that the participants begin to raise their voices. One side claims that this studied indifference to the problems of racial minorities is racist. The other maintains that African-Americans are seeking special favors, that more such favors will only encourage further dependency, and that racial minorities have no one to blame but themselves for their problems. Both sides end up appealing only to their own supporters. Neither is able to invoke a shared understanding, such as a meaningful nondiscrimination principle, that might actually be useful in changing someone's mind.

We would like to propose some way around this rhetorical dead end, but before we can even begin to think about solutions, we must have a clear understanding of the problem. Our goal in the remainder of this chapter is therefore considerably more modest. We will confine ourselves to providing some explanations for the intractability of this problem. Our specific claim is that the difficulties we experience in formulating convincing arguments about race constitute a special case of the broader problem with constitutional argumentation that we have outlined in the preceding chapters.

To see how this is so, consider again the issue posed in *Washington v. Davis*. The problem is hard because, at its core, it amounts to the same state action and baseline difficulties that we encountered in chapters 3 and 4. Indeed, the case demonstrates how the two difficulties are linked. We lack a vocabulary to talk seriously about *Washington v. Davis* because we have yet to find a way to resolve these underlying dilemmas left over from the New Deal revolution.

Although the Court did not use the language of state action, its opinion could easily be reformulated in this fashion. Just as Wisconsin was not constitutionally liable for Joshua DeShaney's injuries, so, too, the District of Columbia was not responsible for injuries suffered by the minority police applicants who failed the police department's examination. Because the examination was facially "neutral," the poor performance by African-Americans must be attributable to forces located in the private sphere—forces for which the state bears no responsibility. Even if the state was responsible for providing an inadequate education, it might be said, individuals failed to apply themselves hard enough or failed to seek out supplemental forms of education.

In *DeShaney* Justice Rehnquist insisted that, although the Constitution prohibited the state from taking affirmative measures that harmed its citizens, it imposed no duties to take affirmative measures to avoid harm inflicted by others. Justice White made precisely the same point in *Washington*: Although the state may not harm African-Americans by affirmatively discriminating against them, it has no constitutional obligation to take the affirmative measures that would be required to avoid harm. One can make this point by saying that the Equal Protection Clause requires only neutrality and does not mandate equal outcomes. One can make precisely the same point by saying that the Equal Protection Clause makes the government responsible only for state action and not for the mere failure to act affirmatively to remedy privately inflicted injuries.

For anyone familiar with New Deal jurisprudence, the weaknesses in this argument, however phrased, are glaringly apparent. The argument assumes that we can define a natural and uncontroversial baseline from which departures from neutrality can be measured. But no such baseline exists. Attempting to define the baseline by distinguishing between government action and inaction ignores all of the ways in which the government acts to enforce background rules that are causally linked to the injury in question. Thus, Joshua DeShaney's injuries were caused by a variety of government interventions into the family (most obviously the allocation of children to their biological parents) that made him vulnerable to his father's violence. Similarly, the poor test performance of the African-American plaintiffs in *Washington v. Davis* did not just "happen."

More fundamental, *Washington v. Davis* again raises the question why the government bears no responsibility for "mere" inaction. Put most simply, we are back to the problem of the cedars and the apples. As Justice Stone explained, there is no reason to treat the status quo or "natural" course of events as a baseline. There was therefore no neutral ground between sacrificing the cedars and sacrificing the apples. Doing nothing is also a government choice, and the government must bear responsibility for its decision's consequences. So, too, there is no neutral ground between taking measures to aid African-American recruits and not taking those measures. The government's failure to adjust its testing criteria to yield more African-American police officers is every bit as much a decision as its failure to destroy the cedar trees.

Brown, and the countertradition it represents, can be understood as embodying just this sort of argument, and, in this sense, there is a direct link between *Brown* and New Deal jurisprudence. In *Plessy v. Ferguson,* the case that *Brown* overruled, the Court insisted that separate but equal was neutral and attributed the stigmatization produced by Jim Crow to private forces in much the way that the modern *Washington* and *DeShaney* courts disclaimed government responsibility:

> We consider the underlying fallacy of the plaintiff's argument to consist in the assumption that the enforced separation of the two races stamps the colored race with a badge of inferiority. If this be so, it is not by reason of anything found in the act, but solely because the colored race chooses to put that construction upon it.

The *Brown* Court emphatically rejected this argument from formal neutrality. For Chief Justice Warren, there was no escape from the choice between organizing the public schools in a fashion that advanced black aspirations and organizing the schools in a fashion that maintained black subordination.The government's failure to take the measures necessary to end black subjugation was itself an injury for which the government bore constitutional responsibility.

Brown's special hold over our constitutional culture is no doubt partly explained by its link to powerful strands in New Deal jurisprudence. Yet, as we have noted, for all the emotional resonance it has for us, on a practical level the *Brown* approach has remained subservient to the competing *Washington v. Davis* tradition. Given the obvious weaknesses in that tradition, why has the Court defended it so vigorously?

Ironically, the same baseline difficulty that makes *Washington v. Davis* so unconvincing also dooms the *Brown* approach. The problem for *Brown* is that once the status quo produced by private forces is abandoned as the baseline, it is not readily apparent what to substitute for it. For example, a Court prepared to jettison *Washington v. Davis* would immediately be confronted with the problem of deciding precisely how many African-American police officers to insist upon. Should the examination be adjusted to produce a percentage of black officers equivalent to blacks' percentage in the population? If only a small adjustment is required and if the test is only marginally related to effective police work, that might be acceptable. More substantial adjustments of more significant tests might cause problems, however. At some point, the gain in African-American employment will no longer be worth the cost in competent policing—a cost that may also be borne disproportionately by the African-American community. How should a court go about deciding when that point has been reached?

Moreover, using the percentage of blacks in the population as a baseline hardly seems just if only a small percentage of blacks actually apply for positions on the police force. Perhaps, then, the percentage of new recruits should mirror the percentage of black applicants. But why should current black application rates be treated as a natural baseline? If the government bears responsibility for African-American failures on the test, why isn't it also responsible for the refusal of African-Americans to apply in the first place? And if it bears that responsibility, how can a court possibly decide what is the constitutionally "right" level of African-American interest in police work?

Ultimately, a Court that embarked on this path would need a fully worked out theory of social justice against which to measure outcomes of this kind. In Platonic fashion, it would have to decide what functions individuals were "naturally" best suited for and how much in the way of power and resources they were "naturally" entitled to.

Efforts along these lines contradict another aspect of New Deal jurisprudence. The New Deal's rejection of *Lochner v. New York* was grounded in a deep distrust of natural baselines of this sort. The justices who assumed office after the New Deal believed that there was no noncontroversial natural law baseline from which constitutional violations could be measured and that the Old Court's effort to construct one had masked a profoundly antidemocratic effort to foist a particular narrow ideology on the rest of the country.

When Justice White complains that a contrary result in *Washington v. Davis* would require "far reaching" interference with political outcomes, he is linking himself to this aspect of the New Deal tradition. Our post–New Deal understanding makes his efforts to rely upon the public–private distinction seem unconvincing and question-begging. Yet that same understanding makes the distinction crucial, since without it, the Court would have to invent the very sort of judicially imposed natural law system that the New Deal revolution was fought to overturn.

The conflict between categorization and caste reflects a similar ambivalence inherited from the New Deal. On one level, the New Deal can be understood as elevating opposition to caste over opposition to categorization. Before the New Deal, courts sometimes stymied government regulation by insisting on individualized judgments about those subject to it. According to this theory, the government violated important individual rights when it categorized large groups of people according to traits possessed by only some of them.

New Dealers understood that effective government control of private power would be impossible so long as this ban on categorization was in force, and they set about dismantling it. An important part of their argument was that the supposed freedom of individuals to act apart from the groups to which they belonged was largely illusory. Thus, individual bakery workers forced to bargain for themselves had no real freedom to turn down the contracts that *Lochner* protected. On the contrary, it was only through government intervention in support of collective action (in the form of unions and regulatory intervention) that the economic caste system could be dismantled.

Brown is also linked to this aspect of New Deal jurisprudence. The *Brown* decision was not about any particular plaintiff's individual rights. The Court's strategy was group-based and rested on a willingness to override individual preferences. Thus, it came as no surprise when the Warren Court rejected "freedom of choice" plans that stymied school segregation by making individual black parents choose between integrated and segregated education. This "choice" was no different from the "choice" of individual bakery workers to work long hours at subsistence wages.

New Dealers were not prepared entirely to let go of the idea of individual freedom, however. They could not do so without slipping into the abyss of nihilism. The whole point of collective intervention was to produce the background conditions that would make individuals "truly" free. The Warren Court saw desegregation in much the same light. Desegregation was required precisely because it was necessary in order to give black children a chance to make meaningful choices about their lives.

Once this much is conceded, it becomes difficult to avoid contradiction. The moral force of opposition to caste is derived from the obligation to take the possibility of individual freedom seriously. Yet advocates of group intervention refuse to take seriously the choices actually made by those they wished to protect.

Perhaps only a few African-Americans have applied for police jobs because they really do not want to be police officers. Perhaps many of them fail the examination because they have made a considered choice not to study harder for it. There is a sense in which denying these possibilities serves to demean those supposedly being protected by affirmative action. It suggests that they should be treated as special wards of the state, incapable of the kind of responsibility expected from the rest of us.

It is also true that what seems like choice is often constrained by background conditions that substantially limit the real options available to suppressed minorities. But we have now come full circle. Trying to specify the background conditions that would make these choices "truly" free returns us to the morass of natural law baselines that New Deal jurisprudence was intended to escape.

This contradiction lies at the heart of one of the Court's most important decisions on affirmative action. In striking down a city's program that set aside 30 percent of its subcontracts for minority entrepreneurs, the Court chastised the city for assuming that African-Americans would—in a world free of discrimination—choose to enter the construction business at the same rate as whites (*City of Richmond v. J. A. Croson Co.*, 1989). The mere fact that relatively few African-Americans were in fact in the business was not enough to establish discrimination, the Court said, because that pattern might result from "both black and white career and entrepreneurial choices. Blacks may be disproportionately attracted" to other businesses.

Contrast this with another opinion by Justice Sandra Day O'Connor, the author of *J. A. Croson*. In upholding a challenge to race-conscious districting for Congress, Justice O'Connor founded her constitutional analysis on the argument that it is an "impermissible racial stereotype" to assume "that members of the same racial group—regardless of their age, education, economic status, or the community in which they live—think alike, share the same political interests, and will prefer the same candidates at the polls" (*Shaw v. Reno,* 1993).

In striking down the set-aside program, the Court relied on a strong principle of color blindness, which derives its moral force from the assumption that African-Americans and whites are fundamentally alike in all matters relevant to government decisions. In short, African-Americans and whites are alike enough to require a strong principle with respect to color blindness. But they may be different enough to make affirmative action unconstitutional.[5]

The rhetoric used to describe America's tragedy of race relations is filled with the imagery of separation. We are said to be two societies, separate and unequal, riven by race prejudice and unable to bridge a huge gulf of culture, class, and worldview.

If the argument we have made in this chapter is correct, these images reverse reality. The problem with constitutional debates about race is not that we have separate worldviews with no points of contact. It is rather that we all have the same worldview but that this worldview is self-contradictory. People on both sides of the racial divide share a commitment to the New Deal's contradictory impulses toward the possibility of collective change and the commitment to individual freedom.

It is therefore hardly surprising that both sides of the race argument resort to the same nondiscrimination principle. Nor is it surprising that resort to the principle fails to advance the argument. The principle supports both positions because they are both the same position—a position that perfectly reflects contradictions that lie at the core of modern constitutional thought.

5. Perhaps the Court will ultimately distinguish between career choices, where African-Americans and whites differ, and political choices, where they do not. We would not want to be asked to draft the opinion doing so.

It follows that it is precisely wrong to suppose that our race predicament will be solved by finding a common language to bridge the gap between racial groups. There already exists a common language. The problem is that the language no longer serves anyone. If we are to solve the problem, we need to develop a new language that will create real conflict by challenging the paradigm shared by all participants in our current debates. Sadly, the task of inventing such a language has not even begun.

6

Pornography and the Financing of Political Campaigns

Our experience with race discrimination suggests that even when people purport to agree on matters of fundamental principle, internal contradictions within the principle can generate unproductive and vitriolic debate. A similar pattern mars efforts to think seriously about freedom of speech.

Attempts to regulate the financing of political campaigns and the availability of pornography provide a telling example. Such attempts have created odd and overlapping alliances.

Some conservatives want to regulate sexually explicit material because they believe it undermines traditional gender roles; they find themselves allied with those feminists who want to regulate the material because they believe it reinforces traditional gender roles. Some conservatives who support regulation of pornography decry campus hate speech codes as exemplifying how political correctness leads to suppression of free speech; then they discover that the most forceful advocates of such codes also support suppressing pornography. Some liberals who think free speech means that the government should not regulate the distribution of pornography also think that free speech means that the government *should* regulate campus hate speech and campaign finance.

When constitutional analysis produces alliances like these, people ought to pay attention. The alliances suggest that just as there is no "deep" conservative or liberal constitutional theory, so, too, conservative or liberal theories of free speech are not really driving the analysis. They suggest that, instead, people decide what policies they favor and then adjust their constitutional theories so that those policies are constitutional. In one sense that ought not be bothersome: Why should anyone be committed to a theory that produces results she finds deeply troubling? A sensible way to deal with such results is to see if the theory can be adjusted to preserve the results the advocate cares about. The real difficulty is that far too many people use this strategy far too frequently—that is, whenever they run across a policy they like that seems inconsistent with the theory they had the moment before. When that happens, the theory is doing no work whatever; everything depends on the results. And yet, advocates pitch their cases on the high constitutional ground, not on the ground—which is what is really at work—that society would be better off with the policies the advocates favor.

Not all conservatives and liberals find themselves in these peculiar alliances (and, of course, what seems peculiar depends on one's overall set of values—from one perspective, the American Civil Liberties Union's opposition to campaign finance regulation, antipornography laws, and campus speech codes seems consistent, while from another it may seem to lump together quite disparate issues). Sometimes, too, people try to distinguish among the problems. For example, some people maintain that the government should have more latitude to regulate sexual speech than to set limits on political speech.[1]

We think that approaching the problems from the other side produces valuable insights. Instead of focusing on what is being regulated, we focus on *why* people think regulation might be a good idea. From this side, the problems of pornography, campaign financing, and hate speech are indeed the same.[2] The argument for regulation in each area begins with the identical premise: People start with unequal resources to accomplish their ends. One source of inequality is the way economic power is distributed between rich and poor. Some liberals advocate campaign finance regulation because they are bothered by the impact of the distribution of wealth on public policy. Similarly, some feminists perceive another source of inequality in the way social power is distrib-

1. Feminist proponents of the regulation of pornography ordinarily rely on the perception that "the personal is the political" to point out that what people think about sex has important implications for what they do in politics and in public life. Unfortunately for them, that makes these regulations seem more like regulation of political speech, which makes them more difficult to justify under traditional First Amendment standards.

2. We do not provide a detailed analysis of campus hate speech codes here because that analysis would track the ones we offer for pornography and campaign finance regulation.

uted between men and women. They advocate the regulation of pornography because they are bothered by the impact of this unequal distribution of social power on public policy. Yet another source of inequality is the way power over ideas is distributed between elites and the common people. Some conservatives advocate the regulation of pornography because they are bothered by the impact that elite views have on public policy in this area.

In this sense, advocates of campaign financing regulation and antipornography laws are attempting to use the government's power to rectify what they believe are the bad social consequences of the existing distribution of power (monetary power in one case, sexual or class power in the other). Both groups are the heirs to the New Deal revolution, which taught us that the Constitution did not limit the government's attempts to rectify what political majorities believe to be the bad social consequences of the existing distribution of power. The New Deal revolution was limited in its initial appearance to establishing that the Constitution's economic provisions did not limit such attempts. Recent regulatory efforts raise the question, Why should the Constitution's free speech provision be any different?

Answering that question is made more difficult by two related problems. First, if we limit the scope of the New Deal revolution to the Constitution's economic provisions, we may indirectly betray the revolution's apparent promise that political majorities may adjust the distribution of economic wealth as they choose. Unless regulated, wealthy people can use their wealth to stymie the kind of economic redistribution that the New Deal revolution supposedly permits.

Second, some Supreme Court cases can be read as confirming the widespread intuition that it is wrong to make access to opportunities to persuade others entirely dependent on wealth. Demonstrations on public streets, for example, are important in building political support, and we think that many people would be bothered if the government charged demonstrators for using the streets, even though people who own television stations can charge for broadcast time. Some people would be "priced out of the market" if they had to pay for all free-speech opportunities. Poor people cannot afford to pay for television time, but they can afford to take time out to demonstrate. Making the streets available for demonstrations gives them free-speech opportunities that they would not have if everyone had to pay for such opportunities. This means, however, that the government not only is *allowed* to address the free speech consequences of the distribution of wealth but *must* address at least some of those consequences.

Around the time the New Deal revolution was being fought, the Supreme Court issued some famous opinions that eloquently defended the use of the streets for First Amendment purposes. These decisions are consistent with the premises of the New Deal revolution because they support the government's authority to redistribute resources. Yet they are also in tension with the revolution because they suggest that economic distributions can be mandated by judges and ought not be left entirely to the political process.

The remainder of this chapter explores these problems. After examining what the Supreme Court has had to say about the government's obligation to deal with the free-speech consequences of the distribution of wealth, we will discuss whether campaign financing regulation and antipornography regulation raise different questions. Our answer, in short, is that the only differences among the "demonstration" cases, campaign financing regulation, and antipornography regulation are pragmatic: The three problems do not differ in principle, but they may differ in the extent to which we can trust government regulators—including judges—to do a decent job of actually addressing the real problems that arise from a skewed distribution of social and economic power.

Free-speech law is driven by a series of unremarkable propositions. Advocates of regulation argue that speech can cause harm.[3] A fair amount of free-speech absolutism, in contrast, rests on the proposition that speech never causes harm; it capitalizes on the familiar saying "Sticks and stones can break my bones, but words can never hurt me." Free-speech absolutists often suggest that claims that speech hurts are false or silly or the result of a peculiar oversensitivity. As we will show, the childhood saying on which free speech absolutists rely is demonstrably incorrect. What is correct, however, is that legislatures and other lawmakers (such as juries) not infrequently overestimate the amount of harm speech causes, and free-speech law ought to respond to that problem without asserting that speech can never cause harm.

Different kinds of speech cause different kinds of harm in different

3. More precisely, that legislatures representing the views of a political majority can reasonably believe that speech causes harm.

ways. False and malicious statements about a person's private life may hurt her reputation and restrict her career options. Tobacco advertising may lead some people to do permanent damage to their health. A person who uses a racist term in an angry argument may find his target hitting back. An eloquent speaker who criticizes the government for allowing too much immigration may persuade listeners to attack people who look Hispanic; an equally eloquent speaker who criticizes the government for keeping out too many political refugees may persuade other people to organize a sanctuary movement to hide illegal immigrants whom they describe as political refugees.

Contemporary free-speech law slots these problems into many boxes. Some speech, such as speech about government policy, is "high-value." Other speech, such as false statements about a person's life, is "low-value." Commercial advertising, according to the Supreme Court, falls somewhere in the middle. The Court has made it hard to regulate high-value speech by requiring the regulations to meet tough standards. Legislatures can regulate low-value speech more easily so long as the regulations are reasonable ways to minimize the harms the low-value speech causes. Obviously, the fact that the standards are so different means that a lot turns on how speech is categorized. Typically, the more a type of speech involves rational argument and relates to political and other public concerns, the more likely it is to be classified as high-value. The categories are not sharply defined, however.

Victims of speech are also grouped into different categories. Sometimes speech inflicts harm on an individual or a narrow class. Traditional libel law, which allows a person to recover for damage to her reputation caused by false factual statements, deals with that sort of harm. At the other extreme, some speech is thought to inflict harm on the society as a whole. The classic free-speech cases involve criticism of the government, which prosecutors claim has a tendency to lead to increased lawbreaking. If that claim is right, the entire society is put at risk. In the middle, some speech is construed as harming an identifiable group smaller than the whole society. Such a claim is made by people who support regulation of pornography as a way of advancing women's interests.

What happens when we say that the Constitution bars a legislature from regulating speech? The unregulated speech will cause whatever harm it causes. We might easily describe this as a subsidy for speech: When the Constitution requires that one person suffer harm because of another person's speech, the victim is subsidizing the speaker. The clearest example is libel law. A newspaper that publishes a libelous statement may achieve an increase in its circulation and, therefore, its profits. The damage to reputation is real, and if the victim cannot recover, she has subsidized the newspaper. Moreover, the damage to reputation may affect the victim's speech opportunities; her damaged reputation may lead people to disbelieve what she says.

The idea that free-speech law is a subsidy is quite general. Victims of harms caused by speech almost always subsidize speakers. Why should they? Again, libel law offers an answer. If we could be sure that juries would do no more than require newspapers to bear the costs of their activities, we might not be too concerned. After all, what good is directly served by disseminating false statements about people's lives? According to the Supreme Court, the problem is that regulating speech has a "chilling effect." No matter how hard we try to avoid mistakes, juries are certain to make them: They will find a statement to be false when it actually is true, or harmful when it actually is not, or more harmful than it actually is. Publishers, facing the risk of jury mistake, will publish fewer controversial statements even if they are accurate; they will, as Justice Brennan put it, "steer clear" of the prohibited zone.

Such a policy, however, deprives the rest of us of useful—and true—information about important matters. The remedy in free-speech law is to limit publishers' liability by narrowing the "zone." Instead of being liable for publishing any false statements, they can be made to pay only when they deliberately publish false statements or when they publish such statements without taking adequate precautions. Under this legal rule, victims can still recover damages for some false speech (which adds nothing to public knowledge or discourse), but publishers are less likely to be deterred by the risk of jury mistake from publishing true speech.

Now we can see why free-speech law forces victims to subsidize speech. Constitutional limits on regulation of speech benefit the public as a whole.[4] Libel victims are not really subsidizing newspapers; they

4. Sometimes defenders of free speech say that the public benefits from the publication of false statements, because such statements may generate a useful investigation into what is really true or because their falseness may reinforce our own confidence in the truth of what we already believe. Even here, however, free-speech law requires victims to suffer because the rest of us benefit from constitutional rules that deny them the opportunity to recover for their injuries.

are subsidizing the rest of us, to make it possible for us to receive as many true statements from newspapers as the papers are ready to publish.[5]

Treating free-speech law as a subsidy does not mean, of course, that the subsidy is a good idea. The "chilling effect" explains why speakers should not have to pay their victims, but it does not explain why the victims should bear the speakers' costs. After all, if the public generally benefits from speech (even when that speech causes harm), why shouldn't the public pay the victims? That way, speakers would not be deterred from speaking and victims would not bear the costs of free speech.

Sometimes, the Court has held, an individual victim does not have to bear the costs of free speech. For example, the Court has permitted regulation of demonstrations that target an individual's residence or interfere with a person's access to an abortion clinic. It has been somewhat more willing to insist on subsidizing speech when the cost is borne by the community as a whole. For example, the public as a whole must run the risk of increased lawlessness when the Constitution prevents limitations on the speech of those who advocate it.

This sort of public subsidy is even more apparent when protestors march on a main street or hold a rally in a public park. This activity imposes costs on the rest of us. Our commuting schedules may be disrupted, extra police officers may have to be dispatched to the area to protect the marchers against their opponents, and the city's garbage collectors will have to devote more time to cleaning up the areas than they otherwise would.

Most legal scholars agree that the Constitution requires these sub-

5. If newspapers are really benefiting all of us, one might suppose that newspaper subscribers would be prepared to pay for the benefit in the form of higher prices and that a public subsidy would be unnecessary. The difficulty is that newspapers are unable to charge for the full benefit of the information that they produce. To take an obvious example, once a daily newspaper is sold, the publisher loses the ability to prevent people other than the purchaser from reading the paper or learning the news contained in it. The newspaper cannot charge the individual who picks up a discarded paper on a subway train or the spouse of a newspaper reader who finds out the news in a dinner-table conversation. More broadly, the newspaper cannot charge for the benefit produced by the wide dissemination of information about public events. Without the ability to capture the economic benefit of this dissemination, publishers have an insufficient incentive to engage in it. A public subsidy provides the additional incentive.

sidies. Unfortunately, the Supreme Court's cases are not quite so clear. Some cases do indicate that cities may not completely deprive protestors of access to areas suitable for demonstrations. For example, the Court held unconstitutional a federal statute barring people from demonstrating on the sidewalks surrounding the Supreme Court itself (*United States v. Grace,* 1983). And we are confident that the Court would hold unconstitutional an ordinance that allowed demonstrations on a city's main street only between the hours of 2 and 4 A.M.

These examples suggest that the guiding rule is that cities must make areas available for demonstrations under reasonable conditions—or, to put it in the terms of a subsidy, cities must provide reasonable (although not extensive) subsidies for speech activities. The next step is to consider how this standard might operate when actual money is involved. Suppose a city insisted that demonstrators pay the actual costs borne by the city to clean up after a demonstration. Would this requirement be constitutional?

The Court has never decided that question. Its cases dealing with fees go off on procedural issues.[6] Still, nearly every legal scholar who has written about the matter believes that a city could not require a cost-justified fee, at least in cases where demonstrators were unable to pay it.

The fact that some demonstrators cannot pay cost-justified fees is important to our argument. Rich people usually do not need a city's streets and parks to make their point. They can rent a hall or buy time on radio or television or, in the extreme, even buy a radio or television station or create a cable program. Only the relatively poor or unpopular, who cannot collect enough money to buy airtime, need to use a city's streets for their speech activities.

The Constitution requires a subsidy for speech activities because some people are unable to pay the market-determined price for engaging in those activities and because the activities benefit all of us. The size of the subsidy is open to debate. What matters most, however, is that the Constitution requires governments—that is, the people generally—to take account of the impact of the distribution of wealth on the ability of people to engage in speech activities.

We have described the subsidies that the Constitution requires the public to pay in support of speech activities. Proposals to regulate the

6. For our purposes, we therefore assume that the procedures to determine actual costs satisfy every requirement the Court might impose.

distribution of pornography or the financing of political campaigns raise related questions. Opponents of pornography restrictions and of campaign financing regulation might claim that protecting this speech gives it a similar, constitutionally mandated subsidy. So far, however, we have treated the concept of subsidy as if everyone agreed on what a subsidy was. The New Deal revolution made that agreement elusive. "Subsidy" implies that we know what the "right" or "free market" level of activity is. The subsidy is then what "goes beyond" what the market provides. The New Deal revolution taught us that the free-market level of activity need not be accepted as a given.

Before addressing this difficulty, we must introduce two additional considerations that have affected the structure of free speech law. These considerations involve how speech causes harm. Sometimes it causes harm by persuading people through rational argument that it would be a good idea to do what the speaker says. For example, an eloquent antiabortion activist might convince a crowd of demonstrators to burn down an abortion clinic. Here speech causes harm because it is rationally persuasive. Sometimes, however, speech causes harm without persuading. For example, a racist epithet hurts its victim even if no one is persuaded by it.

These examples also illustrate the second consideration. Sometimes there is a time lag between the speech and the harm it causes. The destruction of the abortion clinic, for example, occurs only after the crowd hears the speech and acts on it. In other instances, there is no such lag; the target of a racist epithet is harmed as soon as she hears the words.

These questions of how, and how quickly, speech causes harm have affected the structure of free-speech law. The Supreme Court has said, for example, that governments can punish speakers when their words are "directed to inciting or producing imminent lawless action and [are] likely to incite or produce such action" (*Brandenburg v. Ohio,* 1969). That formulation crystallized a great deal of history, but for our purposes it is enough to note that the Court's emphasis on "incitement" suggests a concern for words that are not rationally persuasive and that its attention to "imminent lawless action" suggests a concern for the immediate rather than the delayed impact of speech. Similarly, when Justice Holmes disparaged a looser sense of "incitement" in writing, "Every idea is an incitement. It offers itself for belief, and, if believed, it is acted on," he too suggested that governments should not regulate speech where there is a time lag between the speech and the harm it causes. And, in one of the most widely quoted passages in free-speech theory, Justice Louis Brandeis drew together the themes of rational persuasion and the time factor: "If there be time to expose through discussion the falsehood and fallacies, to avert the evil by the processes of education, the remedy to be applied is more speech, not enforced silence."

For political speech at the heart of historical controversies over free expression, both considerations point in the same direction. All speech has some nonrational component, but political speech usually has a higher proportion of rational argument than, say, novels or Hollywood movies. And, of course, ordinarily one political speech can be countered by a reply speech.

What, however, should we do if the two considerations point in opposite directions? What about speech that does not operate through rational persuasion but takes time to work its way almost unnoticed into our thought processes? That is the question raised by proponents of antipornography regulation.[7]

What harms does pornography cause? Feminist proponents of antipornography legislation identify four different harms. First, some women who participate in the production of pornography are abused in the process. Second, women who unwillingly see pornography or simply know of its prevalence in our culture are psychologically assaulted. Third, some men who consume pornography are led to assault women physically. Finally, the widespread consumption of pornography leads men to think that women are not fully human, contributes to a pervasive social atmosphere of sexism, and stands in the way of social and political changes favorable to women.

In many ways the regulation of pornography is easiest to justify as a post–New Deal labor law, protecting participants in the industry against harms associated with producing the material. At least some women who are filmed in pornography are physically coerced, abused in the film itself, or threatened with abuse if they refuse to participate. Although these assaults are criminal acts, a legislature might reasonably suppose that the ordinary criminal processes are unlikely to be completely effec-

7. More precisely, according to these advocates, pornographic speech contributes to a structure of belief that subordinates women; each individual item of pornography might then immediately reinforce that structure.

tive. So, instead of prosecuting only producers who actually abuse women, a legislature might decide to ban the films' distribution.

Opponents of regulation might object that some women participate voluntarily in the production process. Banning distribution of all films because criminal acts occur while some are made is excessive and deprives some women of opportunities they would like to have. After the New Deal, however, that objection has usually been unavailing in the context of labor regulation. Although not all low-wage jobs are abusive in any real sense, minimum-wage laws bar some people from accepting them even though they would prefer that alternative to unemployment.

Nor is the fact that pornography is speech enough to remove it from the domain of labor law regulation. If we discovered that an ink used by publishers to print ads caused cancer in some workers, the First Amendment would not prohibit a statute barring publishers from using that ink even if publishers could not get their message across as effectively if they had to use other types of ink. Similarly with pornography: Banning its distribution because its production harms workers still leaves proponents of the ideas pornography conveys with alternative, although perhaps less effective, methods of getting their messages across.

This example raises another possibility for defending antipornography regulation as a labor law. Some people might be skeptical about the claim that large numbers of women are physically coerced into participating in producing pornography, although they might concede that a few women are. Coercion, however, can take many forms. For our purposes, the most interesting is what might be called "coercion by restricted alternatives." Some women "voluntarily" participate in making pornography because the alternatives open to them do not seem as desirable when they consider salaries, working conditions, and the like.

Since the New Deal, legislatures have been free to determine that this sort of pressure should count as coercion. Again, consider the worker in an industry with hazardous working conditions. A printer might say that, considering the salary publishers offer and her alternative career options, she would rather work with the dangerous ink for higher pay than accept some other job. Still, a legislature can ban the ink on the ground that workers should not be "forced" to choose between working under unsafe conditions and working at some other job. This is true even though some printers will not be able to work as printers at all if the publisher's profit margins go down, as they will when the ink is banned. In the narrowest sense, some printers will be driven out of the industry entirely—just as women would be driven out of the pornography industry by a ban on the distribution of pornographic films.

Indeed, we are confident that post–New Deal legislatures can ban entire industries as unsafe—professional bungee jumping, perhaps—even if some people prefer working in that industry, at whatever they can earn, to the alternatives they have available. In short, what allows legislatures to regulate working conditions is in part the argument that people can be coerced into working by a restriction on the alternatives available to them. Coercion, that is, goes beyond physical assaults.

This argument, while entirely standard in post–New Deal terms, does not rely on all, or even the most important, harms that pornography is said to cause. It might be adequate to deal with the psychological harm inflicted on women who unwillingly view pornography, particularly if we retain the concept of coercion by restricted alternatives. But the most important arguments for regulating pornography connect it to assaults on women outside the industry and to the general subordination of women.

Both sides in these discussions say silly things about the connection between pornography and assaults on women. Viewing pornography is not a trigger for immediate attacks on women, at least not routinely. Viewing some kinds of pornography, however, probably does change some men's attitudes toward women, and it is hardly unreasonable to think that once those attitudes have changed, changes in behavior will follow. Large parts of the advertising industry, after all, rest on that belief: By portraying smokers as people with bad breath, antismoking advertisements try to generate a negative attitude toward smoking in the hope that people who think that smoking is unattractive will not start to smoke. Or, as Chief Justice Warren Burger once suggested, in a society whose education policy endorses the belief that reading good books may make people behave better, a legislature could reasonably think that reading bad books—or viewing pornography—may make people behave worse (*Paris Adult Theatre* I *v. Slaton,* 1973).

Assaults on women and the belief that women ought to occupy a subordinate place in society have sources other than pornography. And, as opponents of antipornography regulation regularly point out, many published materials, including films and advertisements, carry the message of subordination without the sexual explicitness of pornography. Perhaps, too, there is some deeper cause at work that leads men both to consume pornography and to assault women or believe they should be subordinated.

None of those observations weighs heavily against the case for regulating pornography, however. If pornography is one among many causes of the harms, legislatures ordinarily would be allowed to act against it without having to act simultaneously against all the causes: Congress can ban one particular cancer-causing chemical without banning all such chemicals.

Perhaps legislatures should act against the more important causes of sexual violence and subordination rather than the less important ones. That, however, is a strategic and political judgment that courts have generally left to legislatures. Moreover, there may be a constitutional reason for limiting regulation to pornography. We have repeatedly used words like "reasonable" to describe judgments about causation. In core areas of free-speech law, however, courts have been far more rigorous, usually requiring a much closer connection between speech and harm. Those areas are usually described as involving high-value speech. When the speech falls into a different category, courts allow regulation if legislatures can reasonably believe that there is a causal connection between speech and harm. So, if pornography is low-value speech and the other sources of sexual violence and bad attitudes toward women are high-value speech, the reasons given by proponents of regulation might be strong enough to justify regulation of pornography but not of the other sources.

We have already described how free-speech law distinguishes between high- and low-value speech. Most commentators agree that pornography falls near the low-value end of the spectrum: It has a rather low proportion of rational argument (if it has any at all), and neither its producers nor its viewers really think that it is about political issues in any serious way. So, if pornography is low-value speech and if governments can regulate low-value speech when they can show that it is reasonable to think that the speech causes harm, antipornography regulations should be constitutional.

We have outlined an argument supporting antipornography regulation that emphasizes the connection between pornography and women's subordination. That argument has usually been described as an "equality" argument. That description may be misleading, however. Women's subordination has many aspects: It shows itself through lower wages for women workers, in verbal harassment of women as they walk to work, and—importantly—in judgments by many men that what a woman has to say need not be taken seriously. Pornography, according to this view, might then cause harm not just to women's equality but to their right to free speech as well; antipornography regulation might thus be a way of *protecting* speech rather than (or in addition to) regulating it.

Consider again our description of free-speech law as a subsidy to speech. Since some speech will be sacrificed whether or not pornography is regulated, it is no longer clear who is subsidizing whom. Just as the government must inevitably choose between the cedars and the apples (as we discussed in chapter 2), it must choose between two speech regimes. Traditional civil libertarians who oppose antipornography regulations deny legislatures the power to change the status quo under which men have social power in a form that makes their views more credible than women's views. But the New Deal revolution stands for the proposition that the Constitution does not require us to accept the status quo as a baseline. We might, for example, imagine a world in which men and women have equal social power. According to this view, the Constitution might actually *mandate* antipornography regulation as an obligatory means of subsidizing the speech of women.

Put more directly, in the constitutional world after the New Deal it is misleading to say that one side in the controversy over pornography seeks to "regulate" its distribution while the other wants to maintain "freedom" in distributing pornography. What is at stake are different systems of regulation. Critics of proposed regulations often say that the regulations would suppress speech. So, however, does the system of "non"-regulation. It is only that different speech is suppressed. Nor, finally, will it do to say that pornography may suppress some speech but only because of choices people make in the market, whereas the government itself suppresses speech under antipornography regulation. That is a state action argument that, as we showed in chapter 3, can no longer be sustained.

Thus, the ultimate question is, Which system of regulation exposes the society to the widest range of views? Because the status quo suppresses some views, or at least limits their exposure, that question cannot be answered by a mindless civil libertarian position that "regulation of speech" is a bad thing. It could be that, all things considered, the traditional civil libertarian position, which would make it impossible for society to deploy the power of government against pornography, does indeed expose the society to the widest range of views. But it could be otherwise.

Advocates of the regulation of campaign financing, like proponents of the regulation of pornography, argue that the Constitution permits legislatures to regulate the speech consequences of the status quo distribution of power. With campaign financing the status quo is the distribution of wealth resulting from whatever general system of property holding we have in place.

Proposals to regulate campaign financing fall into four categories. First, legislatures might provide money for campaigning. Second, they might limit campaign contributions. Third, they might limit campaign expenditures. Finally, they might combine a system of public campaign financing with the other kinds of limits, saying that candidates can receive public money for their campaigns only if they agree to limit their expenditures or the contributions they accept. For the purposes of our introductory discussion, the details of campaign financing regulations do not matter, although they will play an important part when we return to the issue at the end of this chapter.

Why do some people think that the system of campaign financing should be changed? Typically, they offer three reasons: corruption, alienation, and equality. The concern with corruption is straightforward. Historical experience shows that individuals or corporations that make large contributions to a legislator's campaign can sometimes persuade that legislator to vote for the contributor's position—even if that position is contrary to the public interest or, less pejoratively, contrary to what the legislator would have done if she had taken a detached view of the public policy issues at stake. Even if a legislator's vote is not actually changed in this fashion, we might still be concerned that it may *seem* to be changed. The Supreme Court has agreed with this reasoning and has upheld the constitutionality of limits on campaign contributions.

The problem of alienation is more difficult. It occurs because "ordinary" people, seeing how expensive it is to mount a serious campaign for office, begin to think that politics is a game for the well-to-do and the well-organized. They lose interest in politics and fail to communicate their views to their representatives or to mount campaigns of their own. The result is a distortion of public policy, as legislators respond to the wishes of the small group that remains interested in politics.

The equality concern is closely related to the problem of alienation. Some potential candidates are simply priced out of the market, knowing that they will be unable to raise enough money to mount a credible campaign. If an underfinanced candidate does decide to run, she may be drowned out by the political advertising that her better-financed rivals can distribute.

Alienation and equality concerns are both connected to the huge amounts needed to run a decent campaign. They could be alleviated if legislatures limited campaign expenditures. The Supreme Court has allowed legislatures to combine limits on expenditures with public financing: It upheld the federal system dealing with presidential campaigns, in which candidates who choose to accept public financing must limit what they can spend. It has not allowed legislatures to limit campaign expenditures directly, however, and it has even barred Congress from limiting expenditures supporting candidates who accept public financing if those expenditures are made independently of the candidates' campaigns (*Buckley v. Valeo,* 1976).[8]

The Court's analysis centered on several propositions. First, it said, "virtually every means of communicating ideas in today's mass society requires the expenditure of money." It followed that a spending limit "necessarily reduces the quantity of expression by restricting the number of ideas discussed, the depth of their exploration, and the size of the audience reached." Finally, addressing the equality concern directly, the Court said, "the concept that government may restrict the speech of some [in] order to enhance the relative voice of others is wholly foreign to the First Amendment."

Proponents of spending limits disagree with the second and third of these propositions. If some views are "drowned out" by massive expenditures, limiting spending might actually *increase* "the number of ideas discussed" and "the depth of their exploration." Still, if we think about our largely two-party system, it is indeed hard to see that a Democrat's views are "drowned out" by massive Republican spending, or vice versa.[9] The problem here, if there is one, is that small parties cannot get themselves heard. No campaign financing proposals, however, really address that problem. (Indeed, the Court's own cases indicate that legislatures may perpetuate the two-party system by providing public financing only to large parties.)

More troublesome is the notion that the idea of restricting the speech

8. Most observers are skeptical about claims that such expenditures are truly "independent."

9. Of course, even if neither side is completely drowned out, a financial imbalance might still change the results in some elections.

of some "to enhance the relative voice of others is wholly foreign to the First Amendment."[10] Our description of free-speech law as a subsidy indicates the problem. Barring government from regulating campaign financing means that those who are relatively disadvantaged in raising money from private sources have their speech limited—and, in this sense, help subsidize the speech of those who can raise more money. This might not be a matter of concern if the reason the losers could not raise enough money were that their views were unpopular. After all, no one is entitled to have his views accepted by anyone. But at least some proponents of unpopular views are confronted with a vicious circle. If only they had the resources available to their competitors, their views might become popular. Yet the views would somehow have to become popular for them to command the resources.

There is therefore a sense in which both regulation of campaign financing and nonregulation involve subsidies flowing from some individuals to others. In both systems some individuals face greater obstacles to effective communication than others. To that extent, at least, the concept that some speech should be limited to enhance the relative voice of others is hardly "foreign" to the First Amendment. On the contrary, it is an inevitable component of any free-speech regime.

There is a more general point that connects our discussions of campaign financing and of antipornography regulation. Campaign expenditures result from a system of public regulation. It is true that this system is embedded in the general law of property, rather than in statutes dealing with campaign financing. Property law allows people to accumulate wealth in such amounts that they find themselves able to spend money on campaigns in addition to food and shelter. It restricts the speech of some—those who are unable to accumulate enough wealth to make significant campaign contributions—and enhances the relative voice of others.

Defenders of the Court's position might respond that, although general property law has this effect, it does not restrict speech "in order to" enhance speech. Put differently, they might rely upon the distinction between laws with improper motivations and those with merely dispro-

10. This statement does not obviously preclude what we might call "progressive public campaign financing," on analogy to progressive taxation, which would provide more public money to candidates who raised *less* money from private contributions. That does indeed enhance the relative voice of some, but without restricting the speech of others. But, again, progressive public campaign financing is not on today's policy agenda.

portionate impacts. We have already discussed the ways in which the state action and conditional-offer doctrines rely upon this distinction and the difficulties the latter has created in a legal culture dominated by legal realism. It should come as no surprise that the distinction is similarly problematic here: Letting something happen can restrict speech as much as doing something.

The problem with the Court's position on campaign financing is captured in the rhetoric that concludes its most important campaign finance decision. "In the free society ordained by our Constitution," the Court said, "it is not the government, but the people—individually as citizens and collectively as associations and political committees—who must retain control over the quantity and range of debate on public issues in a political campaign." What, however, is "the government" but "the people organized collectively"? And why does the Constitution ordain a free society in which the people organized collectively as associations must necessarily be preferred to the people organized collectively as a government?

As with the issue of pornography regulation, the answer must be, we think, that speech opportunities will be more widely available if the people deny themselves the power to regulate campaign financing (or pornography). That, however, is precisely what proponents of the regulation of campaign financing and of pornography deny. In the campaign financing case, the Court simply stated its position on the question as an unanswerable conclusion, without arguing for it. So, too, do many free-speech absolutists, when they discuss pornography regulations.

After the New Deal we thought we knew that the Constitution gives legislatures a free hand in modifying the economic status quo. Our discussion of free-speech, however, suggests that we were wrong. True, when legislatures manage to address the economic status quo, the courts will not stand in their way. Free-speech law, however, can impede the political process. If free-speech law prevents the people organized politically from addressing the free speech implications of the status quo distribution of power, they may be unable to mobilize the political force necessary to alter the economic implications of that distribution. If free-speech law requires that the people allow those who already possess economic or social power to deploy that power in the political process, those with power may be able to stop the government from reducing their power.

Why does this happen? After all, we have argued that the standard resources of constitutional argument might readily be used to defend antipornography and campaign financing regulations. Yet, it turns out, they have not been. Here we must return to the second aspect of the transformation of legal analysis brought about by legal realism (described in chapter 3). Our constitutional analysis so far is a simple application of the first aspect of the legal realist transformation, the perception that distributions of power always result from choices between alternative legal regimes. That perception has practical limits, however, because of the second aspect, the application of ordinary categories of political analysis to legal issues and the implications that analysis has for the balance of power between judges and legislators.

We begin with a stripped-down model of a political and constitutional process involving two groups. The first group benefits from the status quo. From its point of view, there is no need for legislation to change the way things are. The only people who do need legislation are members of the second group—those disadvantaged by the status quo—and the only thing legislatures do, therefore, is to change the status quo.

If the second group manages to trigger legislative action, the first group can go to the courts, claiming that its constitutional rights have been violated. The courts may uphold the legislation, of course, but if they exercise their power to strike it down, they have acted to preserve the status quo. In short, according to this model, judicial review is necessarily a conservative force.

The New Deal conception of judicial review was dominated by this simple model, and the New Deal revolution therefore attempted to remove the courts from the process when economic regulation was involved. New Dealers thought that by limiting the power of courts, they could make the legal system less conservative and thereby free the disadvantaged to change the status quo by persuading legislators to act on their behalf.

Unfortunately, New Dealers failed to realize that by limiting the power of judges, they were also making the system more conservative, in another sense. The newly constrained judiciary could no longer be action-forcing. Judges were now prohibited from changing the distribution of social and economic power growing out of property rights defined by common law and statute.

Our discussion of free-speech law suggests why the New Deal model was too simple. Suppose those who benefit from the status quo are particularly influential in selecting judges. We could then expect that judges will be uncomfortable with efforts to change the status quo. What happened in the New Deal shows that when matters come to a head and there is a direct, dramatic, and large-scale confrontation between the status quo and those who seek to change it, judges will be foolish to oppose change openly. If they can impede change indirectly and less openly, however, their preference for the status quo may prevail. Providing free-speech protection to the status quo, thereby making it more difficult for political attacks on the status quo to succeed, may be a sensible strategy.

According to this view, the Court before the New Deal adopted a strategy that could have been expected to fail: Its constitutional doctrine made the connection between constitutional law and the preservation of the status quo too apparent, too vulnerable to political attack. The contemporary Supreme Court's free-speech jurisprudence is a more subtle defense of the status quo, which—precisely because of its lower visibility—is more likely to succeed.

According to New Deal constitutionalism, the fact that every legal decision is "none the less a choice"—as the cedar tree case put it—licensed political action to change the status quo, but not judicial action. The effect has been to disable people from using the political process to change the status quo as dramatically as New Dealers—or their jurisprudential counterparts—might have thought.

The argument we have made is incomplete, however, because it relies on the assertion that those who benefit from the status quo will be particularly influential in choosing judges. The Constitution, however, makes judicial selection part of the political process; federal judges are nominated by the president and confirmed by the Senate. Why can't a group that has enough votes to change the status quo through legislation get enough votes to pack the courts with its supporters?

Sometimes that does happen—when the appointment process becomes politicized. Making that happen, however, is not easy. The United States constitutional culture has a strong element that asserts that judges should be chosen—or at least confirmed by the Senate—after it considers only their professional qualifications. It should come as no surprise that such an approach systematically biases outcomes toward the status quo, in light of the characteristics of lawyers who satisfy merely professional standards.

Although the people can overcome that preference, the process is likely to take a long time. As we argued in chapter 2, the New Deal revolution, often described as a dramatic and sudden shift in constitutional doctrine, actually rested on a sustained effort—in politics and in the legal academy—to develop political and theoretical challenges to the status quo and the legal theory that supported it. The Court's resistance to the New Deal was the catalyst for the change, but the elements were already in place.

Our analysis suggests that the kinds of changes sought by proponents of antipornography and campaign financing regulations will be achieved through a process that moves back and forth between the politics of legislation and the politics of judicial selection. Paying attention only to the first will allow defenders of the status quo to prevail when they mount constitutional challenges. And experience suggests that the politics of judicial selection is harder for those who challenge the status quo.

What does our argument imply about contemporary proposals for the regulation of pornography and campaign financing? Our constitutional analysis suggests that the only real constitutional issue is whether the current regime provides greater speech opportunities than the alternative regulatory regime, which at first appears to be more openly regulatory. Our political analysis suggests some skeptical questions about whether such regulation will actually change the status quo.

Proponents of regulation contend that the status quo is unjust and, particularly in connection with campaign financing, that the political process is unresponsive to efforts to change it. Yet they are seeking to use that very political process to transform itself. One might fairly be skeptical about the likely benefits of what the untransformed process will produce.[11] Campaign financing regulations, for example, often appear to be incumbent-protecting laws whose conservative implications are found in the details of regulations offered to the public as reforms. Similarly, antipornography regulations may be used to suppress material intended to challenge the sexual status quo—especially feminist or gay–lesbian materials.

Our analysis also suggests that we ought to be skeptical about whether

11. As political scientist Mark Graber puts it, "For an anti-silencing ban on speech to be enacted and appropriate, members of group A must have the private power to silence members of group B in a community where members of (or persons sympathetic to) group B have the political power necessary to silence members of group A. Such a disjunction between private and public power is philosophically possible, but practically unlikely."

such regulations will actually succeed in changing the status quo even if they are enacted. To the extent that they threaten to do so, courts—as yet untransformed—are likely to stop them, finding the proposals unconstitutional or construing them in ways that reinforce rather than undermine the status quo.

In theory, constitutional law's built-in conservatism might be overcome. Courts might interpret the Constitution in an ''action-forcing'' way. They might determine that the Constitution guarantees ''positive'' rights, that is, entitlements to particular outcomes or distributions, an issue we discussed in chapter 5. They might find that the Constitution actually *compels* antipornography and campaign financing regulation. Proponents of these positions might point out that the courts have never given the First Amendment an absolutist interpretation and that failing to make an exception for antipornography and campaign financing regulations (when many other exceptions have already been made) is a form of discrimination that might well be unconstitutional.

The general structure of these arguments is familiar from the cedar tree case: Governments violate the Constitution, the arguments go, by failing to respond to the ''natural'' or market-based distribution of wealth and social power. This is, of course, the state action question in another form.

In practice, however, arguments of this sort run up against the entrenched conservative bias in constitutional law—a bias that has managed to survive the New Deal revolution. Indeed, in an important sense the bias is a part of the legacy of the New Deal. New Dealers distrusted judicial power, and they revolted against the Old Court precisely because it had attempted to constitutionalize broad areas of social policy, thereby frustrating efforts at legislative reform. Ironically, the New Dealers put in place a conservative judicial ideology because at the time it seemed the best way to open up the space for promising possibilities of liberal legislative action.

This legacy confronts modern political activists with a difficult choice. On the one hand, they might attempt to utilize the existing political process, which inevitably reflects the status quo in important ways, to undermine the status quo. Although the deck seems stacked against such efforts, sometimes the unlikely happens. On the other hand, they might attempt to use constitutional rhetoric to circumvent the political process. Although the New Deal revolution provides the analytic tools for accomplishing this task, the conservative bias of constitutional law makes it difficult to find judges willing to use them.

The fundamental question for proponents of the regulation of pornography and campaign financing must be, Do they believe that the political process in which they are engaged is likely to work better than efforts to circumvent it? Unfortunately, that is the kind of question to which political activists caught up in the immediate struggle are unlikely to know the answer—or even to think relevant to their political activities. That, we suspect, contributes to the unenlightening rhetoric about whether these proposals subvert or promote the First Amendment.

7

Death and the Constitution

The American experience with capital punishment is filled with ironies, paradoxes, and contradictions. Here are a few:

- In 1946 Louisiana botched the electrocution of Willie Francis, a sixteen-year-old African-American convicted of murder. The portable electric generator failed to produce sufficient electricity to kill Francis. "Let me breathe!" Francis cried, and the officer, who moments earlier had strapped him to the chair, rushed to remove the mask that threatened to asphyxiate him.
- The United States is the only country in the Western world that regularly imposes the death penalty. It is also the only Western nation in which abolitionists have mounted a successful constitutional challenge to capital punishment.[1]
- Although bitterly divided about capital punishment, both proponents and opponents of the death penalty agree that mutilation and torture are cruel and unusual punishments prohibited by the Eighth Amendment.[2] Yet if the prisoners for whose protection the Eighth Amendment was written were offered the choice, many of them would surely prefer at least some forms of mutilation or torture to death.

1. The Hungarian and South African supreme courts also held the death penalty to be unconstitutional.

2. The Supreme Court has held that, under some circumstances, even assaults that don't produce serious or lasting injuries fall within the prohibition. (See *Hudson v. McMillian*, 1992).

• When asked by polling organizations, overwhelming majorities of the American public strongly support the death penalty. Yet juries return death sentences in only a tiny fraction of the cases in which defendants are eligible for them. In recent years some federal court judges have reserved some of their harshest rhetoric for lawyers and other judges who obstruct the implementation of capital sentences. Yet the federal courts continue to reverse an extraordinary percentage of death cases that come before them. Between 1986 and 1991 the Supreme Court decided thirty-nine capital punishment cases and vacated the death sentences in nineteen.

How are we to explain these anomalies? In this chapter we will explore the relationship between Americans' ambivalent attitude toward capital punishment and the constitutional rhetoric that has been used to debate it. The transformation of legal thought produced by the New Deal revolution is, once again, central to our analysis. These changes made less plausible the arguments that fuel both sides of the death-penalty debate. As a result, the constitutional dispute has been channeled away from the real controversy and into a technocratic and procedural wrangle that has helped perpetuate capital punishment in a form that has left advocates on both sides of the argument deeply unsatisfied.

A brief history of the Supreme Court's modern encounter with the death penalty sets the stage for our discussion. Although the Supreme Court began to express some misgivings about the death penalty in the 1960s, it seemed unlikely that the Court would move decisively to prohibit it. These expectations were confounded in 1973 when, in *Furman v. Georgia,* a closely divided Court invalidated all death-penalty schemes then in effect.

Immediately after *Furman,* many abolitionists believed that the battle had been won and that the death penalty would never again return to the American scene. This prediction, too, turned out to be wrong. Only two of the justices in the narrow five-justice majority—William J. Brennan and Thurgood Marshall—clearly stated that the death penalty was unconstitutional under all circumstances. The other three—Potter Stewart, Byron White, and William O. Douglas—voted to invalidate the statutes before the Court, but each indicated that his views were premised, at least in part, on the haphazard, discriminatory, and random manner in which the penalty was inflicted.

Equipped with a road map provided in Chief Justice Warren Burger's *Furman* dissent and prodded by public opinion polls showing growing support for the death penalty, many states responded to *Furman* by revamping their death-penalty statutes to meet objections to the haphazard use of capital punishment. The reforms took two forms. Some states tried to eliminate discrimination by making the death penalty mandatory for certain crimes. Others instituted a system of "guided discretion" under which juries were instructed to consider specified aggravating and mitigating factors before reaching the ultimate life-or-death issue.

The Court responded to these new statutes in a series of lengthy and confusing opinions handed down in 1976 (*Gregg v. Georgia*). Although no single position attracted majority support, shifting majorities and pluralities on the Court invalidated the mandatory schemes but upheld systems of guided discretion. This outcome might, perhaps, be defended as a statesmanlike compromise. Like many compromises, however, it does not stand up well to close examination.

The prevailing justices had to work hard to explain why mandatory death penalties did not eliminate the problem of discrimination that doomed the *Furman* statutes. They argued that mandatory statutes are discriminatory because they treat all murderers as if they were equally culpable when, in fact, there is a wide range of culpability. According to this view, discrimination can be avoided only by individualized consideration of particular facts about the defendant and the crime he or she committed. Yet any scheme that provides this sort of particularized judgment threatens to reintroduce the discretion that the *Furman* Court found objectionable.

The justices thought they had an answer to this problem. They said that states must "guide" jury discretion by asking the jurors to decide whether there were aggravating or mitigating factors that should influence the outcome. It is not obvious that this approach is really different from the mandatory sentencing scheme that the Court invalidated, however. To the extent that it is different, it seems to reintroduce the unbridled jury discretion that the Court also disapproved.

Consider first the Court's insistence that the jury find an aggravating factor before imposing death. This requirement simply reintroduces mandatory sentencing through the back door. Suppose, for example, that the state requires the death penalty for all persons convicted of murdering a policeman. Because this sentencing scheme treats all guilty persons in the same inflexible fashion despite differences in their culpability, it would appear to be unconstitutional under the 1976 compromise. But is it really different from a scheme that makes death a permissible penalty for murder and then lists the fact that the victim is a police officer as an aggravating factor that requires a death sentence? The Court drove home the point when it upheld a death-penalty statute that required juries to return a death sentence if they found one aggravating circumstance and no mitigating ones.

The justices required that juries consider mitigating factors, too. Those factors make the analysis more complicated, but they do not really solve the problem. The 1976 opinions did not make clear whether the state could restrict the mitigating factors considered by a jury to a predetermined list or whether the jury had to be instructed that it could consider any mitigating factor it thought appropriate. If the list is limited, then the result, once again, is a disguised version of the mandatory, automatic sentencing scheme the Court purported to outlaw. In effect, a closed list creates a mandatory death penalty for substantive crimes defined by the presence of the listed aggravating factors and the absence of the listed mitigating factors.

In cases decided since 1976 the Court has acknowledged this problem and has held that juries cannot be limited to the consideration of previously specified mitigating factors (*Lockett v. Ohio,* 1978). Instead, jurors must be left free to consider any mitigating factor that seems relevant to them in deciding whether to spare the defendant. This open-ended approach avoids the problem of mandatory sentencing, but only by reviving the problem of unbridled discretion and discrimination. A jury that is empowered to spare the defendant on any ground it chooses is hardly "guided" in the exercise of its discretion. The result is therefore a return to the pre-*Furman* regime.[3]

The Court has continued to wrestle with these contradictions. Predictably, the effort has produced a law of capital punishment that has grown increasingly intricate, to the point where it now rivals the Internal Revenue Code in complexity and obscurity. Predictably, too, states have regularly run afoul of these rules, and defense lawyers have been able to

3. On the surface, it may seem that "unbridled" discretion can operate only in favor of life, but the appearance dissolves when we consider the defendant whose jury exercises its discretion to ignore mitigating factors that another jury might have used to impose a life sentence.

take advantage of government missteps to avoid the execution of some of their clients and to delay imposition of the death penalty for many others.

The result has been a legal and political impasse that leaves no one happy. Most studies of the death penalty show that it continues to be imposed in the starkly discriminatory patterns that marked the pre-*Furman* era. Defendants sentenced to death are almost always poor and almost always have inadequate counsel. Juries frequently act after death hearings that take no more than a few hours—sometimes no more than a few minutes—and at which little defense testimony is presented, even when minimal investigation would have uncovered important mitigating evidence. There are some indications that African-American defendants are sentenced to death more frequently than whites and overwhelming evidence that death sentences are used against criminals who kill whites far more frequently than against criminals who kill African-Americans.

In exchange for minimal improvements in the fairness of death adjudications, we have ended up with an extraordinarily unwieldy, lengthy, and cruel legal process. In recent years the Supreme Court has grown impatient with the pace of executions and has instituted some procedural reforms to speed them up. These changes will accomplish little, however, unless the Court simplifies the underlying law embodied in the 1976 compromise. Although so far doing little to "clear up" the huge backlog of condemned prisoners, the Court's new impatience has led to the disturbing and recurring spectacle of defendants paying with their lives for trivial procedural mistakes made by their lawyers. Over time the Court's insistence on haste will certainly result in the execution of some demonstrably innocent defendants. Both of these developments squander the moral force of the message death-penalty advocates hope to communicate.

Meanwhile, the death-row population continues to grow. These prisoners are held for long periods in terrible conditions and under unbearable psychological pressure. There are not nearly enough lawyers to help them navigate the complexities of the system, and the shortage regularly produces the unseemly spectacle of desperate, last-minute legal challenges certain to yield frustration and poorly thought-out legal decisions.

We will argue that the Court's ambivalent stance regarding the issues of certainty and discretion that has produced this mess is directly traceable to our difficulties in assimilating the results of the New Deal revolution. It is important to understand, however, that the problem runs deeper than the particular legal rules formulated by the Court to channel death penalty decisions. The burgeoning numbers of death-row prisoners suspended for years in a netherworld between life and death reflect a more fundamental ambivalence about the use of extreme violence to punish criminals and deter crime. In our anger and despair, we cannot stop sentencing these defendants to death, yet we lack the stomach actually to impose the sentence on more than a handful. The particular legal regime imposed by the Court is more a symptom than a cause of this dilemma.

This more fundamental ambivalence is also causally related to the problems with constitutional argument in the post–New Deal period. To see why this is so, we need to examine in more detail the arguments regularly offered for and against capital punishment.

We begin our discussion by examining the arguments about the death penalty that pack the most emotional power. On both sides, these arguments are grounded in the discourse of rights. In this sense, both proponents and opponents of capital punishment are working within the same tradition and speaking the same language. For reasons we will explore later, rights arguments are sometimes transmuted into the less volatile language of public policy analysis. For the most part, however, it is not disagreement about policy analysis that causes people to get angry about capital punishment. To an extraordinary extent, people are emotionally engaged in the death-penalty debate not because of what capital punishment does but because of what it seems to stand for. The death penalty matters because it speaks to fundamental concerns that transcend particular policy outcomes and relate to our fundamental character as a society.

Proponents of capital punishment believe that criminals have invaded the fundamental rights of their victims—the very rights that the state was created to protect. For them, capital punishment is essential because only the supreme punishment is adequate to convey the seriousness with which society views the invasion of these rights. Only death is sufficient to set things right.[4]

4. Death-penalty advocates, relying on arguments made in the nineteenth century by the German philosopher Immanuel Kant, also ground their argument in the perpetrator's rights. Kant argued that only the severest punishment takes the defendant seriously as a choosing, moral agent.

Opponents of the death penalty insist that criminals also have rights. Their opposition is premised on the belief that there should be significant limitations on the extent of permissible state coercion. Even if the death penalty could be shown to reduce crime, these benefits ought not be achieved in ways that deny the worst and the least powerful among us the essential dignity owed to every person. According to this view, the death penalty is wrong because it constitutes an effort to exile individuals from the human community.

This rights orientation has two important consequences for the argument over the death penalty. First, it takes the issue outside the realm of ordinary politics. Although disagreeing about whether there ought to be a death penalty, both sides are united in the belief that there is only one way to resolve the issue in a just society.

Second, it means that the outcome of the death-penalty debate ought not turn on the real-world consequences of capital punishment. To argue that the death penalty should be retained because it deters crime is to miss the heart of the abolitionist position. Abolitionists insist that condemned criminals have a right to live precisely in the sense that their claim to life ought not to depend on whether it would be useful to kill them. Similarly, those who insist that the death penalty should be abolished because it does not deter misunderstand the retentionist position. Retentionists share the abolitionist aversion to treating criminals as mere means to the ends of the state. Only by subjecting murderers to the most extreme penalty do we treat them as human, moral agents, capable of choice and entitled to respect as ends in themselves.

Each of these characteristics of the death-penalty debate is in tension with an important aspect of the New Deal legacy. The insistence that there is a mandatory answer to the death-penalty problem rings hollow in light of the New Dealers' successful struggle to expand the domain of ordinary politics. The *Lochner* era had been marked by a judicial insistence that the resolution of many issues of social policy was mandatory rather than discretionary. The *Lochner* Court claimed that these questions had objectively ''right'' answers that any person of good will could derive from uncontroversial postulates. New Dealers objected that this approach was arrogant and obscurantist. Policy differences reflected differences in value that could not be papered over through any process of syllogistic reasoning. The defeat of the Old Court was a victory for the view that the effort to saddle the country with one set of values unjustifiably interfered with the domain of discretionary, democratic politics.

The disregard of consequences on both sides of the death-penalty debate is also in tension with the jurisprudential world created by the New Deal revolution. The New Deal was populated by pragmatic social engineers who rejected the rhetoric of natural rights as retrograde ideology that obstructed the search for practical solutions in a time of crisis. They were uninterested in intellectual abstractions and determined to find policies that worked in the real world. They would have been profoundly uncomfortable with the view that the death penalty's morality could somehow be separated from judgments about its effects.

Given this disjunction between the rights-oriented impetus for the death-penalty debate and the policy-oriented intellectual milieu in which it must be conducted, it is not surprising that many rights-oriented arguments are vulnerable to the critiques first developed to attack the Old Court.

Consider first the abolitionist position. Abolitionists claim that the death penalty is wrong because executions invade the inalienable human rights of those condemned to die. It is ironic that this position is advanced almost exclusively by political liberals. More than half a century ago, liberals effectively demolished the distinctions between misfeasance and nonfeasance and between a public and a private sphere. Abolitionists who claim that the death penalty violates basic human rights fail to understand that their argument cannot be maintained unless these distinctions are somehow reconstituted.

The cedar tree case once again provides a useful analogy. Justice Stone was unmoved by the plaintiff's argument that state destruction of the cedar trees violated his rights. As he saw the case, the state could not avoid "the necessity of making a choice between the preservation of one class of property and that of the other." It was "none the less a choice" if the state did nothing, thereby causing the destruction of the apple trees. It followed that the issue in the case was not *whether* property rights should be respected but *whose* property rights should prevail. Whatever the state did or failed to do, some property would inevitably be destroyed. Absolute, nonconsequentialist claims of right were therefore simply beside the point. The case could be resolved only by balancing the value of the apples against the value of the cedars.

As we discussed in chapter 2, Justice Stone's insight subverted not only the feasance–nonfeasance distinction but also the distinction between private and public spheres. Once it was understood that state "inaction" was also a choice, the very notion of an inviolate private sphere became incoherent. If the state failed to regulate the price of labor or the movement of capital in "private" markets, this too was "none the less a choice" made by public officials, for which the state bore responsibility. How to make the choice was a policy question resolvable through an examination of its likely consequences, rather than through a philosophical investigation of natural rights or of an inherently private sphere's preexisting boundaries.

The implications of these insights for the death-penalty debate are obvious. Failure to impose the death penalty, like failure to destroy the cedar trees, is also a choice, even though it is mere "inaction." The government can no more escape responsibility for murders it fails to prevent than for market transactions it fails to regulate. It is therefore wrong to focus solely on the right to life of condemned prisoners. If the death penalty deters, the failure to use it invades the right to life of potential victims. There is no escape from the necessity of balancing these claims against each other.

Of course, this critique of the abolitionist position rests on the proposition that the death penalty in fact saves more lives than it takes. This proposition is hotly disputed—a point to which we will return later in this chapter. For now, it is enough to note that for abolitionists to become enmeshed in this dispute is to give up the moral core of their position. Resting the case for abolition on the absence of deterrence holds hostage the limits on state coercion to the vagaries of social science. It transforms an argument for the essential and universal dignity of each human being into a socially contingent public policy position.

Retentionist arguments are also vulnerable to the critiques developed during the New Deal period. The moral argument for capital punishment depends on simplistic conceptions of responsibility, desert, and freedom that have been implausible since the New Deal revolution.

Consider first the problem of desert. Rights-oriented retentionists must convince us both that condemned prisoners deserve to be punished and that the punishment they deserve is death. Neither of these positions is self-evident. Even if we assume that criminals freely choose to commit their crimes and that it honors their status as choosing agents to punish them, it does not follow that death is the appropriate punishment.

Why isn't life imprisonment sufficient to reestablish the moral balance of the universe? Conversely, why isn't torture or dismemberment necessary?

Technocratic defenders of the death penalty have answers to these questions. Their aim is to calibrate the extent of punishment as precisely as possible so as to achieve the desired level of deterrence at the lowest possible cost. But retentionists who accept this sort of cost–benefit analysis, like abolitionists who dispute the deterrent effect of the death penalty, gut the moral core of their position. The retentionists' argument is attractive precisely because of their stubborn insistence on the justice of the death penalty without regard to its consequences. Unfortunately for them, once the punishment question is cut loose from its deterrent consequences, there remains nothing but unmediated moral intuition to explain why any particular punishment precisely fits the crime.

In the early part of this century, legal realists had a field day attacking conservative judges for assuming that their idiosyncratic moral intuitions were somehow built into the architecture of the universe. The retentionists' argument for death is every bit as dogmatic and unconvincing as these formalist arguments that went out of fashion more than half a century ago.

Moreover, even if we assume that death is sometimes a uniquely appropriate way to punish certain defendants, we must identify the class of defendants for whom it is appropriate. Once again, the death penalty's technocratic defenders have an easier time with this problem. From their perspective, defendants should be punished if, but only if, it is useful to punish them. They might favor killing even innocent, blameless defendants when the punishment is necessary to achieve the requisite degree of deterrence. Our moral revulsion at this prospect suggests why most retentionists are not technocrats. However, defenders of rights-based arguments for capital punishment cannot maintain their moralistic stance without developing a theory of blame and freedom that explains why certain criminals deserve death while others do not.

Difficulties in developing such a theory, once again, stem from our experience during the New Deal. The concept of free will was central to the pre–New Deal ideology embraced by the Old Court, and the Court's critics specialized in debunking it. For example, the *Lochner* Court argued that bakers who agreed to work more than ten hours per day were exercising freedom of contract and that government regulation of such contracts therefore violated fundamental rights. *Lochner*'s critics pointed out that bakers ''chose'' to enter such contracts while caught in a social and economic setting that dictated a particular outcome. Government intervention was justified to control private forces that coerced workers and other vulnerable groups to act in certain ways.

The victory of the New Dealers has left defenders of free-will ideology in an awkward position. After the New Deal, most of the country came to understand that the decision of workers to accept the wage contracts offered by employers had to be seen against a broader social background that substantially restricted their freedom. The decisions of criminals are also made in a broader social setting that may substantially limit their real choices, as well. That understanding, latent though it sometimes is, underlies our society's unease with the statistical association among race, class, and criminality.

One option for retentionists is to turn their backs on the New Deal revolution and to attempt to revive the old free-will paradigm. Most retentionists are not political liberals and therefore may not suffer from the same cognitive dissonance that afflicts abolitionists when they try to reconcile their position with the New Deal's lessons. But embracing free-will ideology only revives the old problem that led to its demise: Retentionists must devise a coherent theory for specifying which murderers ''freely'' choose to kill.

This obligation does not pose much of a problem if one defines ''choice'' very broadly so as to encompass any volitional act. But few retentionists are prepared to go this far. Virtually all would reject the death penalty for extremely young murderers, or for defendants who make good-faith and reasonable mistakes, or for the severely mentally defective, or for persons acting in self-defense or under extreme coercion, even though all of these defendants in some sense ''chose'' to kill. The Supreme Court's 1976 rejection of mandatory death sentences reflects the consensus view that judgments about desert must take some account of the situation in which a defendant finds herself.

This concession leads to determinism's slippery slope. There is a sense in which all decisions are located within a broader social framework that makes some choices more attractive than others and that ''coerces'' the choice that is actually made. This is the problem of ''coercive offers'' discussed in chapter 4 and ''coercion by restricted alternatives,'' discussed in chapter 7.

Although few in our culture are prepared to slide to the bottom of this slope, we have wildly conflicting and inconsistent intuitions about where to dig in our heels. Consider a hypothetical brutal murderer with very low intelligence who is raised in poverty by abusive parents and is diagnosed as suffering from an antisocial personality with poor impulse control. In the absence of a good theory about desert and free will, people are bound to disagree about whether the defendant's social background and emotional disorder sufficiently impinge on his freedom of choice so as to make the death penalty unjust.

Nor is that the end of the problem. It is a mark of the bankruptcy of the free-will paradigm that the very factors that some people believe to be mitigating will be treated by others as aggravating. The defendant's antisocial personality might be characterized as a "mental illness" for which he is not to blame. Or it might be characterized as an indication of his utter depravity, which makes him a particularly appropriate candidate for death. Which characterization one chooses seems, once again, to reflect no more than undefended moral intuition that opponents are asked to accept on faith.

Perhaps there are good theories of desert awaiting discovery that, once articulated, will end controversies of this sort. Even the discovery and acceptance of these theories would not solve the retentionists' problems, however. Retentionists must also deal with the problem of mistake. No matter how carefully the death penalty is administered, it is inevitable that, over time, innocent defendants will mistakenly be executed. Thus, even if we could agree on a theory of desert, it would still be a predictable consequence of a system of capital punishment that some people who do not deserve to die will be executed.

Sometimes, retentionists respond that this risk is more theoretical than real. They maintain that the procedural protections surrounding the death penalty are certain to catch virtually all errors before it is too late. Unfortunately, this sanguine view fails to take into account the disgracefully sloppy fashion in which many states in fact conduct trials for capital offenses.

Moreover, even if the retentionists were right that there are very few errors about ultimate guilt or innocence, there are bound to be many more errors on more subtle questions concerning aggravation and mitigation. Because these errors are every bit as relevant to the issues of desert at the core of retentionist thought, they seriously threaten the moral justification for capital punishment.

Finally, it is important to note that even if we assume (implausibly) that the system makes very few errors of any kind, the retentionist position is still undermined so long as the system is not perfect. Retentionists reason from the moral imperative to give every criminal her due regardless of consequence. It follows from this position that even a single mistake is unacceptable. Instituting a system that permits such a mistake necessarily involves some trade-off between doing justice to a particular individual and avoiding the investment of greater resources in procedural protections that would avoid the mistake.[5] Although post–New Deal pragmatists are perfectly comfortable with this sort of balancing, it cannot be reconciled with the individual rights approach that provides the moral energy behind the retentionist position.

For the reasons we have just outlined, most of the arguments that motivate the death penalty debate have lost their ability to persuade. Their implausibility in a post–New Deal environment has led to a retreat to the kind of instrumental and "value-free" rhetorical moves that are more in keeping with contemporary legal consciousness. We outline some of these argumentative strategies in the following paragraphs.

Our basic thesis is that these are bad arguments. The fundamental problem with them is, by now, familiar: Although the New Deal revolution destroyed the old order's intellectual foundations, it failed to loosen the grip of the prerealist world view. Because it is no longer intellectually respectable to use the pre–New Deal vocabulary to defend their position, the disputants often try to dress up their arguments in modern garb. But the modern arguments are transparent. It is all too obvious that they are offered not because their advocates really believe them but because they must do service for their real beliefs, which they can neither defend nor abandon.

In the death-penalty context, there are three main lines of retreat from rights-based positions. Sometimes, advocates resort to constitutional text. Retentionists claim that the Constitution does not prohibit capital punishment and, indeed, recognizes its existence. In the absence of a textual prohibition, they claim, the matter should be resolved politically. Abolitionists, in contrast, insist that the capacious phrasing of the Cruel and Unusual Punishment Clause was designed to incorporate "evolving

5. Of course, a retributivist might argue for a system that provides more accurate determinations of guilt than the current one does. Still, no system can completely eliminate the risk of error. So long as that risk exists, there is no avoiding the balancing of individual rights against the efficient use of society's resources.

standards of decency'' and that the death penalty does not measure up to these standards.

Social science provides a second escape route. Here, the argument is principally about deterrence. Retentionists claim that the death penalty is justified because it prevents murders and, therefore, saves lives. Abolitionists insist that we could achieve equal or better deterrence through imprisonment of convicted murderers and that the death penalty therefore amounts to pointless slaughter.

Finally, the death-penalty debate is sometimes diverted to issues of equality. This third escape route is utilized principally by abolitionists. Some abolitionists claim that they have no objection in principle to the death penalty. In the real world, however, it is simply not possible to implement capital punishment in a fair fashion. As actually administered, death is reserved for the poor and the powerless and for racial and ethnic minorities—an unconscionable situation.

Each of these arguments has a common structure. The proponent attempts to abstract from controversy about the underlying justice of capital punishment. Instead, the proponent claims, the capital punishment controversy can be resolved by resort to some disembodied, uncontroversial yardstick.

In each case this claim is unconvincing. Arguments of this sort fail to persuade because it is obvious that their proponents are attempting to manipulate rather than convince us. Instead of attempting to justify a position, the arguments serve as rhetorical cover for a predetermined outcome.

Let us first consider arguments from constitutional text. Superficially, it might seem that the text provides powerful support for the retentionist view. Executions were common in the late eighteenth century, and the framers both knew about the death penalty and focused their attention on the issue of excessive punishment. Yet they chose not to include a specific prohibition on capital punishment in the new Constitution. On the contrary, language in the Fifth Amendment's Grand Jury, Double Jeopardy, and Due Process Clauses, adopted contemporaneously with the Eighth Amendment Cruel and Unusual Punishment Clause, seems to presuppose the continued use of the death penalty.[6]

6. The Fifth Amendment requires grand jury indictments before a defendant can be made to answer for a capital offense, forbids subjecting any person to double jeopardy for life or limb, and prohibits deprivation of life without due process of law.

It is important to understand the limits of this argument, however. At the very most, the textual argument precludes *judicial* abolition of the death penalty. Retentionists cannot rely upon the Constitution to support their positions that capital punishment is desirable and that their opponents are wrong to demand its legislative abolition. Retentionist support for the death penalty on the merits must therefore be rooted in some argument independent of constitutional text.

Even as a constitutional matter, the retentionists' textual argument is no more than window dressing unless it does some work not already accomplished by the rights-based arguments. Unless retentionists are satisfied with preaching to the choir, their textual argument must convince some abolitionists that, despite their view on the merits, they ought to oppose judicial abolition. We doubt that the textual argument often accomplishes this task. If it really functioned independently of the merits, one would expect that some who argue that the Eighth Amendment as written permits the death penalty would also spend their energy working to abolish it through legislation.

Perhaps there are such people, although we confess that we have yet to find any. Or perhaps it is simply a remarkable coincidence that virtually all defenders of the textual argument also believe that it is a good thing that the framers were wise enough to leave the capital punishment problem to the vicissitudes of ordinary politics. And perhaps their views are uninfluenced by the fact that in our present political culture they can be fairly confident of winning that political struggle. Yet surely one is entitled to be suspicious when things just happen to work out so neatly. It seems more plausible that they have worked out this way because the textual argument is not really doing the work claimed for it.

Moreover, the retentionist argument from text is not quite as airtight as we have so far assumed. Although the framers did not explicitly outlaw the death penalty, neither did they choose to address the excessive punishment problem by formulating a specific list of punishments that they found objectionable. Instead, they seem to have made a considered decision to leave the standard vague and open-ended in order to permit future judges to decide for themselves whether particular punishments were cruel and unusual. It is therefore not dispositive that the framers themselves accepted the death penalty. Capital punishment might violate the Constitution's general prohibition even if its authors did not recognize this fact.

Thus, good-faith adherence to the text does not automatically support the retentionist position. Textualists are faced with an interpretive choice, and the text itself cannot instruct us on how the text should be interpreted. The need to decide on an interpretation undermines the retentionist claim that we can somehow resolve the death-penalty problem through a mechanical, value-free process that does not implicate our positions on the merits.

It does not follow, however, that textual indeterminacy supports the abolitionist position. Abolitionists too must explain why we should opt for their more open-ended interpretive stance rather than for a narrower view that focuses on the framers' immediate expectations. It strains credulity to believe that this choice is uninfluenced by preexisting commitments on the merits. Imagine, for example, that there was irrefutable legislative history demonstrating that the framers opposed the death penalty and wrote the Cruel and Unusual Punishment Clause with the specific expectation that it would make capital punishment unconstitutional. Is it really plausible that many abolitionists would then insist that contemporary judges should ignore this specific intent and permit executions so long as capital punishment did not violate modern standards of decency? It seems far more likely that abolitionists would accuse a judge who permitted executions in these circumstances of wilful disregard of the framers' specific intent. If this is so, the abolitionists' textual argument is simply offered to justify conclusions its advocates have already reached on other, unstated grounds.

Moreover, even if the abolitionists' textual argument were entirely persuasive and offered in good faith, its effect would still be quite limited. The argument does no more than clear the way for acceptance of the abolitionist position. To support constitutional abolition, it must be supplemented by nontextual reasoning that can convince us that the death penalty in fact violates the standards of decency the Constitution requires.

Some abolitionists—and some retentionists as well—have looked to social science to supply what they need. Like constitutional text, social science findings seem to provide a neutral, noncontroversial set of criteria for evaluating the death penalty. Perhaps unlike textualism, social science holds out the promise of a testable hypothesis about facts in the world rather than ephemeral theories of value and interpretation.

In the context of capital punishment, this hypothesis concerns the deterrent efficacy of the threat of death. Abolitionists claim that the death penalty prevents no more murders than life imprisonment and that it therefore amounts to unnecessary and senseless slaughter. In contrast, retentionists insist that each additional execution deters more than one future murder. According to this view, the death penalty saves lives and ought to be retained.[7]

In principle, it should be possible to put these conflicting claims to a definitive test that would settle the matter. The fact that the argument continues in the face of numerous studies conducted over many years suggests that the problem may not be so simple.

The most obvious difficulty is that there is no way to experiment with various deterrent schemes in antiseptic, laboratory conditions. The best that social scientists can do is examine murder rates in neighboring abolitionist and retentionist states or observe changes in the murder rate within a single jurisdiction after a change in the punishment structure. Unfortunately, these limitations sharply reduce the universe of examples to be studied and make it difficult to generalize from them. Many results are certain to be confounded by a host of intervening variables that may have nothing to do with capital punishment. Although social scientists use sophisticated mathematical techniques for filtering these out, the techniques are no better than the capacity of those using them to imagine the additional variables that need to be accounted for.

In the face of this unavoidable imprecision, the conclusion one draws from the data inevitably depends on how the burden of proof is allocated, and social science offers no neutral, value-free method for making that determination.

Moreover, even if the data unambiguously pointed to one conclusion or the other, this still would not settle the matter. For example, suppose there is no decline in a state's murder rate after it institutes capital punishment. One might conclude from this fact that the death penalty fails to deter and, therefore, ought to be abolished. But the data could be interpreted otherwise: Perhaps capital punishment, as instituted, is inef-

7. Many retentionists insist that the death penalty would be justified even if it resulted in the execution of many guilty defendants to save one innocent life. They argue that the lives of innocent victims are more worthy of protection than those of guilty murderers because murderers have freely chosen a course of conduct that results in their own death. Although this view is perfectly coherent, it requires a specification of which murderers are sufficiently guilty to merit death and therefore leads us back to the problems of desert and free will discussed earlier. Social science provides an attractive solution to the death penalty problem precisely because it seems to avoid these difficulties.

fective because it is imposed too rarely or too humanely. Social science offers no way to refute the claim of death-penalty advocates that significant deterrence could be achieved if only we executed more prisoners or imposed additional suffering.

Conversely, suppose that a state that has instituted capital punishment enjoys a dramatic decline in murder rates. At best, this demonstrates that capital punishment is doing a better job of deterring murder than the system in place before the change. It does not follow that capital punishment is socially optimal, however. The same lower murder rate might have been achieved at less social cost by insisting on solitary confinement for convicted murderers, by instituting gun control, or by increasing expenditures on social programs that attacked root causes of violence and crime. (Even as modest a program as improving ambulance services to get people wounded by gunfire to hospitals more quickly can reduce the murder rate significantly.) Once again, social science offers little that is helpful in evaluating these alternative possibilities. In the face of this uncertainty, one's choice of which hypothesis to accept is bound to be dictated by one's underlying preconceptions, which are unrelated to social science.

Perhaps the most daunting problem for social science is that any model is certain to be incomplete unless these preconceptions are built into it. So far, we have assumed that the death penalty's efficacy depends upon whether it saves more lives than it costs. But a complete calculus of costs and benefits requires consideration of additional variables. For example, friends and relatives of the victim may be led by the sort of rights-based arguments we have discussed to favor capital punishment. These views may prevent them from coming to terms with their loss until the perpetrator is executed. Surely, their pain should count for something in a full reckoning of costs and benefits.

In contrast, abolitionists may believe that, whatever its deterrent efficacy, the death penalty brutalizes our society by violating the fundamental human rights of those executed. They too suffer real pain because they must live in a society that tolerates executions, and this pain must also count for something.

For reasons we have already discussed, social scientists are likely to be uncomfortable with these views. Post–New Deal critiques make them hard to defend, and the social science escape route is attractive precisely because it seems to offer a way of settling the capital punishment controversy without resort to the rights-based arguments that the New Deal revolution made implausible. Yet a social scientist whose techniques are truly value-free must acknowledge that large numbers of people in our society continue to hold these views even if they are, in some sense, anachronistic or irrational. We are therefore confronted with the following paradox: To be truly value-free, a social scientist has no choice but to take account of the values of others. Her model must therefore include the very values it is designed to abstract from.

In one sense, arguments from equality are not value-free at all. The abolitionists' passionate appeal to the requirement of fair and equal treatment seems explicitly normative in its focus. Equality arguments are nonetheless "neutral" in the sense that they purport to avoid explosive disputes about the normative merits of the death penalty by appealing to the less controversial norm requiring equal treatment. Abolitionists who reason from the equality requirement are prepared to concede, at least for purposes of argument, that there is nothing objectionable about the death penalty per se. Instead, they claim, the penalty, as actually administered, unfairly discriminates on the basis of race and class.

The resort to equality arguments of this sort is a familiar move in the post–New Deal legal debate. For example, in the immediate wake of the Roosevelt victory over the Old Court, the liberal justices appointed by President Roosevelt needed to distinguish their judicial activism from the *Lochner* Court's "bad" activism, which had been premised on the defense of controversial substantive rights. Some justices resorted to textual arguments of the sort we have discussed. Less frequently, they relied upon social science claims. However, the Roosevelt Court's most enduring contribution to legal discourse was the assertion that judicial review need not implicate the merits of public policy if courts confine themselves to an insistence that the costs of that policy be fairly and equally distributed.

This requirement provides a powerful argument against the death penalty. Despite the Court's halfhearted efforts to police the process, imposition of the death penalty remains random and freakish. The difference between life and death often turns on lawyering skill, unreviewable prosecutorial discretion, the vagaries of plea bargaining, or simply the whims of a particular jury. It is not unusual for the more culpable of two codefendants to receive life imprisonment, while his less culpable colleague in crime is sentenced to death.

Worse still, some of the system's inequality is not merely random but malignant. Throughout much of the country's history capital punishment—especially for rape—played an important part in the system of oppression inflicted on African-Americans. Even today, there is some evidence of racial bias, and overwhelming evidence of class bias, in implementation of the death penalty.

Moreover, troubling problems remain even if we put to one side the race and class of the defendants selected for death. Persuasive studies demonstrate that the victim's race is an even more important determinant of whether capital punishment is inflicted. Juries are most likely to impose death on black defendants who murder white victims. They are somewhat less likely to sentence white defendants to death for killing white victims. They almost never impose the death penalty on white defendants who murder black victims.

This state of affairs would seem to violate the Fourteenth Amendment's Equal Protection Clause in the most literal sense. The disproportionate use of the death penalty to deter crime against whites means that the "protection of the law" received by African-Americans is plainly unequal to that granted to whites. Given the fact that the immediate impetus for adoption of the Fourteenth Amendment was the failure of southern states to take adequate measures to punish the whites who criminally attacked the newly freed slaves, death-penalty critics would seem to have a powerful constitutional case indeed.

Despite all this, the Supreme Court squarely rejected equality arguments against the death penalty (*McCleskey v. Kemp,* 1987). Our purpose here is not to explore the reasons for that rejection, which relate principally to the Court's insistence on proof of malevolent intent in equal protection cases. We discussed the merits of this controversy in chapter 5, and we will not rehearse the issue here. Instead, our claim is that despite their surface appeal, equality arguments against the death penalty, like the textual and social science arguments discussed earlier, are really ways of hiding the ball.

Abolitionists who root their objection to capital punishment in the rhetoric of equality face two problems. First, it turns out that the norm of equality is quite unattractive when separated from the requirement of substantive justice. Suppose, for example, that we stipulate that the death penalty is substantively unjust. Suppose further that Allen is sentenced to death because he is an African-American, while Bob, who commits an identical crime, escapes death because he is white. There can be no doubt that Allen has been treated unjustly, but it is hard to see how his situation is improved if Bob is killed as well. If the death penalty is really unjust, then imposing an additional injustice would seem to make matters worse rather than better.

Conversely, suppose we stipulate that the death penalty is substantively just. If Allen really deserves to die, why should he be spared simply because Bob has wrongly beaten the system? Of course, in a perfect world, Bob would be executed also. But our failure to respond justly to Bob's case hardly explains why we should also fail to do justice in Allen's. Sparing Allen in these circumstances seems to violate the schoolyard maxim that two wrongs don't make a right.

Moreover, even if there were something to the equality argument as a matter of theory, its advocates face a second problem with the way in which it has been used in practice. As a rhetorical device, the argument is ineffective because it is all too clear that most of its supporters do not take it seriously.

Advocates of equality ask us to believe that their argument does not depend upon substantive opposition to the death penalty. If we are to take them at their word, then they can have no objection to the execution of additional defendants so as to make the incidence of capital punishment more equal. But of course virtually everyone who makes the equality argument does object to more executions. In addition, it is striking that those who make the equality argument never seem satisfied with proposed "improvements" designed to make the death-penalty system operate more equally. Equality appears to be an ever-receding goal, which suggests that the true goal is abolition, not the even-handed administration of capital punishment.

In effect, advocates of equality are playing an elaborate game of chicken. They believe that they can use equality as a lever to gain acceptance of their substantive views. They are counting on the fact that if American society is forced to choose between no death penalty at all or a much broader use of the death penalty, it will choose the former.

The best evidence for the instrumental character of their argument is provided by their reaction when their bluff is called. For example, after the Supreme Court invalidated all existing death statutes in *Furman v. Georgia,* some states responded by making the death penalty mandatory for certain crimes. Of course, this change was insufficient to make the death system truly equal. Even a mandatory system does not eliminate prosecutorial and police discretion, jury nullification, or bias built into the definitions of the underlying crimes. Still, from an equality perspective, this broadening of the death penalty was an important step forward. Yet it pleased few of those who complained the loudest about unequal treatment.

This critique of the equality argument should not be misunderstood. It would be wrong to criticize equality advocates for having passionately held commitments to justice. Their anger at the subordination of people of color—especially when the subordination take the form of deprivation of life itself, either by underprotection or overexecution—hardly requires defense.

The dilemma faced by these advocates is not of their own making, and it is merely a particular example of a broader dilemma confronted by anyone who wants to argue about the death penalty in the post–New Deal period.

The struggle over constitutional law that culminated in the New Deal revolution produced two crucial insights. First, it became apparent that people of good will had conflicting and irreconcilable views about substantive questions of justice. The Old Court's confident, magisterial rhetoric could not paper over the fact that some people simply saw the world differently from other people. Propositions that had seemed self-evidently correct were challenged, and the challenge produced a conflict that shook the country.

Second, New Dealers succeeded in demonstrating that there were no winning arguments that logically compelled a particular resolution of this conflict. Arguments that had seemed persuasive before the New Deal were picked apart through critiques like those advanced in the first part of this chapter and elsewhere throughout this book. Their refutation left a void, which New Dealers effectively filled by expanding the scope of discretionary politics.

When these events occurred, they were liberating and transformative. Unfortunately, however, they have left us with an inability to talk seriously about the issues we care about the most. While expanding the space for political discourse, the New Deal revolution also destroyed the means by which this discourse could be conducted. Thus, people who are deeply concerned about the death penalty must face the brute fact that others in our culture have very different views. Confronted by these irreconcilable differences, a natural response is to attempt to mediate the difference through resort to argumentative techniques, such as appeals to text, social science, and equality, that do not depend for their persuasiveness upon acceptance of the very substantive position in dispute. But these efforts are bound to fail. Few people really believe these arguments, and fewer still are fooled by them into changing their substantive position.

It is not surprising, then, that when we try to talk to each other about capital punishment, we end up talking past each other. The New Deal revolution destroyed the normative consensus that permits real discussion to get off the ground. It is more surprising, however, that we cannot seem to implement in a coherent or effective fashion the wishes of the popular majority that, for whatever reason, favors the death penalty. In the face of overwhelming popular approval of capital punishment, why are we still plagued by posturing and paralysis? Even if we cannot talk about the death penalty, why can't we at least act?

This aspect of our current predicament also relates to the difficulty in maintaining an authentic dialogue in the modern period. The absence of honest exchange has led to a situation where opposing sides are increasingly dug in. Because argument is no longer an effective means of communication, there is no hope that the opposition will be brought around by dispassionate discussion. The legal realists taught us that positions on public issues are not dictated by reason. One consequence of this lesson is that argument about issues can no longer be held external from the personality of those advancing the argument. Because public-policy positions are not a consequence of disembodied logic, they must be constitutive.

It is a short step from this realization to the perception that an attack on one's position is not simply a challenge to the coherence of a particular line of argument but an attack on one's core values and identity. One's opponents are not merely "wrong" in the usual sense but positively evil. They seem to be separated by an unbreachable divide of culture and values that makes them irretrievably foreign and threatening.

In this intellectual milieu, symbolism is certain to predominate over substance. Because there is little prospect of actually convincing someone through the force of argument, positions on public-policy questions tend to lose their operational significance. Thus, beliefs about the death penalty have little to do with serious discussion of the social cost of crime or effective modes of crime prevention. Indeed, they have lost their connection to whether anyone is in fact executed. Instead, expression of opinion about capital punishment is a way of defining oneself and signaling to others which side one is on.

The problem is compounded by the fact that most people are on more than one side. Retentionists are angry and fearful about the levels of crime and violence and the social disintegration these forces seem to represent. Their advocacy of the death penalty symbolizes their determination to do something dramatic and forceful to defend our values. But this position, while fervently held, is abstract and general. Because it operates on the level of symbolism, it need not necessarily be acted upon in concrete cases. When confronted with individuals about to be put to death, it sometimes clashes with the competing claims of individualized compassion and understanding.

This ambivalence manifests a deeper uncertainty about the interplay of law and discretion, which is still another a legacy of the New Deal revolution. As we have already noted, the realist critique permanently destroyed the image of law as a series of overarching rules from which results could be deduced with syllogistic certainty. An important response to this critique was the effort to focus more narrowly on figuring out pragmatic solutions to individual problems without attempting to fit those solutions into some grand theory.

Yet here, as elsewhere, the old order never completely lost its emotional hold. It is very hard to live in a world of radical freedom or to give up on the idea of some general principle that legitimates and rationalizes individual decisions. The New Deal's ad hoc-ery therefore produced a deep-seated insecurity, which, in turn, led to a reassertion of the need for order and principle, only now in an intellectual environment in which we could not quite make ourselves believe that these qualities exist.

The Supreme Court has perfectly captured this contradiction by its confused insistence on both generality and particularity in death-penalty adjudications. Juries contemplating death must apply abstract and general standards. Yet they must also focus on the particular individual whose life is in their hands. Their judgments, in other words, must encapsulate the conflicting symbols of order and mercy that drive the death-penalty controversy.

The Court's death-penalty jurisprudence is similarly caught between the conflicting desires for freedom and constraint. Like the formalists of old, the Court wants to bind our hands in advance through general principles that, when uniformly applied, will rationalize our decisions about life and death. Yet the Court also understands that no general rule can ever capture all the considerations that ought to govern a particular case. It therefore does not want to bind us too tightly for fear that we will be not be free to do what we want in an individual case that we failed to anticipate.

Many of the other anomalies that have plagued our experience with capital punishment are also rooted in these conflicting demands of justice and mercy or constraint and freedom. Consider, for example, the odd behavior of the executioner of Willie Francis. Executions can proceed only to the extent that actors in the process tightly bind themselves to their bureaucratic roles. The elaborate ritual surrounding the death process reinforces the imagery of generality and constraint. This imagery is very powerful, and it usually produces the desired effect. But if something goes wrong in the process—and in the Willie Francis case it went horribly wrong—participants are suddenly confronted with the unsettling reality of the particular consequences of their actions and of their own freedom to alter them.

Our society's contradictory response to capital punishment on the one hand and torture or mutilation on the other reflects a similar ambivalence. The finality of death cuts us off from doubts we might otherwise experience about the violence we have inflicted. In contrast, torture and mutiliation are horrible, at least in part, because they are lingering. It is very difficult to torture a prisoner in a bureaucratically antiseptic environment. Because the violence is ongoing, the torturer is confronted over an extended period with the possibility of choice.

Unlike torture, mutilation can be accomplished quickly and even painlessly. But the continuing survival of its victim has a similar impact. The victim's wounds constitute an undeniable and continuous reminder of the consequences of the violence we have inflicted on him. They are an ugly, festering, and specific reality that intrudes on the carefully constructed grandeur and impersonality of the law.

These contradictions and paradoxes, in turn, illustrate the most unsettling insight of all deriving from legal realism. With the loss of faith in grand and overarching jurisprudential theories has come a realization that our views on issues like capital punishment are radically context-dependent.

It is wrong to suppose that most Americans have one, consistent position about the death penalty, just as it is wrong to suppose that one can deduce logical and determinate results from any general theory of law. What people believe about the capital punishment depends upon the context in which they consider the question. They believe one thing if asked as voters to consider the matter abstractly and another when considering the matter concretely as jurors. Before the fact, they want to bind themselves with rigid rules so as not to flinch from the grim necessity of imposing death. Yet when actually confronted with the immediate prospect of execution, they want the wiggle room that will allow individualized justice to the particular person who is at their mercy.

The great lesson of legal realism is that there is no neutral context from which these context-dependent judgments can, themselves, be judged. We must live with a stubborn and irreducible plurality in our own legal views.

If this were all there was to the matter, the New Deal revolution might have produced a kind of skeptical tolerance for opposing positions. One would suppose that the realization that positions on capital punishment are reflections of context, rather than manifestations of unalterable truths, would soften the hard edges of debate. At this point, however, we are confronted with still another duality. Paradoxically, the realization that deeply held views are a manifestation of context coexists uneasily with the continuing fact that the views are deeply held.

We have therefore ended up with the worst of both worlds. The lessons of legal realism have deprived us of our belief that argument drawn from grand theory can resolve the capital punishment debate. Yet our failure to assimilate those lessons fully means that we cannot give up on our emotional commitment to one side or the other. The New Deal revolution destroyed forever the possibility of genteel discussion within an elite that agreed on a common set of premises. In its wake, we find ourselves shouting louder and louder at our opponents, all the while certain that no one is listening.

8

The Structural Constitution

The great hope for constitutional law is that it might provide a common language that would allow us to discuss and resolve our differences over contested political issues. Advocates of constitutionalism believe that we might transcend our seemingly hopeless disagreements about specific questions—affirmative action and equality, pornography and campaign financing, the death penalty—by agreeing on a common set of premises and commitments on a higher level of generality.

In their most optimistic moments, these advocates hope that agreement at this higher level might ultimately produce agreement at the lower level. Arguments derived from the agreed-upon generalities might actually convince one's opponent—or oneself—to modify initial positions respecting contested specifics.

Even when this version proves too optimistic and the disputants remain unreconciled, constitutional law is not altogether useless, its proponents maintain. Dialogue conducted in a shared language builds bridges between people by drawing them into a common activity—the dialogue itself. Moreover, the perceived allegiance to a common set of general commitments softens the edges of the disagreement by emphasizing what is shared rather than what is contested. Some of these salutary effects survive even when people remain in bitter conflict over the appropriate conclusions to be drawn from the commitments.[1]

1. The yearning for common ground of this sort is palpable. Consider, for example, the efforts of some prochoice and prolife groups to bridge the gap between them by working together on programs such as pregnancy prevention.

Before the New Deal revolution, the general commitments thought to produce these good consequences were a set of substantive values. It seemed possible that a shared belief in individualism and freedom could yield determinate outcomes that would command nearly universal assent. Moreover, where such assent proved unattainable, the belief nonetheless provided a framework and vocabulary that facilitated discussion and bounded the disagreement.

Of course, even in the pre–New Deal period, this vision remained partial and elitist. In the country at large, there was never anything like universal assent to political outcomes or, for that matter, to the premises from which the outcomes were supposedly derived. Indeed, some have suggested that it was the pressure generated by growing social discord that stimulated turn-of-the-century efforts to systematize and rationalize constitutional thought as a bulwark against disintegration.

Still, pre–New Deal jurists seem to have sincerely believed that constitutionalism could indeed be such a bulwark. This belief made sense only if at least some people were convinced—or at least given pause—by constitutional argument. These jurists may have been deluding themselves in thinking that they were talking to anyone outside their own circle, but within the legal and intellectual elite, where "rational" discussion was thought possible and where constitutional law was actually fashioned, broad agreement existed.

The New Deal revolution blew apart this genteel consensus. It would be a serious mistake, however, to suppose that New Dealers rejected the validity of the commitments that underlay pre–New Deal constitutional discussion. New Deal skepticism never went all the way to the bottom. On the contrary, the moral force of the New Deal complaint against economic and social injustice derived from abiding commitments to the ideals of individual freedom and dignity.

Instead of attacking the commitments themselves, New Deal lawyers attacked the conclusions thought to flow from them. They brilliantly deployed the corrosive techniques of legal realism, first developed a generation earlier, to eat away at the iron chain linking shared premise to contested conclusion. By recharacterizing disputes as involving the public rather than the private, feasance rather than nonfeasance, and coercion rather than freedom, they managed to make the old arguments run in the opposite direction.

If our analysis in the preceding chapters is correct, this hybrid character of the New Deal revolution has had a demoralizing effect on constitutional argument. By holding to the initial commitments but demonstrating that clever lawyering could make them support virtually any conclusion, New Dealers left us in a position where we can neither abandon constitutional argument nor use it constructively. Constitutional argument cannot be abandoned, because to abandon it is to leave the field to nihilists who would turn issues of justice into issues of power. Yet constitutional argument cannot be used constructively, because realist manipulation of the relevant categories can produce any answer a clever advocate wants to argue for.

The upshot is that instead of bringing us together, constitutional argument drives us apart. Everyone understands that the arguments are used instrumentally to support preordained conclusions that have nothing to do with the arguments themselves. Instead of persuading adversaries, the arguments divide them into camps, each of which claims to unite all fair-minded and rational people.

The immediate heirs to the New Deal revolution were not unaware of this unsatisfactory state of affairs, and the post-*Lochner* period has been marked by a more or less desperate casting about for a way to reconstruct constitutional argument. Among the most important of these efforts has been the attempt to create a structural constitution.

Advocates of constitutional structuralism are prepared to forsake the old hope of reasoning from shared substantive value judgments to determinate outcomes. Constitutionalism can nonetheless be saved, they maintain, by reasoning from shared commitments about value-free constitutional structure to determinate outcomes.

The post–New Deal period has seen the flowering of a rich variety of theories based on constitutional structure. Three structuralist arguments have been especially influential: textual, democratic, and functional. In the next section, we briefly outline each of these theories and explain the source of its attraction to post–New Deal jurists. In the concluding sections we explore some of the reasons why, despite these attractions, structural arguments have failed to resolve the crisis in modern constitutional thought.

Perhaps the most venerable structural argument is textualism, whose most powerful and dedicated champion for more than thirty years was Justice Hugo Black.

Of course, textual arguments long predated Justice Black's appointment to the Court. From the beginning, Supreme Court justices explained their decisions in terms of constitutional text. Undoubtedly the most famous such explanation appears in *Marbury v. Madison* (1803), in which Chief Justice John Marshall argued that the text of Article 3 deprived him of the power to enforce a section of the 1789 Judiciary Act.

The conservative justices who resisted Franklin Roosevelt's New Deal also relied upon constitutional text. For example, in *United States v. Butler,* a case invalidating Roosevelt's first Agricultural Adjustment Act, Justice Owen Roberts explained that

> when an act of Congress is appropriately challenged in the courts as not conforming to the constitutional mandate the judicial branch of the Government has only one duty,—to lay the article of the Constitution which is invoked beside the statute which is challenged and to decide whether the latter squares with the former.

Before the New Deal revolution, however, no justice made textualism the centerpiece of his judicial philosophy. No justice needed to do so. Although Chief Justice Marshall relied upon constitutional text in *Marbury,* he never suggested that text was the only source of judicial power. In other cases, he was quite prepared to invalidate legislation on the basis of principles of natural justice that stood independent of constitutional text. And although Justice Owen Roberts invoked the image of a mechanical, textual jurisprudence in *Butler,* it is doubtful that he applied the technique even there and beyond question that he joined other opinions that frankly proceeded on nontextualist grounds.

In contrast, Justice Black's long and distinguished judicial career was almost wholly defined by a commitment to the enforcement of constitutional text. Justice Black *needed* to rely upon text, because textualism was necessary to bridge the contradictions in New Deal legal thought.

As veteran of the revolt against *Lochner,* Black fervently believed that unelected judges had no business entrenching contested value judgments. It did not follow that all public policy should be left to the realm of unconstrained politics, however. Although Black shared the New Deal aversion to judicial enforcement of values, he was hardly a nihilist prepared to conflate law and power. Judges had an important, but limited, role to play: They were to enforce the constitutional text faithfully and diligently.

For Black, commitment to text served as the functional equivalent of the pre–New Deal commitment to substantive values. Like the values that animated substantive due process, text seemed to provide a new common ground on which people who differed over immediate political issues might agree. Textualism therefore reconciled New Deal skepticism about judicial supremacy born of the *Lochner* experience with New Deal faith in the possibility of "right" answers to political questions.

Justice Black was best known for deploying textualist arguments in defense of free speech during the McCarthy period. When the First Amendment says, "Congress shall make no law . . . ," Black proclaimed, "'No law' means 'no law.'" He also argued that the Fourteenth Amendment's text showed that state governments had to comply with the restrictions that the Bill of Rights placed on Congress.

It is easy to see why Justice Black saw textualism as an attractive approach to these problems. A "principled" and value-free insistence on enforcing the literal text of the First Amendment allowed him to defend the left from vicious attack without associating himself with leftist substantive values—an association that was especially distasteful (and politically counterproductive) when those under attack were communists.

Similarly, Black's argument that the Fourteenth Amendment, properly understood, incorporated Bill of Rights protections brilliantly papered over some of the important tensions in New Deal jurisprudence. On the one hand, the incorporation doctrine meant that the states had to comply with federal norms governing fundamental rights. The doctrine thus advanced the New Deal's nationalizing and equalizing agenda. On the other, the claim that the Court was doing no more than enforcing literally and in good faith the intent of the Fourteenth Amendment's framers positioned Justice Black to continue the New Deal's withering rhetorical assault against substantive due process and judicial value judgments.

A second variety of structuralism plays off the country's supposed commitment to democracy. According to this view, precisely because people differ about which values are fundamental, the choice of values should be left to the political process. This process serves the same function as constitutional text in Justice Black's jurisprudence. Like text, it is thought to be value-free and therefore seems attractive as a means by which people with different values can settle their disagreements.

In its simplest form, this approach leads to a stance of judicial deference toward political outcomes—a deference associated (albeit inconsistently) with Felix Frankfurter. For Frankfurter, the great triumph of the New Deal had been the expansion of the political sphere. For him, politics was associated with pragmatism and instrumentalism and stood in sharp contrast with the deadening ideology and a priori reasoning foisted on the country by the Old Court. The triumph of the administrative state, with which he was closely associated, amounted to a displacement of judicial power. Administrators, like judges, sometimes decided cases, but they did so on the basis of expertise, good sense, and experience instead of ideology and doctrine.

Frankfurter was less successful than Black in reconciling the New Deal's contradictions, however. His celebration of the political sphere was linked to a deep reverence for courts and for the rule of law. Frankfurter's problem was that total abdication to the political branches would have conflated law and politics—precisely the reduction that he and other New Dealers wished to resist. His belief in pragmatism, rationality, and reformism made him an erratic democrat at best. When democracy produced outcomes that could be so characterized, he was prepared to defer. But when it failed to do so, he wished to assert judicial power. Whereas Black maintained a separate sphere for law by finding refuge in constitutional text, Frankfurter had nowhere to hide. Although often deferential to the political branches, he insisted on a residuum of judicial power to invalidate political outcomes when they violated ill-defined fundamental principles of fairness, justice, and good sense. Despite his pained insistence that these qualities were discoverable through the principled exercise of judicial craft, they ended up sounding very much like the old substantive due process formulations that the Court had abandoned under pressure from New Dealers.

Some of the most obvious difficulties with Frankfurter's approach were resolved by more complex theories of democratic structuralism presaged by Justice Stone's famous footnote 4 in *United States v. Carolene Products* (1938)—a case decided in the immediate wake of the New Deal revolution—and developed with great sophistication in our own time by Professor John Hart Ely. These theories—sometimes rather ponderously labeled ''representation reinforcement''—achieve critical leverage by driving a wedge between political and democratic outcomes.

Where political outcomes are truly democratic, representation reinforcement counsels Frankfurterian restraint. But not all political outcomes are democratic. Political incumbents wishing to entrench their own power sometimes contaminate the political process by erecting barriers to democratic change. Moreover, majorities sometimes undervalue the preferences of certain unpopular minority groups—groups that are systematically outvoted and therefore get none of the power even though they have some of the votes.

Advocates of representation reinforcement argue that courts act legitimately when they "purify" the political process by removing or countering these defects. For example, courts might legitimately enforce free speech and voting rights (to allow democratic challenge to incumbents) or "strictly scrutinize" laws that discriminate on racial or other "suspect" bases (to ensure that the laws are not the result of a prejudiced or unthinking undervaluation of political outsiders' welfare). Representation reinforcement thus avoids question-begging substantive value judgments on the one hand, while giving courts a job to do and thereby avoiding the conflation of law and politics on the other.

Still a third structuralist theory rests on ideas about constitutional function. Functionalists maintain that people who disagree about fundamental values might nonetheless come to agree on which government institutions are best equipped to resolve the disagreement. Functionalism is doubtless the most sophisticated and subtle structuralist response to modern difficulties with constitutional argument. Developed by a group of influential legal academics in the postwar period, it has obvious roots in the policy science, technocratic side of the New Deal revolution.

For New Dealers who believed in rationalizing government, literalistic devotion to constitutional text proved too constraining to provide answers to the problems of the modern state. The growth of federal power and of executive agencies, so obviously necessary to administer the modern welfare state in a rational and humane fashion, could not be justified in terms of a document that reflected the best of eighteenth-century thought.

Democratic theory, even in its most sophisticated form, also proved too crude a tool to resolve modern value disputes. It makes good sense for a democratically elected legislature to formulate broad social goals and policy direction. But it is naive to suppose that these general decisions can be translated directly into the details of public policy. If the realists taught anything to New Dealers, it was that general principles did not decide concrete cases. Broad legislative directives always contain gaps and ambiguities that only officials exercising discretion can fill.

The defense of discretion was a central problem for New Deal jurisprudence. This was true not only because New Dealers had to assimilate the realist insight that legal texts were always and inherently ambiguous and indeterminate but also because the deliberate creation of ambiguity was an essential component of the New Deal strategy for government regulation. New Dealers understood that the welfare state could function only if the Constitution were read to permit broad delegations of authority to executive officers who would then have the flexibility to respond to complex and quickly changing problems. But if these officials had discretion—if a variety of different and contradictory choices were all within an administrator's legal authority—in what sense was the administrator constrained by the rule of law? Wasn't an official whose discretion was unbounded in this fashion simply exercising power over others?

Functionalism provided an attractive solution to this difficulty. Functionalists rejected the simplistic view that the rule of law amounted to strict adherence to a set of specific substantive commands. Government decisions could be lawful without a specification of *what* should be decided so long as they conformed to a set of jurisdictional and procedural rules concerning *who* should decide and *how* decisions should be made. These decision-making principles were legitimate because rational people who might disagree about the ultimate decision could nonetheless agree on questions of decision-making techniques.

One group of decision-making principles related to federalism. Most functionalists conceded to the states broad background authority to formulate primary rules of conduct. Federal legislation was necessarily exceptional. Significantly, however, the appropriate realm for federal intervention was not determined by constitutional text or the framers' intent. Rather, it depended on the existence of a federal interest, usually premised on the need for uniform solutions to "national" problems.

A second group of principles related to separation of powers. Most functionalists took the New Deal revolution to stand above all for the proposition that the political branches were best equipped to formulate rules concerning economic regulation. Paradoxically, they also believed that the legislature was best equipped to resolve disputes concerning the very jurisdictional rules that gave the system legitimacy.

Courts, in contrast, were best suited to the task of mediating between the general principles articulated by legislative bodies and the individual cases that came before them. In part, this task required the enforcement of individual rights against the government. Perhaps more significant, it also required filling in the gaps and ambiguities that inevitably accompanied any legislative command.

According to this view, it was foolish to try to eliminate discretion from the system, since every legislative command necessarily included a delegation of discretionary authority to those who carried it out. Because no legislator could imagine in advance every application of her command, judicial and administrative lawmaking was inevitable.

Although it was important to functionalists that this lawmaking was not unbounded, the constraints on it were procedural rather than substantive. Functionalists argued that judges should engage in a process of "reasoned elaboration" and assume that the legislature consisted of reasonable people acting reasonably (in one famous formulation) and intending to conform to the functionalist limits on its own power. Individual judicial decisions should then be explained and justified in terms of this presumed purpose and these presumed limits. Judges should decide like cases alike and justify each decision in terms of what has gone before and in ways that connect to some general principle that the judge was prepared to defend and apply across the board.

An important consequence of this functionalist account of the rule of law was that decisions were insulated from substantive criticism when these jurisdictional and procedural standards were followed. For example, once it was determined that a certain sort of decision was within Congress's jurisdiction, a court should not upset that decision simply because it was "wrong" on the merits. To say that Congress has jurisdiction over the matter *is* to say that Congress should have the last word when there is disagreement on the merits.

This strong conception of jurisdiction made only paradoxical and not contradictory the view that Congress should have jurisdiction over the enforcement of the functionalist rules that made Congress's decisions legitimate. Disagreement about the content of these meta-rules was like any other disagreement: Some institution had to have final authority to settle the dispute. Because the jurisdictional rules derived from practical questions of governance rather than from abstract principle, they were best formulated by legislators rather than by judges. Although not judicially enforced, the rules were nonetheless binding on legislatures. Moreover, they had an important residual impact on judicial decisions: Because judges were supposed to presume that the legislature was acting rationally, they were obligated to fill in the gaps in statutes by presuming that the legislature meant to follow the rules.

Like textualism and democratic theory, functionalism thus aspired to repress destabilizing disagreement about the merits of public policy. It suggested a way that argument could be terminated before it spun out of control. Once people of good will had agreed on a sensible allocation of law-making authority, they would have to accept the law produced by that authority even when these outputs seemed profoundly wrong.

All this appeared reasonable and civilized to the academics who formulated functional theories. And yet, in the face of these theories, political argument during the postwar period stubbornly kept spinning out of control. Indeed, the most striking fact about all the structural arguments we have discussed is their near-total failure to suppress and control the most destabilizing substantive disagreements.

The theories work well enough when the disagreement is not destabilizing. Most of us recognize that most issues confronting the country can be resolved in a variety of ways without implicating our fundamental values. Just societies have many different methods of delivering health care and strike different trade-offs between competing goods such as environmental protection and industrial expansion. When public policy questions are discretionary in this sense, we are prepared to accept the decisions on the merits simply because they are the result of the operation of a fair structure.

Structuralism is successful in settling these issues precisely because they are not of constitutional dimension. Because the issues are not fundamental, we are prepared to see them resolved by ordinary political processes. Those of us who are not nihilists are unwilling to treat all issues as discretionary, however. There are some questions that do implicate fundamental values. The problem is that not everyone agrees about which questions are fundamental or about how concededly fundamental questions should be resolved. Disagreement at this level is most likely to be destabilizing precisely because people care so much about the outcomes. These are therefore the issues that we need constitutional law to settle in a fashion that does not unravel the social fabric.

Unfortunately, these are also the issues that structuralism has been least successful in resolving. For example, contrary to functionalism, opponents of the Vietnam War were unwilling to change their views or temper their opposition because the decision to go to war was made by the kind of "experts" functionally best equipped to decide. Contrary to textualism, supporters of abortion rights have not been persuaded to abandon their constitutional arguments because the word "abortion" does not appear in the constitutional text, and, contrary to democratic structuralism, supporters of fetal rights have not given up their position when their views have been rejected by democratic majorities.

This is not to say that structuralism plays no part in modern constitutional debate. On the contrary, structural arguments are all around us. The structuralists have been quite successful in altering the vocabulary of constitutional argument. But the arguments are not doing any real work. Like the other arguments we have discussed, structuralism is used instrumentally.

It is therefore not unusual for individuals advancing structuralist positions to get caught in contradictions when the political valence of the argument shifts. Some liberals who hailed the growth of presidential power during the glory days of the New Deal and the Great Society suddenly saw the virtues of checks and balances when conservative presidents used that authority to cut federal spending without congressional authorization or to mount an undeclared war in Nicaragua. Some senators who made elaborate textual and functional arguments against the independent counsel law during the Iran-Contra affair somehow managed to overcome their constitutional scruples when scandal struck a Democratic administration. Even on the Supreme Court, some justices who belittled federalist arguments against congressional meddling with state decisions about criminal justice, welfare reform, and education celebrated federalist values when the Reagan administration attempted to require hospitals to treat severely deformed newborns (*Bowen v. American Hospital Ass'n,* 1986). Conversely, some justices who argued most forcefully for state autonomy when the federal government attempted to implement redistributive programs argued for the primacy of federal authority when states attempted to redistribute resources through affirmative action plans that aided racial minorities (*City of Richmond v. J. A. Croson Co.* Some of the same justices abandoned that principle when they decided to strike down a federal affirmative action program (*Adarand Constructors Inc. V. Penn*, 1995).

In short, structuralist arguments have produced the same sort of depressing posturing that has dominated other branches of constitutional argument in the modern period.

Why has structuralism failed? Perhaps because it depends upon a discipline and honesty that participants in constitutional debate have been unwilling or unable to muster. Advocates of constitutional structuralism usually depict themselves as high-minded sorts, prepared to act in principled and self-restrained fashion even when this restraint produces short-term losses. For those less principled and less restrained, there is a tremendous temptation to cheat on the deal; it seems to them that they can insist on fidelity to structural solutions so long as they produce the "right" outcomes, while breaking free from the agreed-upon structure when adherence to it would lead to victory for their opponents. In short, according to this view there is nothing wrong with structuralism itself. We simply need a better class of citizens.

But surely this will not do. In the first place, constitutional theory must take the world as it is. To paraphrase Madison, if people were angels, no constitutional theory would be necessary. The task of structuralism, or of any other constitutional theory, is to encourage people to behave in a fashion that promotes the public good. It is hardly a defense of structuralism to say that it might work in an imaginary, utopian world where people already behave in such a fashion.

More fundamentally, there is something odd about labeling as "unprincipled" political actors so dedicated to substantive principle that they are prepared to override procedural constraints in order to achieve their conception of justice. From this perspective, Abraham Lincoln and Martin Luther King rank among the least principled figures in American history, while sticklers for structural regularity, such as James Buchanan and some of the academic critics of *Brown v. Board of Education,* should be counted as heroes.

This anomaly suggests that the difficulties with structuralism may be rooted in the theory itself, rather than in the deficiencies of the people applying it. It suggests that structuralists have failed to provide a convincing and coherent account of the relationship between constitutional structure and substantive values. In the next section, we will explore this problem and suggest some reasons why, in the long run, it has doomed the structuralist argument.

Although structuralism gained special prominence after the New Deal revolution, the theory is not new. It played a central role in the founding of the Republic. The founders' structuralism was significantly different from modern versions of the theory, however, and it is important that we understand the differences if we are to understand the relationship between value and structure.

The very act of drafting the Constitution demonstrated a faith in structuralism. The delegates who met in Philadelphia obviously thought they were doing something important and lasting. The point of their efforts was to provide a structure that would limit and channel future political debate.

The theory behind the Constitution was structural as well. The *Federalist Papers* is an extended argument about constitutional structure. In common with other Enlightenment thinkers, its authors believed they could establish institutions that interacted to preserve republican virtue and suppress factional strife.

The framers' conception of the relationship between structure and substantive values was very different from that of modern structuralists, however. Whereas modern structuralists hope to bridge value disagreements through constitutional structure, the framers intended structure to protect and implement certain substantive outcomes.

The Constitution's treatment of slavery provides the most notorious example. Although the word "slavery" nowhere appears in the Constitution, many of its provisions were frankly motivated by a desire to protect slaveholders. This is most obviously true with respect to the clause requiring free states to return runaway slaves and the provision preventing Congress from obstructing the slave trade until 1808. The slave states were also successful in inserting more subtle, structural protections into the document. For example, the infamous three-fifths compromise ensured permanent overrepresentation of the southern states in Congress.[2]

Other structural provisions were designed to produce outcomes that seem more defensible to us today. As the authors of the *Federalist Papers* explained, the Constitution's complex system of overlapping authority, staggered elections, and different constituencies was designed to prevent temporary majorities from interfering with the rights of property and contract. At the same time, the central government was given new powers that allowed it to foster economic growth by overriding sectional rivalries and jealousies.

The framers understood that these substantive outcomes could best be protected indirectly by biasing the structure to produce them automatically rather than directly by enshrining them in the Constitution. Like the clockmaker god envisioned by contemporary Deists, the

2. The compromise ensured greater representation than would have occurred had the slaves not been counted as "persons" at all, but it provided for less overrepresentation than would have occurred had slaves been counted as "full" persons.

framers imagined themselves as first movers who could set up a "machine that would go of itself" without need of external guidance or correction.

By the time modern structuralists developed their theory, these eighteenth-century structural views had been largely discredited. One problem with the eighteenth-century version is illustrated by the example of slavery. For a while, a structural solution served as a workable compromise that allowed people with deeply antagonistic views to join in a common enterprise. Whereas northerners might have had difficulty accepting direct protections for slavery, indirect, structural protection respected northern sensibilities and held out a least a slim hope of using the (admittedly biased) structure to achieve change over the long run.

A structural compromise of this sort is fragile, however. When people come to feel strongly enough about the underlying value questions, they no longer have reason enough to accede to a structure deliberately created to produce outcomes they despise. For example, some abolitionists rejected the structure imposed by the Constitution precisely because it was intended to protect slavery.

The crisis of 1937 reflected (albeit less dramatically) a similar weakness in structuralism's older version. Many of the Old Court's decisions striking down New Deal measures were structuralist in form. The Court held that Congress had exceeded its authority under the commerce and spending clauses when it enacted New Deal legislation and that standardless delegation of legislative authority to the president violated the constitutionally mandated separation of powers. The revolt against the Old Court was, in large measure, a revolt against structuralism. New Dealers understood that this structure had a purpose; having rejected that purpose, they rejected the structure as well.

These problems are exacerbated by a second, related weakness in structural theory: It is exceedingly difficult to maintain a structuralist stance when the structure fails to vindicate the values it is designed to protect. For example, despite a constitutional structure designed to protect slavery and freedom of contract, slaveowners perceived themselves as losing the political struggle in the mid-nineteenth century, and capitalists felt similarly embattled during the progressive era half a century later.

Structuralists might respond to these defeats by stubbornly adhering to the structure even in cases where it fails to do the job intended for it. But this stance seems wooden and pointless. If the outcome is important enough to justify a structure designed to protect it, why not provide direct protection when the structure fails?

Because the Supreme Court saw no reason why not, it provided direct protection for slavery and free-market capitalism in its notorious decisions in *Dred Scott v. Sandford* (1857) and *Lochner v. New York.* Both these decisions ultimately led to disaster, partially because they demonstrated to the Court's opponents the hypocrisy of structuralism. They showed that the deck was firmly stacked against advocates of different values. Even if they played by the rules of the game and somehow overcame the built-in biases of the system, the Court still stood ready to undo their hard-won political victories.

These problems fueled the New Deal revolt against structuralism. Why, then, were structuralist arguments so popular with New Dealers after the revolt succeeded? The answer lies in a subtle shift in the function of structuralism. Whereas the framers saw constitutional structure as a method of indirectly enshrining substantive values, New Dealers imagined that structure could serve as a substitute for substantive values.

Each of the modern structural theories we have considered has value-free pretensions. It was emphatically not Justice Black's position that fidelity to text was justified as the best means of implementing any particular political program. On the contrary, the moral force of Black's position was derived from fervent opposition to judicially imposed value judgments. Significantly, Professor Ely's famous book on representation-reinforcement begins with a devastating assault on the efforts of some judges to read their values into the Constitution. His theory is offered as a method of justifying some forms of judicial review without resort to these judgments. Postwar functional theory, too, was explicitly premised on a belief that policy science could make value disputes obsolete. Functionalism was premised on the belief that people with radically different values could agree on a system for settling their disagreements.

Unfortunately, however, a commitment to structure is virtually impossible to maintain once it is cut loose from value judgments supporting the commitment. There are two sorts of problems. One is that it is hard to choose between structural theories or to give the theories determinate content without reference to disputed value judgments. The other is that it is hard to motivate people to adhere to the theories unless they are also convinced that the theories promote their substantive commitments.

Although many other cases tell essentially the same tale, we will explore in the next section the Court's troubled encounter with supposed federalism and separation of powers limitations on Congress as a particularly powerful example of the predicaments created by value-free structuralism.

Constitutional conflicts between the president and Congress have occupied a great deal of public and scholarly attention recently. Structuralists have tried to resolve these conflicts, but their arguments are transparently political.

The spectacle of liberal academics, who had roundly condemned Richard Nixon's attempts to secure immunity from prosecution, devising ingenious legal theories to explain why Paula Jones could not sue Bill Clinton simply confirms what most people have already learned: Structural separation of powers arguments have no content apart from the underlying merits of the contested issues they are designed to abstract from.

It is hardly an accident that in the modern period liberals have vigorously defended the constitutionality of administrative agencies and raised doubts about the president's war-making power, while conservatives have taken precisely the opposite tack. Delegation to administrative agencies is at the heart of the liberal strategy for government economic intervention at home, while, at least until recently, a powerful and independent presidency was at the heart of the conservative strategy for fighting communism abroad.

It requires some fast footwork to supply the structural argument supporting each of these positions. Conservatives try to discredit liberal domestic activism through textual arguments. They point out that the Constitution creates a single executive and makes no provision for congressional delegation of authority to a quasi-independent fourth branch of government. Liberals respond with functional arguments, pointing out that only administrators possess the flexibility and the expertise to implement complex regulatory schemes.

When the subject is international affairs, the participants neatly change sides. Now it is liberals who rely on constitutional text to argue that the framers intended Congress to play an important role in making war and in foreign affairs, while conservatives advance functional arguments for presidential power, relying on the need for secrecy, flexibility, and unity when dealing with other nations.

Neither the textual nor the functional arguments do the work intended for them. The constitutional text is too open-ended, and modern conditions too different from those at the time of the framing, to provide determinate outcomes. Functional arguments simply reproduce the disagreement on the merits. For example, unity, secrecy, and flexibility in the conduct of foreign affairs are virtues only if one favors a vigorous foreign policy. Similarly, the expertise that allows administrative agencies to regulate the economy is a good only for those who favor government regulation.

Perhaps, then, the Court should defer to democratic outcomes. But which outcomes? When the president and Congress are in conflict, both can, and usually do, claim to speak with the voice of the people. There is no obvious way to sort through these claims without becoming enmeshed in the dispute on the merits.

The result of these difficulties is that the Court has been unable to articulate and maintain a consistent position with regard to conflict between Congress and the president. It has made sporadic efforts to referee these conflicts, only to back away when the task of formulating a doctrinal response independent of the merits proves too daunting.

Although separation of powers conflicts may attract more public attention and concern, the modern Court's struggle with the other basic issue of government organization—federalism—more clearly displays the difficulties with structuralist theories.

Before 1937 the Court regularly invalidated federal legislation on the ground that it exceeded Congress's enumerated powers under Article 1 of the Constitution. As part of the transformation of constitutional law that accompanied the New Deal, the Court pretty much forswore its power to police the boundary between state and federal authority.

Throughout this period, however, a lingering sense has remained that there was some theoretical limit beyond which Congress could not go in preempting local authority. Although belief in such a limit was important, the Supreme Court's efforts to give it determinate content have not exactly inspired confidence.

The saga begins with *United States v. Darby,* a 1941 decision upholding federal wage and hour protection for private workers against the argument that the legislation exceeded Congress's power to regulate commerce among the states. In the 1960s Congress amended these statutes to cover state and local government workers as well. In *Mary-*

land v. Wirtz (1968), the Court upheld the constitutionality of these amendments.

Eight years after *Wirtz,* the Court changed course, reversing *Wirtz* by a 5–4 vote. In *National League of Cities v. Usery* (1976), the Court purported to leave untouched *Darby*'s holding that wage and hour legislation was within the boundaries of Congress's commerce clause authority. It nonetheless struck down the law's application to state workers engaged in "traditional governmental functions" because, it said, this application violated the inherent sovereignty of the states protected by the Tenth Amendment.

On its face, this holding was puzzling. The Tenth Amendment provides: "The powers not delegated to the United States by the Constitution, nor prohibited by it to the States, are reserved to the States respectively, or to the people." The Court's recognition that the Fair Labor Standards Act came within the scope of Congress's commerce clause authority seemed to establish that the power to enact the law was "delegated to the United States by the Constitution" and that the Tenth Amendment by its own terms was inapplicable.

Moreover, even if one were prepared to recognize some implied, nontextual limitation on Congress's powers, the Court did little to explain the scope of this limitation. The Court's subsequent efforts to provide an explanation quickly demonstrated that the entire enterprise was unmanageable.

For example, *National League of Cities* provided that state immunity from federal legislation was available only when the legislation touched upon a "traditional governmental function." This led the Court to distinguish between subway workers—Congress could not protect them according to *National League of Cities,* because running subways is a traditional governmental function—and workers on government-owned railroads—Congress could protect them because railroads are not traditionally operated by the government (*United Transportation Union v. Long Island Railroad,* 1982).[3]

3. As residents of Washington, D.C., we are struck by this anomaly: Our Metrorail system operates both below and above ground. Apparently Congress can protect workers in the bright sunshine of the Rhode Island Avenue stop but suddenly loses its power as the Red Line train pulls into the below-ground Union Station. Of course we do not believe that any court would ever reach that bizarre result, but the fact that the Supreme Court's distinctions allow us to make this joke suggests how people can manipulate their characterizations of what is involved to reach the results they prefer for other unstated reasons.

The Court also intimated that it was necessary to balance the state interest against the federal one. This led to a distinction between the Fair Labor Standards Act, which the Court found insufficiently important to justify federal intervention, and the Age Discrimination in Employment Act, which it found more significant and therefore constitutional (*EEOC v. Wyoming,* 1983).

After nine years of struggling with these difficulties, the Court threw in the towel. In *Garcia v. San Antonio Metropolitan Transit Authority* (1985), a new five-justice majority overruled *National League of Cities* and rejected "a rule of state immunity from federal regulation that turns on a judicial appraisal of whether a particular governmental function is 'integral' or 'traditional.'"[4]

Even this turnabout did not quite end the story, however. In *New York v. United States* (1992), the Court appeared to reverse field again. It relied upon federalism principles to strike down sections of a federal statute that required states to develop disposal sites for radioactive waste. The statute provided that states making inadequate progress toward waste disposal were required to take over the waste within its borders, thereby making them liable for all damages the waste caused. The Court purported to distinguish *Garcia,* holding that although Congress had the power to make states liable under generally applicable laws, it lacked the power to force states to administer federal programs.

New York was followed by *United States v. Lopez* (1995), where the Court, for the first time since the New Deal revolution, invalidated a federal statute as beyond the scope of Congress's Commerce Clause powers. The Court held that a statute prohibiting the possession of a gun near a school regulated neither commercial nor interstate activity and was therefore unconstitutional.

It is too early to know how significant *New York* and *Lopez* will be or whether the distinction between *Garcia* and *New York* can be successfully maintained. It is noteworthy that the *New York* and *Lopez* opinions are larded with the same kinds of qualifications and equivocations that helped undermine *National League of Cities*.[5] One can easily

4. Justice Blackmun, who had provided the crucial fifth vote in *National League of Cities,* authored *Garcia.*

5. For example, the *New York* Court intimated that federal funding made conditional upon a state's willingness to enact a regulatory program would not violate its newly crafted principle and that the principle also permits Congress to offer states a choice between complying with a federal mandate and having the area preempted by federal law. In

imagine subsequent cases seizing upon these qualifications to eviscerate *New York* and *Lopez* results in the same fashion that *National League of Cities* was subverted.

Whatever the future of *New York* and *Lopez,* it is safe to say that the Court's modern encounter with federalism limits on the powers of Congress constitutes something less than a monument to the virtues of judicial review. Why has it proved so difficult for the Court to articulate and adhere to structural rules defining the powers of Congress vis-à-vis the states? Why does the Court cycle between brave efforts to put teeth into the structural rules and embarrassed confessions of weakness accompanied by humiliating retreats?

Part of the problem can surely be explained by the shifting composition of the Court, by changes of heart on the part of individual justices, and, perhaps, by the effort to manipulate doctrine and precedent for short-term advantage. But this is not the whole story. The opinions in these cases exhibit good faith efforts to deploy structural arguments. In some sense, each of them, taken in isolation, is sensible and convincing. Yet they have produced wildly unstable results.

This discouraging record suggests that structuralism simply lacks determinate content. As we have discussed, structuralism comes in a variety of flavors, and different structural arguments push in different directions.

For example, a textualist faced with a problem about the scope of Congress's commerce clause powers might want to adhere to the original understanding and therefore sharply constrain federal power, even if two hundred years of industrialization and nationalization makes this result radically impractical. In contrast, a democratic structuralist might well oppose judicial interference with political outcomes formulated by Congress, at least in the absence of a strong argument that these outcomes are undemocratic. A functionalist might occupy a middle position, favoring federal intervention in cases where a federal interest requires a national solution but preserving an area of local autonomy in other cases.

How is a conscientious structuralist to choose among these competing structural approaches? If structuralism were grounded in the desire to

---

addition, the Court purported to preserve Congress's power to force state courts, as opposed to executive agencies, to administer a federal program.

vindicate a particular set of substantive values, we would know, at least in theory, how to proceed. We would then do our best to choose the structural theory that does the most to advance those values over the long run. But the modern defense of structuralism rests on a desire to avoid controversial value judgments. Without such judgments, we are left entirely at sea.

Moreover, even if we were somehow to settle on a particular structural theory, further problems remain. Each of the theories themselves yields indeterminate outcomes. For example, it is not obvious that a textualist need oppose the modern expansion of federal power. Although the framers doubtless imagined a far more limited federal government, they lived in a preindustrial society. Advocates of federal power can argue that the text of Article 1 was written broadly enough to permit federal expansion when the need arose.

It is, once again, hard to know how to choose between a narrow approach that focuses on what the framers specifically intended and a broader approach that focuses on their open-textured language without evaluating the merits of the outcomes each approach produces. Indeed, democratic and functional theories were developed precisely because it came to be seen that judges were manipulating these ambiguities in textualism to implement their political agenda. Unfortunately, however, both democratic and functional theories also contain ambiguities that can be resolved only by resort to contested political premises.

For example, although we assumed earlier that a democratic structuralist would favor judicial abstention when the federal government preempts state authority, there are also arguments from democracy that favor judicial intervention. For present purposes, we will put to one side the daunting task of deciding when an outcome is "truly" democratic and when it is the product of the kind of defect in the political process that judges should correct. "Democracy" is also a contested concept without determinate meaning in our political culture. But even if we assume this problem away and stipulate a particular version of democracy, the fact remains that a court faced with a federalism controversy will inevitably countermand a democratically derived decision whatever it does.

True, when Congress chooses to regulate in an area traditionally left to local authorities, its decision is in some sense democratic. The problem is that when a state chooses not to regulate, its decision is democratic as well. Whether the Court acts or fails to act, it is upsetting a decision supported by the voters of one political unit or another. The Court cannot decide the case without some meta-theory about what the appropriate unit of aggregation should be—about *which* democratic majority ought to prevail. It is hard to see how such a theory could be generated without a view about what it is that we are trying to accomplish in the first place.

Functional theories face similar problems. On the one hand, a functionalist might support judicial intervention to police a federalism boundary defined by practical considerations of relative competence and function. On the other hand, precisely because the boundary is so defined and is not marked by a timeless, judicially discoverable principle, a functionalist might be inclined to cede to Congress jurisdiction over the boundary-setting function. If Congress is allowed to set its own limits, it is hard to see how it is meaningfully constrained. Yet if the limits are enforced by courts, judges become enmeshed in issues of practical politics and governance that, functionalists insist, they lack the competence to resolve.

In light of the difficulties in giving determinate content to value-free structuralism, no one should be surprised that the cases using the approach are inconsistent. And there is an even deeper problem. Even if value-free structuralists could show that their approach yielded determinate and uncontroversial outcomes, that fact alone does not provide an incentive for anyone to use the approach. Unless the theory is entirely circular, the reasons for being a structuralist must be rooted in some normative position outside of structuralism—the very sort of normative position that structuralism is designed to avoid.

Consider, for example, the Court's structural explanation for its decision to overrule *National League of Cities* and forgo Tenth Amendment supervision over the federal-state boundary. The majority advanced two structural arguments favoring judicial abstention.

First, it argued that the judiciary lacked the competence to determine the appropriate boundary between state and federal authority. With newfound modesty born of bitter, recent experience, the Court doubted that it could ultimately "identify principled constitutional limitations on the scope of Congress's Commerce Clause powers over the States merely by relying on *a priori* definitions of state sovereignty" and rejected "as unsound in principle and unworkable in practice, a rule of state immunity from federal regulation that turns on a judicial appraisal of whether a particular governmental function is 'integral' or 'traditional.'"

Second, the Court argued that political checks and balances built into the system provided automatic, nonjudicial protection for the state sovereignty.[6]

Each of these arguments is firmly rooted in modern structural theories. The first insists on the kind of judicial agnosticism concerning fundamental value choices that is the hallmark of modern structuralism. The second invokes the image of a self-correcting political sphere where outcomes are legitimated by the process that produces them.

Unfortunately, the majority does not seem to have noticed that the two arguments conflict with each other. If we are to take seriously the Court's insistence that judges cannot know the appropriate boundary between state and federal power, then we cannot also take seriously its assertion that the political process has provided adequate protection for the states. Conversely, if the Court knows that the current balance between state and federal authority is the "right" balance, why does it lack the competence to formulate judicially enforceable rules that will ensure that this "right" balance is maintained?

This contradiction goes to the core of all modern structural theories. The attraction of these theories is that they seem to provide an escape from the searing struggle over fundamental values that has so badly damaged constitutional argument in the late twentieth century. Yet to the very extent that these theories succeed in this aim, they deprive their potential adherents of any reason for embracing them.

Ultimately, the problem is as simple as it is insoluble. We have a choice between constitutional theories that rest on controversial value judgments and constitutional theories that steer clear of such judgments. To the extent that we choose theories of the first type, they will be unacceptable to those who do not already share the theory's basic value orientation. To the extent we choose theories of the second type, the normative emptiness of the theories will mean that citizens will have no

6. In the majority's view,

> The principal means chosen by the Framers to ensure the role of the States in the federal system lies in the structure of the Federal Government itself. . . .
>
> The effectiveness of the federal political process in preserving the States' interests is apparent even today in the course of federal legislation. On the one hand, the States have been able to direct a substantial proportion of federal revenues into their own treasuries in the form of general and program-specific grant in aid.
>
> [A]t the same time that the States have exercised their influence to obtain federal support, they have been able to exempt themselves from a wide variety of obligations imposed by Congress under the Commerce Clause.

reason to adhere to them. In either event, the theories will not succeed in bridging disagreement over the things we care about the most.

In the post–New Deal period, structural theories have dominated constitutional discourse. The reason is obvious. Despite their flaws, these theories provide the last, best hope for rescuing constitutional argument from the dead end produced by the partial assimilation of the realist critique. To give up on these theories is to give up on constitutionalism altogether, and virtually no one wants to do that. So we cling to the structural theories, even as they repeatedly fail.

The process is unending because each end point seems unacceptable: To give up on constitutional discourse is to give up on the possibility of mediating our most significant disagreements through a commitment to a common set of premises; yet to embrace constitutional discourse is to suppress the destabilizing realist arguments that have become a central part of our intellectual and cultural universe.

Is there an escape from this cycle? In the concluding chapter, we discuss the possible futures of constitutional argument.

9

Conclusion: The Case for Skeptical Commitment

Constitutional rhetoric is the language of American politics.

Or at least it used to be. Could it be that our ancient obsession with constitutional argument is finally coming to an end?

Consider, for example, President Clinton's first two nominations to the Supreme Court. Superficially, it might appear that the president's extended public agonizing over these appointments reflects the continuing importance of constitutional law. We believe it suggests just the opposite.

One might have supposed that President Clinton would treat these appointments as especially significant. He is a lawyer who began his career by teaching constitutional law, and he purports to care deeply about it. Like many of his generation, he professes a nostalgic attraction to the idealism and moral drama that marked the Warren Court period. His appointments were the first by a Democratic president in almost thirty years, and his campaign promise to end Republican domination of the Court played a role in his election.

Yet the president also faced difficulties in making these appointments. One problem was that no one seemed to want the job. For the first time in recent memory, the president was publicly turned down by several of his top choices—a stunning development that itself suggests the declining significance of constitutional argument in our public life.

A second problem was that no one—least of all the president himself—really desired a return to Warren Court activism. Today, few people in the political mainstream believe that nine justices sitting in

Washington can or should effect important social transformation by the stroke of a pen. A nominee who attempted to go to the Court with an agenda for serious change would be savaged by the Senate and prove nothing but a headache for the president.

Consider instead the positions likely to be held by the most liberal person we can imagine a Democratic president nominating even if the Democrats regain control of the Senate. Such a nominee would be somewhat more receptive to affirmative action than the Court recently has been but would hardly be likely to find affirmative action programs required by the Constitution. Similarly, such a nominee might be somewhat more willing to find programs unconstitutional because they have a disproportionate adverse impact on racial minorities but would be unlikely to invalidate many laws solely because of that impact. No such nominee is likely to find "welfare rights" in the Constitution, despite intimations from the Warren Court along those lines. She or he might be somewhat more skeptical about the fairness with which the death penalty is administered today but would hardly be likely to find it unconstitutional under all circumstances. Finally, such a nominee would probably find some way to defend gay rights under the Constitution.[1] On the whole, this is not an agenda designed to stir the passions of those who found the Warren Court an inspiration.

So President Clinton found himself pulled in two directions. His nominees needed to satisfy liberal nostalgia for the lost youth of constitutional argument, but they also had to reflect the sober and mature second thoughts that come with middle age.

After some initial stumblings, Clinton brilliantly bridged this gap by filling the first vacancy with Ruth Bader Ginsburg. As a pioneer in the legal battle against gender discrimination, Justice Ginsburg had once used constitutional law to accomplish something important. As a cautious and conservative lower-court judge, she had convincingly demonstrated that she would never do so again.

It would be expecting too much to hope to find a second nominee who could so successfully paper over the president's contradictory impulses, and it is not surprising that an extended and public search for such a nominee ended in failure. It speaks volumes that, when forced to make a clean choice between these impulses, Clinton came down firmly on the

1. There is a fair chance that within a decade even the current Supreme Court will find a way to provide at least limited protection for gays.

side of relegating constitutional argument to the margins of public life.

If press reports are to be believed, the president wanted to nominate Bruce Babbitt, his secretary of the interior, to the Court. Although Babbitt is certainly no dangerous radical, his career has been marked by a willingness to depart from the conventional wisdom. For precisely that reason, the prospect of his nomination attracted immediate opposition in the Senate. Most analysts believed that Babbitt would nonetheless have been confirmed, but evidently the president was unwilling to undertake even moderate risk for the sake of constitutional doctrine. Accordingly, he promptly retreated and, with a notable lack of enthusiasm, named Stephen Breyer, another cautious centrist much less likely to rock the boat.

It is not our intention to cast aspersions on Justices Ginsburg and Breyer. They are two of the most thoughtful and competent justices appointed in recent years. Their nominations nonetheless strongly suggest that constitutional argument simply doesn't matter as much as it used to. In the end, even a president who has legal training and knows and cares more about constitutional law than any other president since the New Deal was unwilling to expend any political capital to appoint justices who would make an appreciable difference.

There are other indications that our society has grown tired of constitutional debate. Efforts by the Right to revive the Republican party at its 1992 presidential nominating convention by raising "hot-button" constitutional issues like abortion, gay rights, affirmative action, and school prayer fizzled badly, and the "Contract with America," which was adopted by most Republican candidates for the House of Representatives during the 1994 election, conspicuously avoided these issues.

On the Left, constitutional attacks on gender discrimination have more or less played out. Racial discrimination law and free-speech doctrine, which once energized left-wing politics, have been transformed into tools for conservatives, useful to challenge affirmative action and "political correctness." Constitutional assaults on the unequal distribution of wealth and its effect on political power have failed to so much as dent public consciousness.

Even the Supreme Court seems to have lost interest in constitutional argument. The Court in the mid-1990s decides a little more than half the number of cases per term that it decided a decade ago, and the vast majority of the cases it does decide involve extremely technical issues that interest only specialists.

On the few occasions when the Court addresses questions of real moment, its decisions seem deliberately designed to dampen serious debate. Its recent pronouncements on abortion, for example, have deftly removed the issue from the public agenda, and its decisions on issues such as voting rights, religious freedom, term limits, and affirmative action are opaque, confused, and prolix. Increasingly, the Court appears leaderless and its decisions ad hoc. Justice Scalia alone writes with passion and commitment, and his efforts to engage his colleagues in real debate have led only to his marginalization.

We believe that this loss of interest in constitutional debate is a direct consequence of the difficulties we have outlined in this book. People are finally catching on to the fact that the Constitution does not settle arguments. They have become tired of seeing supposedly bedrock principle manipulated and of hearing rhetoric that divides rather than convinces. Most of all, they seem weary of the politics of polarization—the demonization of opponents and the oversimplification of complex problems that are hallmarks of modern constitutional argument.

There is a sense in which the decline of constitutional debate marks the maturation of American politics. Three quarters of a century after the advent of American legal realism, we are finally beginning to absorb its great lessons: There are no immutable and uncontroversial legal principles that resolve questions of public policy; there is no escape from painful and divisive political struggle.

Perhaps, then, the growing recognition of the emptiness of constitutional argument will allow us at last to talk directly to each other without the necessity of filtering our disagreements through overblown constitutional rhetoric. Perhaps we are on the verge of a reconstituted dialogue, finally freed from the posturing and the moral one-upmanship that accompany constitutional debate and that have prevented true communication for so long. Perhaps, in the long run, we are better off without a Constitution.

Perhaps, but we doubt it. A dialogue of this sort holds real promise, but it poses real dangers as well. For all its deficiencies, constitutional argument would not have played such a prominent role in American public debate for so many years if it were not serving important purposes. We think it likely that these purposes will ultimately reassert themselves and that we will be unable to give up for long our addiction to constitutional rhetoric.

To see why this is so, we have to imagine a world without constitutional rhetoric. In the preceding chapters, we have argued that constitutional argument in the modern context divides rather than unites. It does not follow, however, that without this argument we would be able to transcend our differences. Less appealing possibilities seem more likely. Political argument could devolve into the unabashed efforts of groups to assert raw power over each other, or citizens could retreat to a position of weary and cynical disengagement.

One does not have to look far to find early indications of trends in both directions. American politics more than ever seems dominated by the efforts of narrow interest groups to protect their share of the pie. Increasingly, advocates for these groups find it unnecessary even to pretend to make arguments premised on the public good. They are unwilling to entertain the possibility of shared sacrifice for a purpose that transcends narrow self-interest and are no longer embarrassed to admit that they are simply out for their own.

This politics of self-interest, in turn, produces a splintering of our political culture. Because constitutional argument does not mediate between conflicting worldviews and no longer creates a shared vision for the country, the best we can hope for is a more or less stable division of the booty, supported by an armed truce between sullen factions having nothing in common.

The alternative vision is equally bleak. One important function of constitutional rhetoric is to signal to one's allies and opponents a seriousness of purpose and depth of commitment lacking in ordinary political argument. The realization that this rhetoric is a sham makes it much harder to motivate anyone to take politics seriously. If great and transcendent principles are not really at stake—if constitutional argument amounts to no more than a series of tendentious rhetorical moves—then it is hard to know why one should bother. The result is the retreat to private lives and cynical disengagement that is said to mark the "X Generation" but that runs far deeper through the society.

There is good reason to be concerned that these dystopias lie just over the horizon. Yet each alternative future is so unattractive that we doubt that Americans will be satisfied with either of them for long. The real challenge, then, is not to abandon constitutional argument but to revive it in an intellectual environment that has destroyed its basic premises.

If constitutional discourse continues to play an important role in our politics, how might its pathologies be reduced? One possibility is to devise new methods of talking about constitutional law.

Recently some legal scholars have begun to explore storytelling as a means of improving our understanding of law. On one level, this method surely works: As good trial lawyers have always known, helping people understand how law actually operates in their lives has to improve their ability to develop sensible legal rules. Using stories in that way, however, also runs some risks, as partisans on each side deploy the worst horror stories they can about the positions they oppose.

More promisingly, this narrative jurisprudence might help redefine legal argument. Practitioners of this form of argument go beyond using stories to make legal arguments more effective; instead, the stories *become* the legal arguments.

This new kind of argument might help solve some of the problems with modern constitutional discourse. A story-telling approach might better communicate the subtlety, ambiguity, and complexity of legal problems. By placing the problem within a "thick" context, it encourages empathic identification. Such "argument" (if, indeed, argument is the right word) persuades more gently than standard legal discourse. Instead of attempting to compel one's adversary by the force of logical deduction, practitioners of narrative jurisprudence demonstrate by example how a person located in a certain setting might believe in certain things and act in certain ways.

For these reasons, narrative jurisprudence holds some promise for reconstructing constitutional discourse. There are also reasons for skepticism, however. First, our constitutional culture is recalcitrant enough that the approach is likely to face serious obstacles. It will be a long time before the U.S. solicitor general files a short story, rather than a legal brief, with the Supreme Court.

Second, even if the mode of legal discourse could somehow be transformed, there is no guarantee that the transformation alone would produce the desired results. After all, stories can be just as tendentious as briefs, and, as the current controversy over multiculturalism in public education demonstrates, the struggle over which story gets told can be every bit as divisive as legal argument.

Although narrative jurisprudence makes a valuable contribution by demonstrating how the mood or attitude of those advancing legal positions might be transformed, there is no necessary connection between this transformation and a change in the form of argument. Without the transformation, narrative jurisprudence is likely to be just as tendentious as standard modes of argument. With it, perhaps the standard modes (which lawyers are, in any event, likely to be more adept at using) might be made to serve more constructive purposes. Indeed, as we discuss later in this chapter, there are strengths to standard argument that, properly deployed, might be especially conducive to a change in attitude.

What sort of change is required? In an important book on the legal profession, *The Lost Lawyer,* Dean Anthony Kronman makes some useful suggestions. Kronman sets himself the task of explaining how some public decisions can be "better" than others when disputants cannot even agree on a common metric to measure the benefits of competing outcomes. He argues that persons who are skilled at "legal statesmanship" make better decisions because they are better able to maintain sympathy and understanding for the positions they oppose. This attitude does not necessarily dictate compromise or noninterference. In this approach, there are still winners and losers in political struggle. Yet the decisions are made in a spirit that maintains a sense of political community with one's opponents.

How might Kronman's vision apply to constitutional discourse? One important consequence of his position is to bring into question the intended audience for constitutional argument. Throughout this book, we have assumed that constitutional discourse is directed outward—that it is designed to persuade others of the correctness of one's views. Our central thesis has been that the malleability of the standard techniques of such argument means that it no longer has much persuasive power.

Suppose we had focused instead on the utility of constitutional argument that is directed inward. The kind of constitutionalists Kronman describes as statesmen might be less concerned about the effect of argument on others and more concerned about its effect on themselves and their allies. Instead of attempting to bludgeon opponents into seeing the world their way, they might use the techniques of constitutional argument to see the world from their opponents' perspective.

Viewed in this light, the very characteristics of constitutional argument that have made it problematic in our political culture can be transformed into strengths. For example, we have argued that the destabilizing tools of legal realism have made many of the standard moves in constitutional discourse ineffective. Intellectual understanding of these destabilizing techniques has been coupled with an emotional unwillingness to let go of the prerealist world of rights, privacy, and free will. As a result, advocates can flip back and forth between modes of argument to serve their purposes.

This very indeterminacy, which makes the argument unconvincing when it is directed outward, might serve to advance the cause of political community when it is directed inward. Constitutionalists who truly understand the problems with constitutional argument that we have outlined in previous chapters can also understand why their opponents are not required by some immutable and fundamental principle to forsake their positions.

Conventional forms of legal justification and ordinary techniques of legal education might be made to serve a similar end. Consider, for example, the requirement that judges justify their outcomes by resort to "neutral principles." Many have argued that the neutral-principle requirement does little to constrain because clever judges can always gerrymander a neutral principle to reach the "right" result in the case at hand, without meaningfully limiting their freedom to reach preferred outcomes in other cases.

Even if this criticism of neutral-principles methodology is accurate (and we think that it is), the mental discipline required to fashion neutral principles might nonetheless promote constitutional statesmanship. Judges who honestly go through this exercise must apply the rule they favor in cases where it might produce outcomes they oppose. This requirement, in turn, forces judges to think about shifts in context and encourages reflection about how small changes in circumstances might make the justice of the rule appear very different. Even if judges are ultimately able to manipulate the rule in a way that leaves them unconstrained, this mental exercise is bound to make them more sympathetic to their opponents' points of view.

Properly pursued, classroom techniques like the Socratic method serve a similar function. For example, pro-choice advocates might do their best really to understand what it means to believe that abortion is quite literally murder of an innocent child: Could they construct arguments, compelling from within that framework, to support the proposition that killing one abortion provider is justified under existing criminal law doctrines that sometimes allow a person to break the law to avert a greater evil? Those who seek closer relations between religion and government might do their best really to understand what it means to believe that majority religions are ultimately dedicated to the eradication of religious dissent: Could they construct arguments to assert that no government support of religion whatever is compatible with present understandings of the Constitution's ban on laws respecting an establishment of religion?

The aim of these exercises is to build political community by changing the perspective of people who advance constitutional argument. Reflective people who submit to this discipline in good faith may come to understand that if circumstances had been a little different—if their parents had a different set of values, for example—they might well find themselves believing just as deeply in what they actually reject as they believe what they now accept. As the French author Gustave Flaubert put it a century ago, "I see reasons for holding all opinions; it is not that mine are not sharply defined, but I understand how a man who has lived in circumstances contrary to mine also has contrary ideas." Note that Flaubert was not praising a tolerance grounded on indifference to his own opinions, which he insisted were sharply defined. Rather, he was attempting to hold on to his opinions quite firmly, while simultaneously having enough distance from them to understand that others were just as convinced about their contrary views.

Of course, constitutional argument can never be wholly internal. So long as people engage in political and legal debate, the kind of argument one advances will also have an external impact. In the present climate, this fact presents a real problem for constitutionalists. In a world where constitutional discourse remains polarized, an insistence on the sort of honesty and generosity of spirit we advocate may seem something like unilateral disarmament.

We have often observed that when constitutional advocates talk off the record, their real views are far more textured and subtle than one would guess from their public presentations. When the arguments are over and people have gone off to relax, the best advocates often say that we should not take the forcefulness of their advocacy, their insistence that every possible consideration points in their favor and the like, to mean that their overall approach to constitutional law is quite that hard-edged. As sensible people, they say, they know that constitutional issues are in fact more complex than they can discuss in a public setting. Their difficulty is that in the heat of argument, the admission of any doubt or ambiguity is likely to be seized upon as a sign of weakness. When one's opponent already has adopted a take-no-prisoners rhetoric, honest concessions become the basis for demonizing: "If your position is *that* weak," the opponent will say, "you have to be masquerading your mere policy preferences as constitutional requirements."

The result is what game theorists call a "collective action" problem: People who engage in constitutional discourse would all be better off if they could find a way to lower the temperature; yet the temperature remains high because it is hard for people to reach an enforceable bargain that would accomplish a mutually beneficial objective.

We do not wish to understate the difficulties this problem poses for the revival of constitutional argument. Yet even here, we think, there are at least limited prospects for change. It is possible, for example, that confessions of weakness might actually improve both the quality and the persuasiveness of external debate.

To see why, imagine that with respect to a particular issue (perhaps affirmative action or the death penalty) there is a ''bell-curve'' distribution of opinion. Those at each end care passionately about the issue and are certain they are right, while those in the middle care less and are more open to argument. The debate will probably be dominated by those at the ends of the distribution: They care the most and so have the greatest incentive to participate actively in public discussion.[2]

Much of today's constitutional debate has consisted of efforts by individuals at both extremes to read their opponents out of the political mainstream. In effect, they have expended their energy shouting at each other—over the heads of those in the middle who might in fact be persuaded if the argument were directed at them.

Redirecting constitutional argument toward those in the middle might be more productive. First, and most obvious, these are the people who are more open to persuasion. If advocates actually tried to persuade them, there would be less moral posturing and rallying of one's own troops and more honest exchange of ideas.

Second, because people in the middle are bound to see the problem as more nuanced and ambiguous than are those at the extremes, arguments that concede complexity and that honestly explore weaknesses are more likely to be effective with this group. Advocates might be able to build a sense of identification with the audience in the middle if they were to acknowledge honestly the problems with the positions they espouse. Constitutionalists might actually achieve the good internal effects described earlier without losing much in the way of external persuasiveness.

Finally, if advocates on the distribution's ends stopped shouting over the heads of those in the middle, their new audience might be coaxed

2. This fact alone goes a long way toward explaining why so much constitutional debate is unenlightening: It is conducted by those with the most extreme views, who are the least receptive to persuasion by the other side.

into participating in the discussion. Instead of cynical disengagement, there might be real dialogue, conducted by people who are bound to have less doctrinaire views.

There are some possibilities, then, for a transformation of constitutional argument. Yet there are real obstacles as well. In particular, it is foolish to underestimate the damage an adversary culture has inflicted on our ability to sustain the sort of dialogue we imagine. Constitutionalism must develop a discipline and an intellectual suppleness that are both difficult to master and not much valued in our current environment. What is ultimately required is a kind of dual consciousness—a skeptical commitment of the sort Flaubert described—that few contemporary advocates possess.

Constitutionalists cannot simply forget their hard-won knowledge of the emptiness of constitutional arguments. Yet they must act *as if* the arguments were not empty if they are to energize our politics and give meaning and purpose to our public lives. They must somehow authentically admire the emperor's new clothes, all the while knowing on a different level of consciousness that he is most assuredly naked.

Once again, some of the legal realist teachings that created the problem in the first place may also help us see the outlines of a solution. *Miller v. Schoene* stands for the proposition that all law is choice, that doing nothing is a way of doing something, and that there is therefore no refuge from the obligation of engagement and justification. We are therefore obliged to construct meaning even when we know that it does not exist—to proceed as if constitutional rhetoric were meaningful, even when we know that it is not.[3]

How, then, might adherents to skeptical commitment behave? They would be committed and engaged because disengagement is "none the less a choice," and a bad one at that. They would continue to make constitutional arguments because, for all its flaws, constitutional rhetoric provides the only vocabulary we have for reaching beyond ourselves and appealing to universal values. Yet this engagement would somehow

3. It follows that the argument for skeptical commitment is not an argument against judicial review. The "none the less a choice" perspective means that *not* exercising the power of judicial review is as much an assertion of authority as is exercising that power. Whatever criteria we have for evaluating how our political institutions operate must be applied to decisions *not* to invalidate statutes no less stringently than they are to decisions to invalidate them.

be linked with skeptical tolerance and an ironic self-awareness of the contingency of one's own beliefs. The hard edge of constitutional debate would be dulled by the unsuppressible knowledge that none of us has unmediated access to universal truth and that when we pretend that we do, as we must, we are nonetheless only pretending.

Adherents to skeptical commitment would reach out to opponents while also confronting them. They would combine anger with empathy, faith with agnosticism, action with reflection.

In short, skeptical commitment requires a kind of maturity, self-knowledge, and tolerance for contradiction that no society in history has been able to muster. Is American society moving in this direction? Our own skeptical commitment leaves us doubting—and believing—that it could be so.

BIBLIOGRAPHIC ESSAY

General

This essay does not purport to be anything like a comprehensive compilation of the thousands of books and articles devoted to the subjects we discuss. We have elected to try to be helpful rather than exhaustive by providing a manageable list of works a reader interested in the subject might consult for further information. We have therefore confined ourselves to listing and describing only those books and articles specifically discussed or quoted from in text or that have especially influenced our thinking. For an overview of constitutional theory, see Mark Tushnet, *Red, White, and Blue: A Critical Analysis of Constitutional Law* (Cambridge, Mass., 1988). A helpful overview of constitutional history, written by a scholar deeply influenced by his understanding of the New Deal revolution, is Robert McCloskey, *The American Supreme Court* (2d rev. ed. by Sanford Levinson, Chicago, 1994).

Chapter 1

For the classic discussion of the dominant role (and conservative impact) of lawyers in formulating the issues in American politics, see Alexis de Tocqueville, *Democracy in America,* vol. 1, at 272–280 (New York, 1945). For an entertaining history of rhetorical use of the Constitution in

American politics, see Michael Kammen, *The Machine That Would Go of Itself: The Constitution in American Culture* (New York, 1986).

For arguments purporting to demonstrate that the framers did not intend anything like the Fourth Amendment regime advocated by Hentoff, see Telford Taylor, *Two Studies in Constitutional Interpretation* (Columbus, Ohio, 1969), and Akhil Amar, "Fourth Amendment First Principles," 107 *Harvard Law Review* 757 (1994). A much more sophisticated defense of the warrant requirement than Hentoff provides can be found in Silas Wasserstrom, "The Incredible Shrinking Fourth Amendment," 21 *American Criminal Law Review* 257 (1984).

The Nat Hentoff column discussed in the text is entitled "Is Congress Going to Bring Back George III?," *Washington Post,* Nov. 9, 1991, at A27. The following George Will columns are discussed in the text: "How Can a Judge Impose Birth Control?," *Newsday,* June 26, 1988, at 10; "Affirmative Action Gets a Good Knock," *Newsday,* Jan. 30, 1989, at 50; "The Flag Dispute: Individualism Redux," *Newsday,* June 3, 1989, at 43; "The Flag Isn't the Only Thing Burned Up," *Newsday,* June 26, 1989, at 51; "Maybe the Second Amendment Should Be Repealed," *Atlanta Constitution,* Mar. 21, 1991, at 19.

Judge Bork's statements quoted in the text are taken from *The Tempting of America: The Political Seduction of the Law* 1–11, 199–206 (New York, 1990), and from testimony at his confirmation hearings. See "Nomination of Robert H. Bork to be Associate Justice of the Supreme Court of the United States," 100th Cong., 1st Sess., at 103–855 (1989). Professor Tribe's statements are from his testimony in opposition to Judge Bork's elevation to the Supreme Court (see id., at 1267–1346) and from Laurence H. Tribe, *American Constitutional Law* iii (2d ed.) (Westbury, N.Y., 1988). For testimony in support of Judge Bork's nomination from serious constitutional scholars, see "Nomination of Robert H. Bork to be Associate Justice of the Supreme Court of the United States," *supra,* at 1354 (statement of University of Chicago Law Professor Michael McConnell), 1369 (statement of Harvard University Law Professor Richard Stewart), 2435 (statement of Yale Law School Professor George Priest), 2926 (statement of Columbia University Law Professor Henry Monaghan). For statements by former and sitting justices supporting the nomination, see id., at 2276 (statement of former Chief Justice Warren Burger); Ethan Bronner, *Battle for Justice* 199 (New York, 1989) (quoting Justice John Paul Stevens's speech to the Eighth Judicial Conference supporting Judge Bork's nomination).

The most comprehensive argument for a sliding-scale approach to equal protection review from the Supreme Court's liberal wing is in *San Antonio School Dist. v. Rodriguez,* 411 U.S. 1, 98–110 (1973) (Marshall, J. dissenting). The Court's adoption of something close to the liberal position in the context of gender discrimination came in *Craig v. Boren,* 429 U.S. 190 (1976).

The article by Professor McConnell discussed in the text is "The Selective Funding Problem: Abortion and Religious Schools," 104 *Harvard Law Review* 989 (1991). The article by Professors Strauss and Sunstein is "The Senate, the Constitution, and the Confirmation Process," 101 *Yale Law Journal* 1491 (1992). For a book-length treatment of the problem along similar lines, see Steven Carter, *The Confirmation Mess: Cleaning Up the Federal Appointments Process* (New York, 1994).

Professor Ely's attack on the Supreme Court's abortion decisions can be found in "The Wages of Crying Wolf: A Comment on *Roe v. Wade,*" 82 *Yale Law Journal* 920 (1973). For scholarly defenses of *Roe v. Wade* on representation reinforcement grounds, see Sylvia Law, "Rethinking Sex and the Constitution," 132 *University of Pennsylvania Law Review* 955 (1984); Donald Regan, "Rewriting *Roe v. Wade,*" 77 *Michigan Law Review* 1569 (1979). For judicial support of these views, see *Planned Parenthood of Southeastern Pennsylvania v. Casey,* 112 S. Ct. 2791 (1992). For a feminist attack on *Roe,* see Catherine MacKinnon, "*Roe v. Wade,* A Study in Male Ideology," in Jay Garfield and Patricia Hennessy eds., *Abortion: Moral and Legal Perspectives* (Amherst, Mass. 1985).

Chapter 2

A collection of primary sources on legal realism is contained in William W. Fisher III, Morton J. Horwitz, and Thomas A. Reed, eds., *American Legal Realism* (New York, 1993). Morton Horwitz, *The Transformation of American Law, 1870–1960: The Crisis of Legal Orthodoxy* (New York, 1992) provides a description of the intellectual and political setting in which legal realism developed. (A somewhat different view of legal realism, emphasizing the thought of a different set of authors, is John Henry Schlegel, *American Legal Realism and Empirical Social Science* [Chapel Hill, N.C., 1995]. We incline to the view offered by

Horwitz, at least to the extent that it describes the background of the arguments we make.) *Miller v. Schoene* is the focus of Warren Samuels, "Interrelations Between Legal and Economic Processes," 14 *Journal of Law and Economics* 435 (1971). Herbert Wechsler's discussion of *Brown v. Board of Education* is in Herbert Wechsler, "Toward Neutral Principles of Constitutional Law," 73 *Harvard Law Review* 1 (1959). This article generated a large number of responses, many of which dealt with Wechsler's general observations about constitutional theory and the requirement of neutrality. For one dealing relatively more with his discussion of *Brown,* see Charles Black, "The Lawfulness of the Segregation Decisions," 69 *Yale Law Journal* 421 (1960). Melvin I. Urofsky, *Felix Frankfurter: Judicial Restraint and Individual Liberties* (Boston, 1991), provides an accessible account of Frankfurter's jurisprudence.

Sunstein's most fully developed presentation is *The Partial Constitution* (Cambridge, Mass., 1993). Tushnet has reviewed *The Partial Constitution:* see Mark Tushnet, "The Bricoleur at the Center," 60 *University of Chicago Law Review* 1071 (1993). Bruce Ackerman, *We the People: Foundations* (Cambridge, Mass., 1993), is the first volume of a projected three-volume work developing his theory. For representative critical commentary, see Michael Klarman, "Constitutional Fact/Constitutional Fiction: A Critique of Bruce Ackerman's Theory of Constitutional Moments," 44 *Stanford Law Review* 759 (1992); Michael McConnell, "The Forgotten Constitutional Moment," 11 *Constitutional Commentary* 115 (1994); amd Robert Justin Lipkin, "Can American Constitutional Law Be Postmodern?," 42 *Buffalo Law Review* 319 (1994). McConnell in particular stresses the difficulties associated with Ackerman's effort to identify only three constitutional moments.

Chapter 3

The DeShaney case has sparked a large literature, most of it critical. Interesting treatments of the case can be found in Martha Minow, "Words and the Door to the Land of Change: Law, Language, and Social Change," 43 *Vanderbilt Law Review* 1665 (1990); Akhil Amar, "Child Abuse as Slavery: A Thirteenth Amendment Response to De-

Shaney,'' 105 *Harvard Law Review* 1359 (1992); David Strauss, ''Due Process, Government Inaction, and Private Wrongs,'' 1989 *Supreme Court Review* 53.

Succeeding generations of constitutional scholars have returned, with obsessive regularity, to the state action problem. For the classic, early realist treatment of the problem of private power, see Robert Hale, ''Coercion and Distribution in a Supposedly Non-Coercive State,'' 38 *Political Science Quarterly* 476 (1920). See also Robert Hale, *Freedom through Law: Public Control of Private Governing Power* (New York, 1952); Robert Hale, ''Bargaining, Duress and Economic Liberty,'' 43 *Columbia Law Review* 603 (1943).

Warren Court activism, especially to remedy racial discrimination, triggered renewed interest in state action. The leading works are Charles Black, ''The Supreme Court: 1966 Term—Foreword: 'State Action,' Equal Protection, and California's Proposition 14,'' 81 *Harvard Law Review* 69 (1967); Jerre S. Williams, ''The Twilight of State Action,'' 41 *Texas Law Review* 347 (1963); Louis Henkin, ''*Shelley v. Kraemer:* Notes for a Revised Opinion,'' 110 *University of Pennsylvania Law Review* 473 (1962).

Modern commentary on state action has been almost unrelievedly negative. Centrist scholars have argued that state action analysis can be folded into the merits. See, e.g., Robert J. Glennon, Jr., and John E. Nowak, ''A Functional Analysis of the Fourteenth Amendment 'State Action' Requirement,'' 1976 *Supreme Court Review* 221; Laurence H. Tribe, *Constitutional Choices* at 255 (Cambridge, Mass., 1985); Cass Sunstein, ''*Lochner's* Legacy,'' 87 *Columbia Law Review* 873 (1987); Erwin Chemerinsky, ''Rethinking State Action,'' 80 *Northwestern University Law Review* 503 (1985).

Scholars on the Left have used the doctrine as a wedge to attack liberal theory. See, e.g., Paul Brest, ''State Action and Liberal Theory: A Casenote on *Flagg Brothers v. Brooks,*'' 130 *University of Pennsylvania Law Review* 1296 (1982); Duncan Kennedy, ''The Stages of Decline of the Public-Private Distinction,'' 130 *University of Pennsylvania Law Review* 1349 (1982).

Feminists have attacked the doctrine as shielding private (male) power from legal control. See, e.g., Frances Olsen, ''Constitutional Law: Feminist Critiques of the Public/Private Distinction,'' 10 *Constitutional Commentary* 319 (1993).

For a classic attack from (what is now considered) the Right on the Court's supposed manipulation of the doctrine, see Herbert Wechsler, "Toward Neutral Principles in Constitutional Law," 73 *Harvard Law Review* 1 (1959).

For an unusual and provocative defense of the doctrine that purports to take account of many of the arguments we make in text, see Larry Alexander and Paul Horton, *Whom Does the Constitution Command?* (New York, 1988); Larry Alexander, "The Public/Private Distinction and Constitutional Limits on Private Power," 10 *Constitutional Commentary* 361 (1993).

There is an extensive literature on the moral and legal status of the more general feasance–nonfeasance distinction. For an entertaining defense of the distinction, see Judith Jarvis Thompson, "The Trolley Problem," 94 *Yale Law Journal* 1395 (1985). See also Ernest Weinrib, "The Case for a Duty to Rescue," 90 *Yale Law Journal* 247 (1980). For an impassioned attack on the distinction that proceeds from utilitarian premises, see Peter Singer, "Famine, Affluence, and Morality," 1 *Philosophy and Public Affairs* 229 (1972).

On the background of the Fourteenth Amendment and Congress's desire to entrench the Civil Rights Act of 1866, see Eric Foner, *Reconstruction: America's Unfinished Revolution* at 257 (New York, 1988); Eric McKitrick, *Andrew Johnson and Reconstruction* at 326–363 (Chicago, 1960); John Frank and Robert Munro, "The Original Understanding of the 'Equal Protection of the Laws,'" 50 *Columbia Law Review* 131 (1950). Justice Bradley's private correspondence on the meaning of the Fourteenth Amendment referred to in the text is quoted and discussed in *Bell v. Maryland,* 378 U.S. 226, 309–310 (Goldberg, J. concurring).

Chapter 4

For press accounts of the McSpadden–Butler controversy, see "'Every Woman and Child' Faces Rape, Judge Says; McSpadden Says Castration Should Be Sex Case Option," *Houston Chronicle,* Oct 13, 1992, at 17A,; "Proposed Castration Called Off, Judge Removes Himself From Case," United Press International, Domestic News, Mar. 16, 1992.

Early scholarly interest in the conditional-offer problem was sparked by the Warren Court's flirtation with the articulation of positive rights.

The leading treatment of the issue from this period is William Van Alstyne, "The Demise of the Right-Privilege Distinction in Constitutional Law," 81 *Harvard Law Review* 1439 (1968). With the fading of Warren Court activism, interest in the problem declined as well. In recent years, however, legal academics have rediscovered the problem, and there has been an outpouring of new articles and books on the subject. Much of this work has been influenced by philosophical literature, especially the article by Robert Nozick discussed in the text. See Robert Nozick, "Coercion," in *Philosophy, Science and Method: Essays in Honor of Ernest Nagel* (New York, 1969). See also David Zimmerman, "Coercive Wage Offers," 10 *Philosophy and Public Affairs* 121 (1981).

For a path-breaking article by a legal academic who incorporated Nozick's insights and first saw the problem in terms of generating appropriate baselines against which offers and threats could be measured, see Seth Kreimer, "Allocational Sanctions: The Problem of Negative Rights in a Positive State," 132 *University of Pennsylvania Law Review* 1293 (1984). Although not insisting upon a single method for generating a baseline, Kreimer defends the "prediction" method discussed in the text. He provides a good discussion of the pre–New Deal conditional offer cases discussed in the text. Cass Sunstein argues that the doctrine depends for its coherence on the acceptance of common-law baselines and that, with the realization that these do not constitute a "natural" state of affairs, the doctrine should be abolished. See Cass Sunstein, "Is There an Unconstitutional Conditions Doctrine?," 26 *San Diego Law Review* 337 (1989). Richard Epstein's book-length treatment of the subject attempts to generate baselines through the use of a bargaining model that focuses on government monopolization of access to certain goods and a desire to minimize externalities. See Richard Epstein, *Bargaining with the State* (Princeton, N.J., 1993). For a persuasive attack on Nozick's coercion model and an attempt to see the problem in terms of the appropriate distribution of power between various groups, see Kathleen Sullivan, "Unconstitutional Conditions," 102 *Harvard Law Review* 1413 (1989). For applications of conditional-offer analysis to particular legal doctrines, see David Cole, "Beyond Unconstitutional Conditions: Charting Spheres of Neutrality in Government-Funded Speech," 67 *New York University Law Review* 675 (1992) (free speech); William Marshall, "Towards a Nonunifying Theory of Unconstitutional Conditions: The Example of the Religion Clauses," 26 *San*

Diego Law Review 243 (1989) (free exercise and establishment); Michael McConnell, "The Selective Funding Problem: Abortions and Religious Schools," 104 *Harvard Law Review* 989 (1991) (establishment, free exercise, and abortion); Albert Rosenthal, "Conditional Federal Spending as a Regulatory Device," 26 *San Diego Law Review* 277 (1989) (spending); Lynn Baker, "The Prices of Rights: Toward a Positive Theory of Unconstitutional Conditions," 75 *Cornell Law Review* 1185 (1990) (public assistance). A useful summary of the various positions can be found in Larry Alexander, "Understanding Constitutional Rights in a World of Optional Baselines," 26 *San Diego Law Review* 175 (1989).

Chapter 5

There is a vast literature on the constitutional law of race discrimination. The summary that follows is limited to a few of the most influential works dealing with the particular topics discussed in the chapter.

For a provocative effort to resolve some of the conceptual difficulties discussed in the text concerning racial discrimination in jury selection, see Barbara Underwood, "Ending Race Discrimination in Jury Selection: Whose Right Is It, Anyway?," 92 *Columbia Law Review* 775 (1992).

For a defense of the "color-blindness" version of the antidiscrimination principle, see William Van Alstyne, "Rites of Passage: Race, the Supreme Court, and the Constitution," 46 *University of Chicago Law Review* 775 (1979). For attacks, see Barbara J. Flagg, " 'Was Blind but Now I See': White Race Consciousness and the Requirement of Discriminatory Intent," 91 *Michigan Law Review* 953 (1993); David Strauss, "The Myth of Colorblindness," 1986 *Supreme Court Review* 99. For a defense of the "race-conscious" version of the principle, see Gary Peller, "Race Consciousness," 1990 *Duke Law Review* 758. An influential defense of the "group rights" version of the principle is found in Owen Fiss, "Groups and the Equal Protection Clause," 5 *Philosophy and Public Affairs* 175 (1976). The "individualist" version is articulated in Paul Brest, "Foreword—In Defense of the Antidiscrimination Principle," 90 *Harvard Law Review* 1 (1976).

A large and growing body of literature criticizes *Washington v. Davis* and an "intent" approach to racial discrimination. Perhaps the most influential attack is Charles Lawrence, "The Id, the Ego, and Equal Protection: Reckoning with Unconscious Racism," 39 *Stanford Law Review* 317 (1987). Much of the criticism argues that supposedly neutral norms in fact reflect white assumptions and values. See, for example, Kimberle Crenshaw, "Race, Reform, and Retrenchment: Transformation and Legitimation in Antidiscrimination Law," 101 *Harvard Law Review* 1331 (1988). For an exploration of the tensions between *Washington v. Davis* and *Brown v. Board of Education,* see David Strauss, "Discriminatory Intent and the Taming of *Brown,*" 56 *University of Chicago Law Review* 935 (1989). For a creative defense of *Washington v. Davis,* see Randall Kennedy, "The State, Criminal Law and Racial Discrimination: A Comment," 107 *Harvard Law Review* 1255 (1994).

Some of the most provocative literature on racial discrimination argues that antidiscrimination law itself serves to legitimate racial discrimination. By far the most influential work defending this position is Derrick Bell, *And We Are Not Saved: The Elusive Quest for Racial Justice* (New York, 1987). See also Alan Freeman, "Racism, Rights, and the Quest for Equal Opportunity: A Critical Legal Essay," 23 *Harvard Civil Liberties-Civil Rights Law Review* 295 (1988); Girardeau Spann, *Race Against the Court: The Supreme Court and Minorities in Contemporary America* (New York, 1993).

Chapter 6

The classic expositions of free-speech law, both from a relatively civil libertarian perspective and both somewhat dated though still quite useful, are Thomas Emerson, *The System of Freedom of Expression* (New York, 1970), and Harry Kalven, *A Worthy Tradition: Freedom of Speech in America* (New York, 1988) (this work is based on published articles and a manuscript left at the time of Kalven's death in 1973).

The arguments that are the foundation for our treatment of pornography regulation are presented effectively in Catharine MacKinnon, *Only Words* (Cambridge, Mass., 1993). Cass Sunstein, *Democracy and the Problem of Free Speech* (New York, 1993), presents his own version of those arguments. The conservative position is presented in Harry Clor, *Obscenity and Public Morality: Censorship in a Liberal Society* (Chicago, 1969).

Useful criticisms stressing the simplifications embedded in MacKinnon's arguments are Susan Etta Keller, "Viewing and Doing: Complicating Pornography's Meaning," 81 *Georgetown Law Journal* 2195 (1993), and Carlin Meyer, "Sex, Sin, and Women's Liberation: Against Porn-Suppression," 72 *Texas Law Review* 1097 (1994). Sunstein's version is challenged in Jeanne Schroeder, "The Taming of the Shrew: The Liberal Attempt to Mainstream Radical Feminist Theory," 5 *Yale Journal of Law and Feminism* 123 (1992). A more traditional civil-libertarian approach, which takes feminist concerns into account, is Nadine Strossen, "A Feminist Critique of 'the' Feminist Critique of Pornography," 79 *Virginia Law Review* 1099 (1993).

The literature on the constitutional dimensions of campaign financing regulation is huge. Much of it focuses on the details of the jurisprudence developed by the Supreme Court in the years since *Buckley v. Valeo*. In many ways, however, the best contributions are among the earliest; both are by Judge J. Skelly Wright: "Politics and the Constitution: Is Money Speech?," 85 *Yale Law Journal* 1001 (1976), and its follow-up, "Money and the Pollution of Politics: Is the First Amendment an Obstacle to Political Equality?," 82 *Columbia Law Review* 609 (1982). A counterview is offered in Lillian BeVier, "Money and Politics: A Perspective on the First Amendment and Campaign Finance Reform," 73 *California Law Review* 1045 (1985). The "Symposium on Campaign Finance Reform," 94 *Columbia Law Review* 1125 (1994), canvasses the problem from various perspectives, both political and disciplinary, but concentrates on the fundamental questions we deal with. The Graber quotation is from Mark A. Graber, "Old Wine in New Bottles: The Constitutional Status of Unconstitutional Speech," 48 *Vanderbilt Law Review* 349 (1995).

Chapter 7

Virtually all of the literature on capital punishment is polemical. For good summaries of the competing positions, see Hugo Adam Bedau, *The Death Penalty in America* (New York, 1979) and Ernest van den Haag and John Conrad, *The Death Penalty: A Debate* (New York, 1983).

Vigorous defenses of rights-based retentionism can be found in Walter Berns, *For Capital Punishment: Crime and the Morality of the Death Penalty* (New York, 1979) and Ernest van den Haag, *Punishing*

Criminals: Concerning a Very Old and Painful Question (New York, 1975). The rights-based abolitionist position is presented in Hugo Adam Bedau, *The Death Penalty in America, supra,* at 123–130, 171–182.

Textual arguments are analyzed in Raoul Berger, *Death Penalties: The Supreme Court's Obstacle Course* (Cambridge, Mass., 1982) and Anthony Granucci, "'Nor Cruel and Unusual Punishments Inflicted': The Original Meaning," 57 *California Law Review* 839 (1969).

The modern debate concerning the deterrent impact of the death penalty begins with Isaac Ehrlich's study purporting to demonstrate that between 1933 and 1967, each additional execution might have saved eight lives. See Isaac Ehrlich, "The Deterrent Effect of Capital Punishment: A Question of Life and Death," 65 *American Economic Review* 397 (1975). Ehrlich's study has been widely criticized. For an especially powerful response, see Richard O. Lempert, "Deterrence and Desert: An Assessment of the Moral Bases for Capital Punishment," 79 *Michigan Law Review* 1177 (1981). See also William J. Bowers and Glenn L. Pierce, "The Illusion of Deterrence in Isaac Ehrlich's Research on Capital Punishment," 85 *Yale Law Journal* 187 (1987); Hans Zeisel, "The Deterrent Effects of the Death Penalty: Facts v. Faiths," 1976 *Supreme Court Review* 317. For Ehrlich's answer to his critics, see Isaac Ehrlich and Randall Mark, "Fear of Deterrence," 6 *Journal of Legal Studies* 293 (1977).

The most significant empirical work on discrimination in the administration of the death penalty has been done by David Baldus and his colleagues. See David C. Baldus, Charles A. Pulaski, Jr., George Woodworth, and Frederick Kyle, "Identifying Comparatively Excessive Sentences of Death: A Quantitative Approach," 33 *Stanford Law Review* 1 (1980); David C. Baldus, Charles A. Pulaski, Jr., and George Woodworth, "Comparative Review of Death Sentences: An Empirical Study of the Georgia Experience," 74 *Journal of Criminal Law and Criminology* 661 (1983). See also Charles Black, *Capital Punishment: The Inevitablility of Caprice and Mistake* (New York, 1981). For a rebuttal, see Ernest van den Haag, *Punishing Criminals, supra*. For a summary of polling data on the death penalty, see James Alan Fox, Michael L. Radelet, and Julie L. Bonsteel, "Death Penalty Opinion in the Post-Furman Years," 18 *New York University Review of Law & Social Change* 499 (1990–91).

The account in the text of the botched execution of Willie Francis is drawn from Arthur Selwyn Miller and Jeffrey H. Bowman, *Death by Installments: The Ordeal of Willie Francis* (New York, 1988).

Chapter 8

For forceful statements of Justice Black's approach to constitutional interpretation, see Hugo L. Black, *A Constitutional Faith* (New York, 1968); Hugo L. Black, "The Bill of Rights," 35 *New York University Law Review* 865 (1960). For less rigid defenses of originalism, see Antonin Scalia, "Originalism: The Lesser Evil," 57 *University of Cincinnati Law Review* 849 (1989); Frederick Schauer, "Easy Cases," 58 *Southern California Law Review* 399 (1985); Owen Fiss, "Objectivity and Interpretation," 34 *Stanford Law Review* 739 (1982). Criticism of originalist approaches can be found in Paul Brest, "The Misconceived Quest for the Original Understanding," 60 *Boston University Law Review* 204 (1980), and Larry Simon, "The Authority of the Constitution and Its Meaning: A Preface to a Theory of Constitutional Interpretation," 58 *Southern California Law Review* 603 (1985).

The best-known modern defense of judicial deference in the name of democratic values is Robert Bork, *The Tempting of America: The Political Seduction of the Law* (New York, 1990).

John Hart Ely's theory of representation reinforcement is set out in *Democracy and Distrust* (Cambridge, Mass., 1980). The book has generated a large literature. For two powerful critiques of Ely's thesis, see Richard Parker, "The Past of Constitutional Theory—and Its Future," 42 *Ohio State Law Journal* 223 (1981), and Laurence H. Tribe, "The Puzzling Persistence of Process-Based Constitutional Theories," 89 *Yale Law Journal* 1063 (1980). For a recent defense of a portion of Ely's theory, see Michael J. Klarman, "The Puzzling Resistance to Political Process Theory," 77 *University of Virginia Law Review* 747 (1991).

The foundational work in the functionalist or legal process tradition is a set of teaching materials written by Henry Hart and Albert Sacks. After existing for several generations in photocopy form, the materials have been published with a useful introduction by William Eskridge and Philip Frickey. See Henry Hart and Albert Sacks, *The Legal Process: Basic Problems in the Making and Application of Law* (Westbury, N.Y.,

1994). See also Alexander Bickel, *The Least Dangerous Branch: The Supreme Court at the Bar of Politics* (2d ed. New Haven, 1986); Herbert Wechsler, "Toward Neutral Principles of Constitutional Law," 73 *Harvard Law Review* 1 (1959). For a useful effort to locate functional theories historically and intellectually, see William J. Eskridge and Philip P. Frickey, "The Making of 'The Legal Process,'" 107 *Harvard Law Review* 2031 (1994). For a less sympathetic appraisal, see Gary Peller, "Neutral Principles in the 1950's," 21 *University of Michigan Journal of Law Reform* 561 (1988).

Applications of the functionalist approach to federalism and separation-of-powers questions can be found in Herbert Wechsler, "The Political Safeguards of Federalism: The Role of the States in the Composition and Selection of the National Government," 54 *Columbia Law Review* 543 (1954), and Jesse H. Choper, *Judicial Review and the National Political Process: A Functional Reconsideration of the Supreme Court* (Chicago, 1980). For some representative critiques, see Andrzej Rapaczynski, "From Sovereignty to Process: The Jurisprudence of Federalism after Garcia," 1985 *Supreme Court Review* 341; J. Gregory Sidak, "To Declare War," 41 *Duke Law Journal* 27 (1991); Larry Kramer, "Understanding Federalism," 47 *Vanderbilt Law Review* 1485 (1994).

Chapter 9

There is a large literature defending and utilizing narrative jurisprudence. For a useful introduction, see Kim Lane Scheppele, "Foreword: Telling Stories," 87 *Michigan Law Review* 2073 (1989), and the symposium of which it is a part. The best example of narrative jurisprudence to date is Patricia Williams, *The Alchemy of Race and Rights* (Cambridge, Mass., 1991). For a skeptical but not altogether unfriendly treatment, see Daniel A. Farber and Suzanna Sherry, "Telling Stories Out of School: An Essay on Legal Narratives," 45 *Stanford Law Review* 807 (1993).

Anthony Kronman's defense of legal statesmanship is set forth in Anthony Kronman, *The Lost Lawyer: Failing Ideals in the Legal Profession* (Cambridge, Mass., 1993).

For an account of President Clinton's awkward search for a Supreme

Court nominee, see "Court Runners-up Drew President's Warmest Praise; Clinton Settled on Breyer as Less Risky Choice," *Washington Post,* May 15, 1994, at A6. We found the quotation from Flaubert in a review by Gabriele Annan, *New York Review of Books,* Dec. 1, 1994, at 19.

TABLE OF CASES

INDEX